Grand Forage 1778

Other Titles in the Series

The Road to Concord: How Four Small Cannon Ignited the American Revolution by J. L. Bell

A JOURNAL OF THE AMERICAN REVOLUTION BOOK

GRAND FORAGE 1778

THE
Battleground
Around
New York City

TODD W. BRAISTED

WESTHOLME
Yardley

Westholme Publishing, LLC
904 Edgewood Road
Yardley, Pennsylvania 19067
Visit our Web site at www.westholmepublishing.com

First Printing April 2016
10 9 8 7 6 5 4 3 2 1
ISBN: 978-1-59416-250-3
Also available as an eBook.

Printed in the United States of America.

CONTENTS

List of Maps   vi

Introduction   vii

  1. Clinton's Conundrum   1

  2. War in Westchester   12

  3. The Woman   27

  4. A Time for Light Troops   41

  5. Food and Forage   56

  6. Bergen County in the Crosshairs   70

  7. The Fog of War   84

  8. Bayonets in the Night   99

  9. The Collection   113

10. Parrying the Thrust in Westchester   130

11. In Quest of Pirates and Poles   142

12. Withdrawal   156

Epilogue   170

Notes   178

Bibliography   206

Acknowledgments   211

Index   215

Maps

1. "Ambuscade of the Indians at Kingsbridge.
August 31st 1778."   22–23

2. Disposition of British troops, with fortifications
north of "Fort Knypehausen" (Fort Washington) to
Kingsbridge and Fort Independence, c. 1778.   34–35

3. Plan of Paulus's Hook and fortifications, 1778.   63

4. "Sketch of the Road from Paulus Hook and
Hobocken to New Bridge," 1778.   78–79

5. "Skecth of the road from Kings Bridge
to White Plains," 1778.   92–93

6. Plan of the country at and in the vicinity
of Forts Lee and "Independency," showing the
position of the British army, c. 1776   120–121

7. New York Island. Military; unfinished, c. 1776   162–163

INTRODUCTION

THE AMERICAN REVOLUTION IS BEST KNOWN FOR ITS FAMOUS battles and campaigns: patriotic Americans acting in harmony against some of Europe's finest soldiers who were fighting for a distant monarch and the preservation of colonial rule. While that is certainly true by way of perception, the reality was perhaps something different. The great armies of both sides did indeed fight large-scale battles that have come down through history and decided the fate of empires, but the norm was a daily routine of fatigue and foraging, frequently interspersed with *petite guerres*, or "little wars," of raids and small expeditions. While not finding their place in the annals of the Revolution as Saratoga and Yorktown did, these expeditions, raids, and minor campaigns often involved as many men as the larger battles and certainly left marks on the country that often survive to this day. This volume seeks to show how these small actions, viewed together for the first time, made up one campaign, one generally not considered as such by many today. Perhaps that is because the objective of the campaign was not conquest of territory or defeat of an entire army but the acquisition of enough supplies, in this case food for humans and horses, to allow for the prosecution of campaigns elsewhere. The premise may seem mundane enough, but the end result was the death, wounding, or capture of several hundred soldiers. The campaign was certainly real enough for them.

The war likewise produced its share of heroes (and villains) who are known to many people today. The exploits of George Washington and Sir Henry Clinton are studied in schools today, but in the hotly contested environs of 1778 New York City, men such as George Baylor, Casmir Pulaski, and Charles Scott squared off against the likes of Charles Grey, Patrick Ferguson, and Wilhelm von Knyphausen, names familiar to the inhabitants there. And for the residents living in these areas, the war was often not about independence or loyalty but subsistence and survival. The farmer who tilled his two hundred or three hundred acres of land in Paramus, New Jersey, or Tarrytown, New York, often did not care if the soldiers encamping on his farm wore blue coats or red; after two years of war in his backyard, he knew that an army, any army, would soon devour his crops and livestock, and that he would lose hundreds of fence rails used for firewood. In a time devoid of social safety nets, a farmer's main concern was the support and maintenance of his family, often by whatever means necessary. That was precisely the case for many in autumn 1778, a time after the major actions at Monmouth and Rhode Island and before a shift to British offensive operations in the south. While overlapping the time of these two actions, particularly the latter, this work does not cover those battles more than in relation to the main focus of the work. These were major engagements, worthy of their own volumes, which have been, and continue to be, subjects of new and worthy books by historians.[1] Knowledge of those engagements is helpful but not necessary for reading this book. The focus here is the smaller engagements during that period, seldom covered in other works, all leading up to the British Grand Forage; seemingly random minor engagements between the lines separating the two armies around New York City culminating in major operations, albeit in the quest for food and provender.

The battlegrounds of 1778 around New York City are today obscured by housing, malls, modern roads, and urban sprawl. It is difficult for a person living in the congestion of Westchester County or even more so in densely urbanized Bergen County to envision a time when the area consisted of sprawling farms interspersed with dirt roads and sandstone houses; when Dutch, German, and a variety of other languages were commonly spoken by the residents; and when one's neighbor might also be an armed enemy, openly or clandestinely. Even to those familiar in passing with some of the Revolution's larger battles, the tendency is to call to mind only the famous and well known, such as Yorktown, Saratoga, and Concord, all national park sites today. Seldom are places like Old Tappan, River Edge, Englewood, Tuckerton, Yonkers, and Dobbs Ferry thought of as battlefields by the people who live and work in those towns today.

One

Clinton's Conundrum

M ARCH 21, 1778. THE WAR IN AMERICA HAD BEEN RAGING for nearly three years. While most British strategic campaign decisions had originated on the ground in America, to be approved in London, 1778 would be different. All the previous campaigns had only to consider the defeat of rebellious colonists, campaigns without worldwide considerations. The situation was now changed. The alliance between France and the United States of America meant Great Britain was once again facing an enemy with the means and capability of attacking it almost anywhere. No longer would British possessions far from America's shores lay protected simply by their geography. Their safety would now require British troops, British warships. For a country already stressed with manpower issues in the war, this was a major problem. One of the greatest myths of the American Revolution is that the British were the greatest military power in Europe or the world when the war broke out. All the major European armies dwarfed that of the British, who relied more on the Royal Navy to safeguard their island nation than a large standing infantry force. The entry of France into the war changed that.

Sitting in his London office that March day, Lord George Germain, principal secretary of state for American affairs, knew the political and military situation possibly better than anyone else at that stage of the war. Sir William Howe, Britain's commanding officer in America since replacing Thomas Gage in 1775, had led a large army in capturing New York and Philadelphia, beating General George Washington time and again along the way. But his time in America was coming to an end. A month earlier, Germain had informed Sir Henry Clinton, commander of the garrison of New York City, that he was to be the new commander in chief of the British army in America. General Howe had requested leave to return to England, which was approved by the king, who likewise appointed Clinton to the command in his place. It was what came after that promotion that led to despair with Clinton: circumstances forced a redistribution of British military power in America. The British army would now be scattered across North America, leaving the commander in chief with few troops to form an army of maneuver to campaign with, as his predecessor had possessed.

"I should now acquaint you with His Majesty's Intentions respecting the Operations of the next Campaign, should another Campaign become necessary," began Germain's lengthy operational plan to Clinton.[1] Troops would be needed to reinforce Nova Scotia, Newfoundland, the Island of Saint John's (Prince Edward Island), Bermuda, and West Florida. Most significantly, two major expeditions were to be launched, both using troops then in America. The smaller expedition would at least keep the troops in America, the king desiring "an attack should be made upon the Southern Colonies, with a view to the conquest & possession of Georgia & South Carolina." Britain's possessions in the south at that point consisted of the two provinces of East and West Florida, the latter stretching from the panhandle to the Mississippi River, while the former was centered on its capital, Saint Augustine. Each province had a small number of British regular troops along with some Loyalist troops, but little offensively had been accomplished the previous three years other than some minor raids into Georgia. Offensive operations to capture lightly defended Georgia alone would require no less than two thousand five hundred men from Clinton's army.

While the reinforcements to the outposts and the Georgia expedition drained troops away, the real blow was losing ten British infantry regiments for an expedition to attack the French in the West Indies. These forces, over five thousand men led by Major General James Grant, represented the core of any offensive force Clinton may have hoped to use in carrying on the war against Washington in the Middle Atlantic colonies. Having just two weeks earlier ordered Clinton to send thousands of troops to reinforce outposts and attack the south, Germain now sent along orders from the king himself that Philadelphia was to be abandoned, Grant's expedition was to attack the French in the West Indies, and Clinton, with his remaining force, was, for all intents and purposes, to sit in New York while a commission led by the Earl of Carlisle concluded a treaty of peace with the Americans, granting them everything but independence.[2] This commission, formed in London in April 1778, was (as far as the British were concerned) a last serious attempt to bring the war to a peaceful conclusion. Consisting of William Eden, George Johnstone, and the earl, the commission was empowered to inform Congress that all objectionable parliamentary laws passed since 1763 concerning America would be rescinded and that America would enjoy many freedoms under British government, but not independence. Knowing the French alliance was at hand, Congress resolved on April 22, 1778, to enter into no agreement with the British that did not include a free and independent United States and the removal of all British troops therefrom. Clinton was added to the commission when it arrived in America.

Its arrival at Philadelphia on the eve of the evacuation of the city by the British, could not have happened at a worse time. Fearing that their sudden arrival and desire to treat with Congress at the exact moment the British army was in retreat would make Britain's case seem extremely weak, the commissioners glumly set off for New York City. Congress forwarded Washington a letter to be delivered to the commissioners, but he was forced to sit on it while they were traveling. Writing to Congress on June 18, 1778,

Washington was actually relieved at their absence:

> The Letter for the Commissioners, I shall transmit by the earli-
> est opportunity; However their departure from Philadelphia will
> prevent their getting it as soon as they otherwise would have
> done. I cannot say, that I regret the delay; for there is no know-
> ing, to what acts of depredation and ruin, their disappointed
> ambition might have led. And permit me to add, that I think
> there was no other criterion for Congress to go by, than the one
> they have adopted. The proceedings of the 22d of April, it is
> probable, have reached Britain by this time, and will shew, that
> the present powers of the Commissioners or [at] least those we
> are obliged to suppose them to possess, are wholly incompetent
> to any valuable end.[3]

The Carlisle Peace Commission remained in America for the
next five months, fruitlessly looking for an opening to accomplish
something or enter into worthwhile negotiations. Clinton, however, was first and foremost a professional soldier, and he resigned
himself to the task at hand:

> The great change which public affairs had undergone, in Europe
> as well as America, within the last six months had so clouded
> every prospect of a successful issue to the unfortunate contest we
> were engaged in that no officer who had the least anxious regard
> for his professional fame would court a charge so hopeless as
> this now appeared so likely to be. For neither honor nor credit
> could be expected from it, but on the contrary a considerable
> portion of blame, howsoever unmerited, seemed to be almost
> inevitable. I was, notwithstanding, duly sensible of the confi-
> dence with which the King had honored me, and I consequently
> prepared with all diligence to obey His Majesty's commands to
> the fullest extent of my ability.[4]

Clinton had shown himself an able subordinate to his predecessor, Howe. Left in command of the troops in New York City while

Howe captured Philadelphia, Clinton showed activity and determination in using his limited forces to the best advantage, while at the same time ceaselessly complaining that he had no forces at hand to launch any operations. That mindset would only worsen with his new orders.

The strategy drawn up in England envisioned the offensive operations taking place away from New York City, a place the British considered too important to ever abandon. That required Clinton to more or less stay put, on the defensive. The new seat of war, at least in America, would be the south. The province of East Florida, sparsely settled and with only enough British and Loyalist troops present to maintain a defense, was thought to be a proper jumping-off point for an invasion of Georgia. The initial plans envisioned one main thrust from a reinforced Saint Augustine, but the plans quickly morphed into a two-pronged invasion, the one from Saint Augustine and a second, seaborne attack on Savannah. Future plans would depend on the success of the initial operations. The initial instructions, however, brimmed with optimism:

> It is The King's Intention, that an attack should be made upon the Southern Colonies, with a view to the conquest & possession of Georgia & South Carolina. The various accounts we receive from those Provinces concur in representing the distress of the Inhabitants, and their general disposition to return to their allegiance. A large supply of Arms will therefore be sent out for the purpose of arming such of them as shall join the King's Troops; and indeed it is The King's Wish that every means were employed to raise & embody the well-affected Inhabitants in all the Provinces where any Posts are maintained or Operations carried on. It cannot be expected that Farmers or men of property accustomed to a life of ease, will engage in the Military Service for an indefinite time, or expose themselves to be carried away to places remote from their own Possessions, altho' they would readily enough take up Arms as an embodied Militia, officered by their own Countrymen.[5]

Over the next several years, Clinton would faithfully carry out these orders, first in Georgia, then in the Carolinas. While many historians have belittled British strategy for believing the south to have a large proportion of Loyalists (a doubt shared by a number of British officers as well, including Clinton), it was in fact the truth, although not as anyone saw it at the time. Many of these "Loyalists" found their political allegiance altogether muted when strong British forces were not nearby. Those espousing an open allegiance to the British government with no British soldiers stationed in a more-or-less permanent manner nearby were risking not only their freedom but their property as well. This was demonstrated when Clinton sent three expeditions to Virginia from April 1779 to December 1780. Before the third one, led by Benedict Arnold, the previous two had stayed less than two months before leaving. When a leading Loyalist in Virginia was asked by a Hessian officer in 1781 why he did not volunteer to raise a militia regiment for local defense, the man replied:

"I must first see if it is true that your people really intend to remain with us. You have already been in this area twice. General [Alexander] Leslie gave me the same assurances in the past autumn, and where is he now? In Carolina! Who knows where you will be this autumn? And should the French unite with the Americans, everything would certainly be lost to you here. What would we loyally disposed subjects have then? Nothing but misfortune from the Opposition Party, if you leave us again."[6]

In spring 1778 however, these expeditions were still to come. What troops that would be left at New York City were to be used by Clinton, in conjunction with the Royal Navy, to attack ports where state privateers operated. These privately owned but government-sanctioned warships wreaked havoc not only on British and Loyalist merchant ships but also on the occasional unescorted military store ship or troop transport. Despite ordering the removal of so many troops (and ships) from Clinton's command, Germain still expected this mode of warfare to be carried out, while British peace commissioners sought to end the war on favorable terms: "I will still hope you may find means, in conjunction with the Squadron that will be left in North America, to keep up an alarm on the Sea Coasts of the rebellious Provinces, & perhaps disable them from materially annoying our Trade."[7] Clinton was promised that thousands of reinforcements would arrive later in the year, along with troops for Canada and Nova Scotia. In the end, only the latter two received any men. Clinton was on his own.[8]

One suggestion Germain made did resonate with Clinton, and he willingly followed through on it before the evacuation of Philadelphia.

During the course of the war, and certainly before Clinton assumed command, the British had taken pains to learn who their foes were, in other words, who the men were who composed the Continental army and where they came from. After the Battle of Brandywine on September 11, 1777, Commissary of Prisoners David Sproat prepared an analysis of the Continentals captured during that engagement. Of the 315 privates, only 82 had been born in America. Aside from a smattering of such nationalities as Russians, Swiss, French, and Germans, the largest single group was the Irish, of which 134 had been taken in the battle. Sproat observed that they were "Chiefly belonging to the Pensylvania, and New Jersey Battalions. Servants imported in the last ships from Londonderry, Newry, Belfast, Cork, &c. who had inlisted to get clear of servitude, and cancel their indentures."[9]

Accordingly, Germain wrote to Clinton in March 1778 "to suggest to you, the great advantage which must follow from drawing over from the Rebels the Europeans in their Service. Especial encouragement should be held out to them to desert & join the King's Forces."[10] The first to seize this opportunity was a young captain in the 63rd Regiment of Foot, Lord Francis Rawdon. This young Irish officer had served in America since the beginning of the war and like several other ambitious officers in the army at that time, he sought fast advancement by raising a corps of Provincial soldiers—American regulars in the service of the British. Upon Clinton's assuming command of the army, Rawdon proposed to raise a corps exclusively of these Irish immigrants that would not only serve the purpose of raising new men for the British but draw soldiers away from Washington. Clinton approved of the plan and on May 25, 1778, formed the Volunteers of Ireland. It would be one of the best fighting units in the army over the next four years.[11]

Among the worst of the orders Clinton received was that he was to retain only one of the two cavalry regiments under his command. Since 1776, he had had at his disposal the 16th and 17th Regiments of Light Dragoons, a total of over 730 cavalrymen in summer 1778.[12] The rationale for cutting the cavalry in half was "to free the Army of every unnecessary impediment to its expeditious removals."[13] The move was immensely shortsighted. Even under the plan of operations laid out by Germain, a regiment of cavalry would have been highly useful for the intended expedition to Georgia. Instead, Provincial cavalry would have to be raised in each successive year of the war, both in the north and the south, and at a much higher cost than it would have been to simply retain both regiments of British light dragoons. Indeed, one of the first actions Lieutenant Colonel Archibald Campbell took after capturing Savannah was to form two troops of light dragoons under British officers.[14]

Before any expeditions could be made, there was still the matter of evacuating Philadelphia and concentrating forces at New York City. The majority of the heavy baggage and stores, excess provisions, heavy artillery, invalids, and Loyalist civilians with their belongings would require transport ships for the voyage to New York. That left over twenty thousand men, women, and children to march across New Jersey in the heat of June.[15] Then there was the threat of Washington and his newly revitalized army, trained over the winter by a professional Prussian officer, Major General Friedrich Wilhelm Baron von Steuben, and brought up to strength by the recent addition of thousands of temporary soldiers, known as levies, to fill out the Continental regiments.

Washington kept himself well informed of British preparations. There was little Clinton could do to mask what was going on. One spy reported to Washington in early June 1778:

200 Waggons landed, 800 Barrels Pork, 3000 Sacks Biskets in Stables; to morrow the rest of the Provitions and Waggons will

be over, next day the troops. This day all the Sick and Wounded went on bord, yesterday a number of Cannon broke and throne of[f] the warf, Likewise thousands of broken muskets and a large Quantity of Barrels Pork and Beef was throne over and not less than 4000 Blankets burnt that came out of the Hospitle. By Procklamation the Shipping is to be all gone Down to morrow by Sun set, and all friends to Goverment is to go with the fleet.[16]

Washington was not the only consideration for the British at this time. Unknown to Clinton, but well known to Germain, the French were on their way to America. Already fearing an attack on Nova Scotia, the British had ordered three regiments of infantry directly from Great Britain to Halifax: the 70th, 74th, and 82nd, the last two newly raised corps.[17] Arriving in Halifax on August 12, 1778, under convoy of the frigate *Thetis*, these troops in some measure only replaced the Corps of Marines, which was ordered from Halifax to man the fleet because of the French war, the Royal Navy having no pressing need for them before that time.

Official word of the French sailing for America was sent to Clinton on June 5, 1778, well after he had learned of it through other channels.[18] The French—consisting of a fleet of eleven ships of the line, a fifty-gun ship, and five frigates, with three thousand infantry under Count Charles Hector D'Estaing—had slipped past British-held Gibraltar on May 16, 1778, and were seen taking the southern passage to America.[19] The shipping from Philadelphia, however, arrived safe at New York, with Admiral D'Estaing's fleet not arriving in America until a week afterward.

The British army's march across New Jersey commenced Wednesday, June 17, 1778.[20] It took thirteen days to march through the sandy soil of south central New Jersey, under temperatures reaching one hundred degrees. Frequent skirmishing, plundering, and desertion were all hallmarks of the passage. No fewer than three Provincial officers—a lieutenant of the Maryland Loyalists and two captains of the Roman Catholic Volunteers—were court-martialed for plundering horses and cattle, with both captains found guilty and cashiered.[21] The climax of the march was undoubtedly the Battle of Monmouth on June 28, 1778. While most historians today consider the battle a draw, in 1778, both commanders took credit for victory, but in different ways. Clinton, always one to take things personally, took to the pen after the war in publicly explaining why he believed he won, and in strict strategic terms, he was probably correct:

> Nothing, surely, can be more ridiculous than the claim to advantage which Mr. Washington and Mr. [Charles] Lee have set up in their respective accounts of this day's action, wherein they are pleased to assert "the King's army received a handsome check." For besides the manifest misapplication of that term to an army whose principle is retreat, and which accomplishes it without affront or loss, there does not appear to be the slightest foundation for a claim to advantage on the side of the enemy at any one period of the day, the transactions of which may be summed up in a very few words. The rear guard of the King's army is attacked on its march by the avant garde of the enemy. It turns upon them, drives them back to their gross, remains some hours in their presence until all its advanced detachments return, and then falls back, without being followed, to the ground from which the enemy had been first driven, where it continues for several hours undisturbed, waiting for the cool of the evening to resume its march. And so apprehensive are the enemy of approaching its position that not even a patrol ventured near it until twelve o'clock of the next day.[22]

The army ended its march on the Heights of Neversink, from which it took ships from Sandy Hook to Staten Island, Manhattan, and Long Island. Within a week of the army's arrival back in New York, D'Estaing and his fleet appeared off Sandy Hook, where Clinton had left several British regiments and the Provincial West Jersey Volunteers making fortifications to secure the vital bay and passage into New York Harbor. "Count d'Estaing, after having completely blocked up the port of New York for twelve days and making prize of every vessel that approached it in that time, weighed anchor at last on the 22d and disappeared."[23] The logical next place for the appearance of the French was the less-well-defended garrison of Newport, Rhode Island, and its valuable port.

The garrison of Rhode Island had already been twice reinforced in 1778. At the end of May, a large Provincial regiment, the Prince of Wales American Volunteers, was transferred from New York.[24] On July 15, before the arrival of the French and Continental force that would besiege Rhode Island, four more units arrived from New York: the British 38th Regiment of Foot, the Provincial King's American Regiment, and the two German regiments of Anspach.[25] With four thousand additional men ready to relieve Rhode Island if necessary, and even adding the 23rd Regiment of Foot to act as marines on Howe's warships, Clinton felt himself prepared to deal with any attack on his New England garrison.

After safely arriving in New York from the march across New Jersey, even while dealing with the matter of the French, it took Clinton only a week to start his plans for embarking troops for the new expeditions. After reading a message from General Grant, his commander for the West Indies, he realized there was an issue at hand that might need to be addressed. He instructed his adjutant general to reply to Grant, which was done July 11, 1778:

"His Excellency . . . agrees to your having Ten Regiments, viz 4th, 5th, 15th, 17th, 27th, 28th, 40th, 46th, 49th, & 55th. Such a number of Regiments will be drafted, as will complete the Effective Rank & File of those above mentioned to the destined number. With regard to Provisions, the Commander in Chief fears he cannot (with the attention necessary to his own situation) supply you so largely as you have demanded: He will, however, make your stock as great as he can with prudence."[26]

The problem Clinton would have to deal with was food, for both men and horses. Issuing provisions to a static garrison that could be regularly supplied was one thing, but having to issue out food for humans and forage for horses for weeks in advance for troops traveling onboard ship was very much something else. And without a speedy acquisition of more supplies, Clinton simply did not have enough on hand.

Two

War in Westchester

WITH THE BRITISH EVACUATION OF PHILADELPHIA, GEORGE Washington was left to guess at General Clinton's next move at New York City. It was an exciting time for the Continental army's senior military officer. The capital of the fledgling United States had been liberated without a shot being fired, and word of an approaching French fleet promised immediate dividends from America's new European ally. The target of this French assistance was not to be New York City, whose narrow channels and heavy fortifications would have been problematic for the large warships of their navy to have traversed; rather, it was Rhode Island and its five-thousand man garrison under Major General Robert Pigot.[1] In the event of the French not being able to attack the Royal Navy at New York, Washington had proposed an operation against Rhode Island.

On July 22, 1778, Washington set his plan in motion, sending two brigades of Continental troops from Westchester for Rhode Island, where they would join an army forming under Major General John Sullivan, to whom Washington wrote, "You will I am well assured pursue every measure in your power that can render the enterprize happy and fortunate, and as its success will depend in a great degree on the promptness and energy of its execution, I trust the conduct will answer the spirit and hopes of the expedition."[2]

Indeed, expectations for success were high, given the thousands of Continental and militia forces gathering under Sullivan, joined to a French fleet with additional troops fresh from Europe. On August 10, 1778, Sullivan's troops crossed from the mainland and occupied the recently abandoned northern posts of the British. Admiral Richard Howe's fleet arrived off Newport soon after, causing French admiral D'Estaing with his ships and troops to sail out and seek battle. Sullivan, not wishing to prosecute a vigorous attack without the aid of his ally, settled in for a siege. Writing to Washington on the same day, Sullivan informed his commander in chief, "It is out of my Power to inform You when we shall make the Attacks on the Enemy as it is uncertain when the French Fleet will return and I think it necessary to wait their Arrival as their Troops are on board."[3]

While events transpired in New England, Washington took his forces and established a position at White Plains, in Westchester County, New York. There, north of the British lines at Kingsbridge, the Continental army was in an excellent position to await events, whatever they might be. While Washington had a force of some twenty thousand Continentals at his disposal, his force was inadequate to seriously challenge the British in their fortifications while the Royal Navy still controlled the surrounding waters.[4] Organized into sixteen brigades and supplemented by cavalry, artillery, and militia, Washington's main body was screened by a force of three thousand light troops drawn from the different brigades. Formed for the "Safety and Ease of the Army," the light infantry was "composed of the best, most hardy and active Marksmen and commanded by good Partizan Officers."[5] To the light infantry would be added detachments of cavalry drawn from the regiments of light dragoons with Washington.[6] The whole was put under the command of thirty-nine-year-old Brigadier General Charles Scott of Virginia.

This corps of light infantry was reflective of the army (and country) as a whole, drawing men together from New England to North Carolina. At a time when people identified with their state above the greater concept of a unified country, the experience could be fairly labeled a culture shock. Such was the case of Private Joseph Plumb Martin. He was a teenager from Milford, Connecticut, a veteran of about a year and a half's service in the 8th Connecticut Regiment of infantry. The war, and the army, gave him an opportunity to meet his countrymen in a way he probably could not have imagined growing up:

> There were three regiments of Light Infantry, composed of men from the whole main army. It was a motley group—Yankees, Irishmen, Buckskins and what not. The regiment that I belonged to was made up of about one half New Englanders and the remainder were chiefly Pennsylvanians—two sets of people as opposite in manners and customs as light and darkness. Consequently, there was not much cordiality subsisting between us, for, to tell the sober truth, I had in those days as lief have been incorporated with a tribe of western Indians as with any of the southern troops, especially of those which consisted mostly, as the Pennsylvanians did, of foreigners. But I was among them and in the same regiment too, and under their officers (but the officers, in general, were gentlemen) and had to do duty with them. To make a bad matter worse, I was often, when on duty, the only Yankee that happened to be on the same tour for several days together. "The bloody Yankee," or "the d——d Yankee," was the mildest epithets that they would bestow upon me at such times. It often made me think of home, or at least of my regiment of fellow Yankees.[7]

The duties of Scott's corps consisted of patrolling the Westchester countryside between Washington's headquarters and White Plains, preventing desertion from his camp, gaining intelligence of British movements, and perhaps ambushing an unsuspecting foray of British troops. The ground they covered in Westchester has often been referred to as the neutral ground, meaning an area between the warring parties. The term is somewhat misleading, as the inhabitants living there definitely favored one side or another; the hard part for Scott's men was determining which side that was. How divided the loyalties of the inhabitants were is best exemplified by the fact that the county had two competing militia forces, both highly effective, one fighting for the United States under Colonels Joseph Drake, James Hammond, Thomas Thomas, and Pierre Van Cortland; and one fighting for Great Britain under Colonel James DeLancey, Lieutenant Colonel Isaac Hatfield, and Major Mansfield Baremore. These men on each side would fight each other regardless of the presence of large standing armies that would otherwise subvert their actions to the main army's campaign, but for now they simply added another layer to the greater civil war raging around them.

Sullivan's failure to act in Rhode Island without the assistance of the full French force gave Clinton the time to undertake an expedition to relieve General Pigot and the British garrison. For his part, Clinton could deploy his own light troops to counter Scott's, keeping Westchester in a state of turmoil. While Clinton would be taking the two battalions of British light infantry among the four thousand troops in his relief of Rhode Island, the forces he left behind at Kingsbridge were among the most active in the army, under very capable commanders. While regular battalions of British, Hessians, and Provincials manned the fortifications and lines anchored on Fort Knyphausen, formerly Fort Washington, the light troops screened the front of Kingsbridge, the northernmost outpost of British-held New York City. Of the four corps that composed this light force, none were British, but rather Hessian and Provincial. The German contingent consisted of foot and mounted Jägers (riflemen), while the Provincials fielded the Queen's American Rangers (commonly known as the Queen's Rangers), British Legion, and Emmerick's Chasseurs, all of which had infantry and cavalry components. The esprit of these units was exemplified by the words of the British Legion's commander, Colonel Lord William Cathcart, who described his corps as "ready at all Times to be *Enfants*

Pardus—to be like Fireships to expose themselves for the rest of the Army."[8]

That the two sides would meet and clash was inevitable. Washington was desperately seeking information on Clinton's movements, particularly as they related to the ongoing Siege of Rhode Island. Spies, officers, and ordinary residents made constant sightings of ships heading east in Long Island Sound, some with troops, others with forage. One observer, George Hurlbut of New Rochelle, New York, reported to Washington on August 30 that he had counted, at different times during that day, eight sloops, one schooner, one transport, and a twenty-gun warship heading east through the sound.[9] Minor skirmishes between Scott's light infantry and detachments of Emmerick's Chasseurs and the Hessian Jägers had already transpired as the Continental troops extended farther and farther toward the British lines to gather intelligence on these movements. On August 31, however, each side would be bloodied in turn in one of the more unusual encounters of the war.

Early that August Monday morning, a detachment of 115 Hessian Jägers under Captain Carl Moritz von Donop headed north from the British lines. In what is now Yonkers, along the Hudson River, about two miles or less from the manor house of Loyalist Frederick Philipse, there lay in ambush a force of Continental light infantry commanded by Colonel Mordecai Gist of the 3rd Maryland Regiment. Waiting until the Hessians were within range, the Continentals rose up and fired into the green-coated riflemen. According to Jäger captain Johann Ewald, this surprise killed six and wounded six more, with four others being taken prisoner.[10] Wishing to extricate himself from the trap, Donop led his survivors rapidly back the way they had come, fighting their way through and retreating to Kingsbridge.

Unfortunately for Scott's command, their moment of triumph was short lived. The light corps of the British assembled at Kingsbridge were commanded by some of Britain's most active officers, men never looking to shirk a fight. The three Provincial light corps at Kingsbridge—the Queen's Rangers, British Legion, and Emmerick's Chasseurs—although raised in America over the previous two years and composed principally of Loyalists, were all commanded by European officers. Provincial units had been raised in the colonies throughout the eighteenth century as necessity required, most recently during the French and Indian War. Unlike the standing army of Great Britain, Provincials were raised only during times of hostilities and disbanded at the end of the year or the end of the conflict. When rebellion broke out in 1775, London had no doubt it could raise thousands of men once again in America, and, to one degree or another, it was correct. These units were uniformed, armed, paid, provisioned, trained, and disciplined the same as the British regular troops, but their term of service was only for the duration of the war.

While the majority of the officers were American Loyalists, the British used the opportunity to advance deserving junior officers from the regulars into Provincial units. This benefitted the new corps by giving them experienced, professional officers and likewise expedited the officers' promotions to higher positions. The Queen's Rangers, a corps originally raised in 1776 by the veteran Robert Rogers, had gone through a succession of regular officers after Rogers proved unfit for command, culminating in the appointment of John Graves Simcoe, a captain in the 40th Regiment, to command the corps.[11] Simcoe initially jumped from captain to major, and in less than a year, Clinton not only promoted him to lieutenant colonel but antedated his date of rank to supersede all other Provincial officers of the same rank to ensure his seniority.[12]

Simcoe's newest close friend was another regular officer promoted to lieutenant colonel in the Provincials, Banastre Tarleton. The son of a wealthy Liverpool family and a twenty-two-year-old cornet in the 1st Dragoon Guards, Tarleton volunteered for service in America because his own regiment remained in Great Britain. Attaching himself as a volunteer to the 16th Light Dragoons, Tarleton made a quick name for himself by aiding in the capture of Continental major general Charles Lee at Basking Ridge, New Jersey.[13] Appointed major of brigade to the two cavalry regiments, he no doubt became friends with William Cathcart, a captain in the 17th Light Dragoons. Like Simcoe, Tarleton was recognized as a talented officer in need of much higher rank than the British army could provide at that time. His friend Cathcart was a fellow up-and-comer, and together in July 1778 they raised a Provincial regiment, the British Legion, with Cathcart promoted to colonel and Tarleton as his lieutenant colonel.[14] Simcoe, only two years older than Tarleton, immediately bonded with the dashing young cavalry officer. "[I]n Tarleton, he had a colleague, full of enterprise and spirit, and anxious for every opportunity of distinguishing himself."[15]

The third Provincial commander was radically different from Tarleton and Simcoe. Andreas Emmerick (or Emmerich) was a forty-one-year-old professional German officer, a veteran Hessian partisan who had served against the French in the Seven Years' War. Prior to the American Revolution, Emmerick was in England serving as deputy surveyor general of His Majesty's Woods and Parks, after having served in a similar capacity in Westphalia. Emmerick apparently volunteered in April 1776 to carry dispatches to America and serve as a volunteer in whatever capacity was available.[16] He arrived in time to take part in the New York City Campaign, and General Howe appointed him to command the corps of Guides & Pioneers, where he was praised for his "Spirit, Diligence & fidelity."[17]

Returning to England in early 1777, Emmerick requested to raise a corps of one thousand men in Germany, consisting of three hundred chasseurs (light infantry), three hundred hussars (light cavalry), and four hundred grenadiers (heavy infantry).[18] Conceiving that the corps would cost a fortune to raise, and probably not having confidence in Emmerick to complete it, the British declined the offer, and Emmerick went back to America to once again serve as a volunteer.[19] His chance to lead a light corps came on August 21, 1777, when Clinton, commanding at New York in the absence of Howe on the Philadelphia expedition, appointed Emmerick to command one hundred men drawn from existing Provincial units then serving at Kingsbridge.[20] In April 1778, after eight months of constant attrition, Emmerick was granted a warrant to raise a corps of two troops of light dragoons and six companies of infantry.[21] Even though the corps of Simcoe, Tarleton, and Emmerick more or less resembled each other as cavalry-infantry units, the friendship that existed between the first two men does not seem to have been extended to the third, with Emmerick perhaps feeling a sense of professional resentment with men much younger than him serving as his equal or, in Simcoe's case, his superior.

On the heels of the ambush of the Hessian Jägers, Simcoe, Tarleton, and Emmerick convened a quick meeting to see if there was an opportunity to turn the tables on Scott's Continental light troops. That afternoon, Simcoe, as senior officer, led the three Provincial light corps, along with a detachment of about seventy-four officers and men of the 2nd Battalion, DeLancey's Brigade, and two companies of Jägers in support, clandestinely to Valentine's Hill, just north of Mile Square in Westchester.[22] Using the hill and surrounding woods to advantage, Simcoe sought to lure any rebel patrol down the road intersecting the country, while Provincials made their way behind them as they passed. The plan went awry almost immediately. Directed by Simcoe to lie in ambush at the home of Frederick Devoe, Emmerick advanced his corps to the left of the hill and halted at the Devoe house. Unfortunately for Emmerick, this was the Daniel Devoe house, not the Frederick Devoe house, which was farther ahead and more suitable for getting in the rear of an advancing enemy. To compound the mistake, Emmerick sent a small patrol directly on the road, which would have tipped off any enemy coming down the road from advancing into the trap. The patrol, not encountering any enemy force, returned to Emmerick, who put his rifle, light infantry, and chasseur companies on the left, and his two troops of light dragoons and some light infantry behind and to the right as a reserve, with the two companies of Jägers in between. The two troops of British Legion cavalry (a third was not present) and the Queen's Rangers were concealed in the woods to the right. It is not known what position DeLancey's Brigade took, but it may have been in reserve or covering another avenue of advance or retreat.

One Continental corps in particular under Scott's command was especially dreaded by some of the men in Simcoe's force. Eleven days before the intended ambush, Emmerick had led a patrol of his light infantry company under Lieutenant George Welbank toward East Chester, where it was set upon by a party of Indians in the Continental service.[23] Hearing the firing from Emmerick's patrol, about sixty-five Hessians under Captain Ewald of the Jägers and some Queen's Rangers under Simcoe raced to his assistance. Catching sight of the reinforcements, the Indians withdrew. Ewald, in his usual manner of inflating numbers, wrote that Emmerick had lost over twenty men, but the newspapers and muster rolls agree the number was one killed and three wounded or taken.[24] News of the new enemy force operating under Washington spread quickly among the British troops around Kingsbridge. "Lt. Col. Simcoe understood that Nimham, an Indian chief, and some of his tribe, were with the enemy; and by his spies, who were excellent, he was informed that they were highly elated at the retreat of Emmerick's corps, and applied it to the whole of the light troops at Kingsbridge."[25] Now, on August 31, Ewald well remembered the Indian force: "[T]he enemy was said to be two thousand strong and had the Indian tribe, toward which our men showed some fear because it had been described to them as more dangerous than it really was."[26] Who were these Indians in a theater so far removed from the frontiers of New York and Pennsylvania, fighting on the side opposed by the majority of native tribes?

Certainly one of the more unusual groups of Washington's army in summer 1778 was a small band of forty to sixty Stockbridge Indians. These men were primarily Mohicans, settled in Stockbridge, Massachusetts, during the mid-1700s. These warriors were commanded by a father and son, Daniel and Abraham Nimham, their chief sachems, or leaders. If Congress found uniforming soldiers difficult, it knew next to nothing about supplying the needs of an Indian tribe. Abraham Nimham personally traveled to Philadelphia to petition Congress for clothing: "[T]hey are at present not fit to go into the service, for want of comfortable Cloathing. We Indians have no wool nor flax, nor do we understand how to manifacture them to supply our own . . . neither can we find it any where about us for money."[27] Captain Ewald would soon have an opportunity to examine the warriors of this corps close up, and wrote of them:

> Their costume was a shirt of coarse linen down to the knees, long trousers also of linen down to the feet, on which they wore shoes of deerskin, and the head was covered with a hat made of bast. Their weapons were a rifle or a musket, a quiver with some twenty arrows, and a short battle-axe which they know how to throw very skillfully. Through the nose and in the ears they wore rings, and on their heads only the hair of the crown remained standing in a circle the size of a dollar-piece, the remainder being shaved off bare. They pull out with pincers all the hairs of the beard, as well as those on all other parts of the body.[28]

It was this small corps, joined to about forty light infantry under Major John Stewart of the 2nd Maryland Regiment, that would be so unfortunate as to encounter Simcoe's force that August day.

Emmerick, by placing his infantry at the wrong Devoe house, enabled Nimham's force to discover and push it at the start of the engagement. Stewart left the Indians on their own, his men taking a position on their left, but not engaged with Emmerick's corps. Following his original instructions to draw the enemy in, Emmerick and his infantry retreated "by degrees" until the Indians were close to the rest of the Crown forces. Simcoe, wanting a good view of the battlefield, climbed halfway up a tree, on the top of which was a young drummer of the rangers feeding his commanding officer information. Sensing the time was right to move, Simcoe ordered the rangers infantry to move ahead, while Tarleton and his two troops of cavalry and one troop of Queen's Rangers hussars moved off to the right to clear a line of fences in his front. After diverting the bulk of the rangers infantry under Major John Ross to advance toward Stewart's light infantry, Simcoe personally took the grenadier company of the rangers and advanced on the flank of the Indians, getting within ten yards without being perceived. Intent on attacking Emmerick's corps, the Indians did not notice Simcoe until too late. Turning and giving "a yell," the Indians fired and

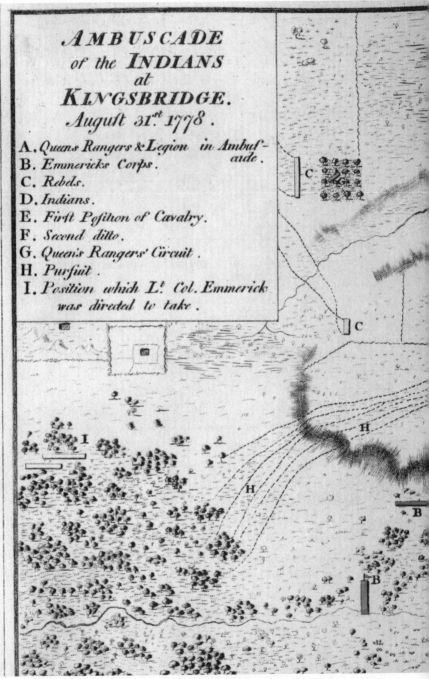

MAP 1. "Ambuscade of the Indians at Kingsbridge. August 31st 1778."

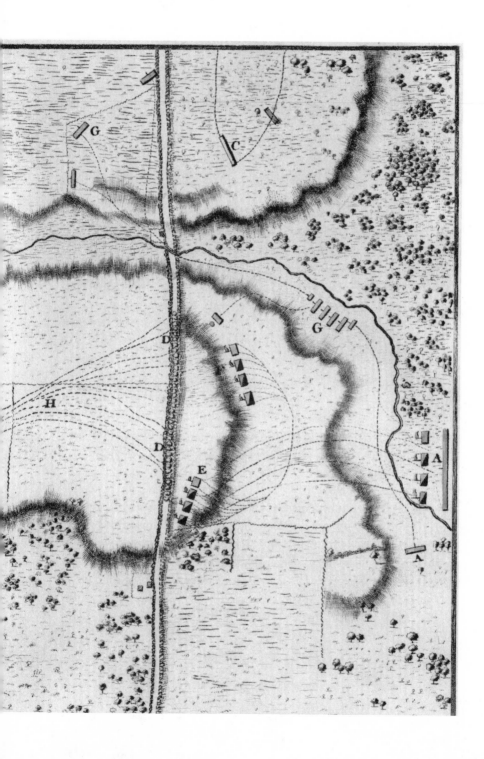

wounded four grenadiers, and Simcoe himself was wounded by Daniel Nimham.[29] Calling to his people, the chief yelled at them to fly, "that he was old and would stand and die there," which he then did, struck down by Simcoe's orderly, Private Edward Wight of the hussars.[30] It was then that the cavalry struck.

Accounts of the cavalry attack differ. An officer of Emmerick's insisted that Emmerick himself "ordered a charge by his own dragoons, accompanied by those of the legion."[31] Simcoe would later make no mention of Emmerick or his cavalry. Ewald noted the cavalry of Emmerick and the legion in the attack, but made no mention of the troop of rangers.[32] Whatever the case, the Indians now had to contend with approximately 175 saber-wielding cavalry crashing down on them, supported by infantry. The Indians fought back heroically, as credited by all those who fought against them. Tarleton, at the head of his cavalry, was unseated by an Indian while in the act of striking at him and was only saved because the Indian had no bayonet on his unloaded musket. The cavalry broke the Indian line, which then gave way and attempted a retreat to the woods. For most it was too late; they were cut down where they stood. Simcoe, though wounded, rejoined the rangers infantry and pushed after Stewart's light infantry, which fled after being attacked by at least seven times its number. Stewart's force left a wounded Captain Nathan Goodale of the 5th Massachusetts Regiment behind, a prisoner to Simcoe's force.[33]

By the end of the day it was all over, except to count the casualties. Accounts of the Indians' losses vary widely, generally from seventeen to thirty-seven killed, including both Nimhams and the rest of their leaders. Captain Johann Heinrichs of the Jägers wrote to Germany that "Twenty seven Indians with their captain were cut down with the sabre."[34] Thomas Devoe, a descendent of the Devoe family that lived at the battlefield, in 1880 recalled a conversation he had fifty-five years earlier with a woman who had been living there at the time. She told him:

Several of the wounded soldiers were taken to the houses of Frederick and Daniel DeVoe, where their wounds were dressed and cared for, and one poor Indian was brought to the latter's house—a most distressing looking object—having one side of his head or face cleaved down by a sabre cut almost to the chin; here he was nursed several weeks, when he was able to get away to some of his comrades north, where he finally got well, but with a face frightfully disfigured. Others were afterwards found maimed; the old Chief, Ninham, was so badly wounded that he must have soon after died; yet before his death he was able to crawl down the hill to a running brook, towards Jesse Husted's house, where his body was afterwards found by the peculiar action of the house dogs, which led to the suspicion that they had eaten human flesh. They were followed, when the remains of Ninham's body, which had been nearly devoured by the dogs, were found, and also the mutilated bodies of two or three more; all of which were buried in the "Indian Field," and a number of large stones piled on their graves, not as a monument, but to protect the bodies from further desecration.[35]

The action was not without cost to Simcoe and his command. Six of the Queen's Rangers were wounded besides Simcoe, who received a blow to his arm.[36] Two cavalrymen in the British Legion were killed, Sergeant Thomas Wood and Private Thomas Mullen, both of whom had only just enlisted and had a combined four weeks of experience in the army.[37] From Emmerick's Chasseurs, twenty-one-year-old John Crawford, a Connecticut carpenter turned cavalry corporal, lost his left arm in the action, a wound that did not necessitate his discharge from the army for another fourteen months and did not stop him from being promoted to sergeant.[38]

The first that General Scott knew of the affair was when the initial survivors trickled into his camp. After dispatching three hundred men under Colonel Richard Parker of the 1st Virginia Regiment to secure the remainder of Stewart's command, Scott wrote bleakly to Washington to inform him of the defeat:

"There are not more than fourteen Indians Yet com in. Among the missing is Capt. Nimham his father and the whole of the officers of that Corps. Majr. Steward tells me that he misses a Capt.,

Sub[altern] & about twenty men from his parties. I am in Hopes it is not so bad as it at Present appears But I cant promise myself that it will be much Short of it."[39]

British lieutenant general Charles, Lord Cornwallis, in a letter written to the still-absent Clinton, reported twenty to thirty of the enemy killed, "mostly Indians," and a New England captain and a few others captured. He particularly noted Tarleton and his cavalry "sabred many."[40] With no formal casualty report having been made out, and with no two British reports close to agreeing, it is unknown what the final losses to Scott's command were.

No reply from Washington to Scott has been found. In the grand context of the war, the skirmish was inconsequential. Given Washington's plans, or perhaps hopes, for the days and weeks ahead, the issue probably faded from mind quickly.

Three

The Woman

W ASHINGTON COULD AFFORD TO SHRUG OFF THE DEFEAT OF
Nimham's and Stewart's light troops that August day, for
his thoughts were strategic, not tactical. The British commander in
chief and thousands of his troops were off attempting to rescue
Rhode Island from General John Sullivan's besieging forces and
their new French allies. Reports from spies and deserters indicated
that another, much larger embarkation was imminent. Was the
Revolution about to end victoriously, and relatively quickly, for the
new United States? Washington's task at hand was to figure out
how to take advantage of the situation and hasten the end of the
war.

That last week of August, Washington drafted an audacious plan
for his army at White Plains to seize northern Manhattan and hope-
fully New York City itself. After leaving guards and garrisons in the
Hudson Highlands and other critical locations, Washington could
probably field an army of fifteen thousand to eighteen thousand
men with which to attack the British. Included in this would be
artillerymen, cavalry, boatmen, and wagoners, besides militia and

followers of the army. With the absence of Clinton and his four thousand men sent to the relief, hundreds more soldiers serving as marines in Admiral Howe's fleet, and a thousand Provincials and militia off on Long Island's east end foraging in Suffolk County under Major General William Tryon, the British may have actually appeared vulnerable to Washington. British troops were scattered in camps throughout western Long Island, Brooklyn, Staten Island, Paulus Hook (modern-day Jersey City), Sandy Hook, and of course Manhattan Island. The troops left behind, present and fit for duty, exclusive of Tryon's force, amounted to about seventeen thousand five hundred.[1] In addition, the British could embody perhaps twenty-five hundred Loyalist militia and volunteer companies in the areas they controlled, but much like the militia serving under Washington, their zeal, discipline, and reliability would vary widely.

The British strength in defending New York had never relied primarily on the army but rather the rivers, creeks, bays, and sounds that surrounded their islands, and the warships that patrolled them. The Royal Navy had been indispensable in allowing the army under General Howe to defeat Washington and capture New York City. It allowed Howe the flexibility to strike at places and times of his choice, never allowing Washington to concentrate his force or take the offensive. After the fall of Fort Washington at the northern end of Manhattan, the British had a complete barrier of water around their New York possessions. The two British posts in New Jersey—Paulus Hook along the Hudson opposite Manhattan and Sandy Hook at the northern end of the Jersey Shore—were never in serious danger of being overwhelmed as long as the Royal Navy was there to support, or, if need be, evacuate them.[2] Whatever fleet of galleys and small ships was at Washington's disposal in 1776 was mostly lost during that campaign, and other than boats to transport men and material across the river in the Hudson Highlands, no shipping on hand could challenge British dominance on the water.

Washington's full plans for an attack on the British lines are not known, but a partial draft does exist among his papers. Washington's hopes would be placed on two thousand men in two divisions, one commanded by General Scott, the other by Brigadier General Anthony Wayne, and the whole under Major General Alexander McDougall. Scott was already an experienced commander of light troops. Wayne was a Chester County, Pennsylvania, surveyor and politician who, on January 1, 1776, was commissioned colonel of the 1st Pennsylvania Regiment. After he served that year in Canada with the Northern Army, the following year saw him fighting much closer to home. On September 20, 1777, at Paoli, his command was surprised in a night attack by the British light infantry under Major General Charles Grey and was severely defeated. Wayne continued his aggressive style of command for the remainder of the war, in 1779 successfully surprising and taking the impressive British fortifications at Stony Point, but the following year suffering considerable losses to a much inferior force of Loyalist woodcutters at Bulls Ferry, New Jersey.[3] McDougall was a forty-seven-year-old native of Scotland whose family settled in New York in 1740. An original firebrand of the Revolution, McDougall raised the 1st New York Regiment in 1775, then was promoted to brigadier general the following year and major general the year after that. McDougall later went into politics. He died in 1786.[4]

The task of these officers would be Herculean if executed. Not only were these troops to capture all the outer works and forts above and below Fort Washington (renamed Fort Knyphausen by the British, in honor of that officer's role in taking the fort), but they were to go after that major fortification itself, with a detachment to "Land in the Cove under Fort Washington & endeavour to surprise it." McDougall was to capture the forts below, in the neighborhood of today's northern Central Park, "then act from Circumstances, keeping these as places of security & retreat." Artillerists were to accompany the troops, to man the captured guns of each fortification. It was only then that the three main divisions of the army under Washington would advance to attack the even-more-numerous forts, redoubts, and blockhouses ringing Kingsbridge, one "to endeavour to surprise the Redout No. 1—a Detach. from the 2nd line is to attempt Fort Independence" and so on. The entire plan depended not only on complete surprise but on little or no opposition by the thousands of British, Hessian, and Provincial troops manning the works and on there being no British vessels in the river to engage these troops. What was to be done after all these forts were taken is unknown, as the draft ends there.[5]

Washington was not so foolish as to decide on something this bold on his own. Seeking the advice of all the generals then present with his army, he laid out all the facts of the situation in a council of war, one of many he convened during the war. Prior to setting forth his proposals, he briefed the officers on the current state of affairs and the latest intelligence of the enemy situation. Setting forth the options left open to the army as he saw them, he then asked the generals for a written reply with their thoughts, opinions, and more or less a vote on how to proceed. The defeat of the detachment under Nimham and Stewart was of relatively minor concern given the more important news Washington received on August 31 and shared at his council of war at White Plains the following day, namely, that a dispatch had arrived from General Sullivan, commanding at Rhode Island, informing him that his forces had given up the siege and retreated to the mainland after a hard-fought battle against the pursuing British at Quaker Hill. The raising of the siege and withdrawal of Sullivan's force, coupled with the removal of D'Estaing's storm- and battle-damaged fleet, left Clinton free to act offensively with his four thousand embarked troops at a time and place of his choosing. Washington therefore asked each of his general officers these questions:

> 1st Whether any operations can be undertaken at the present juncture by this Army, and of what kind? Whether a movement of the whole or a principal part of it to the Eastward, will be advisable and afford a prospect of advantage?
>
> 2nd In case a movement to the Eastward should be thought proper what measures and precautions should be taken for the security of the Highland passes?
>
> 3rd Or whether an attempt with such a probability of success as will justify it, can be made upon New York in its present circumstances?[6]

Whether he truly wanted a bold stroke at New York or simply wanted to test the temper of his senior officers, the answers that came back showed a streak of caution that perhaps surprised Washington. Of the nineteen generals present, all but two returned their answers the following day.[7] While a few supported moving a few brigades toward Rhode Island, only Major General Benjamin Lincoln favored moving the bulk of the army to the east, thinking, as several did, that Boston may be a target of Clinton and his reinforcement.[8] Most thought that any raid Clinton could muster would be accomplished before Washington's troops would be near enough to intervene, and if Boston was an object, Sullivan's force and New England militia would suffice. The common view among the generals was that there were no compelling reasons for Clinton to attack New England.

If the prospect of moving toward Rhode Island generated little enthusiasm, the idea of attacking the lines at Kingsbridge was met with almost universal disapproval. Major General William Alexander, also known as Lord Stirling, spoke for many when he wrote that any attack on the British lines was "futile and extremely dangerous."[9] The generals correctly observed that an attack on the lines at Kingsbridge would serve little to no strategic purpose, as any works captured could not be held because of the rivers controlled by the Royal Navy. A second factor was the want of intelligence in knowing precisely what Clinton and his four thousand men would do now that Rhode Island was secure. Many felt he would simply return to New York, in which case a move by Washington's force against the British lines was in danger of being taken in the flank or rear by the returning British. Accurate intelligence was not wanting just concerning Clinton's movements but for all other aspects of the Crown forces at this time, particularly the overall strength of the British forces, where exactly they were, and a precise knowledge of the works at Kingsbridge.

Whatever may be said for Washington's spy rings during the war, during this period, the edge in intelligence gathering definitely tilted toward the British. General Scott, commanding the light infantry on the lines, was tasked with gathering whatever intelligence could be

gained from Long Island and New York City. To this end, he
employed senior Continental army officers in the hazardous task of
going to the lines, or behind them, either gaining firsthand knowledge or meeting spies who had come out from British-held territory. On September 3, Scott made a familiar report to Washington:
"Capt. [Eli] Levensworth returnd last night but Was not able to
procure any Intelligence material, he Is again gon to meet another
person whom he expects from Whitestone. Colo. [Morris]
Grayham also expects to meet a person from New York this
Day."[10] The previous day, Scott had conceded that no one could be
prevailed on to actually go onto Long Island to gather information.[11] For the time being, the army of the United States would rely
on what it could see from its lines, the occasional British deserter,
and newspapers smuggled out of New York City.

The British, on the other hand, had an extensive network in place
to give them up-to-date information on Washington's movements
and the state of his army. The most numerous sources were escaped
prisoners, residents bringing goods into New York for trade or sale,
and deserters from the Continental army. Responsibility for conducting interviews and collating the various accounts rested with a
small cadre of officers in the British Adjutant General's Department,
along with a handful of senior Provincial officers such as Colonel
Beverley Robinson of Dutchess County, New York. Robinson, an
old friend of George Washington's when both men lived in Virginia,
had been late in declaring for the British, not joining them until April
1777. When he did step forward, however, he did so wholehearted-
ly, raising a corps, the Loyal American Regiment, composed primarily of his Dutchess and Westchester neighbors and including numerous members of his own family.[12]

The reliability of information gleaned from deserters is always
problematic: are they relating an accurate picture of the army they
left, a snapshot of their immediate situation, or simply saying what
they believe their new superiors wish to hear? The British seldom
relied on one or two accounts to formulate any opinions; rather,
they gathered all the accounts into books and looked for a prepon-
derance of accounts, or patterns. In other words, if one deserter

said his regiment had five hundred men but five others put it at four hundred, the accounts of those five would outweigh that of the one. An example of what the British were learning from Washington's former soldiers is well exemplified by three deserters from Scott's command who arrived at the British lines in late August 1778:

Thos. Bradly Irish man 2nd Battn. Pensylvania Regt. Col. Walter Stuart—above 2 years in the Service, that 9 or 10 Days ago there was a Detachment formed from the army consisting of Nearly 2500 which are comd. by Gl. Scot marched from the W[hite] plains & are Encamped 5 miles from thence, which place he left last night Saturday 22nd [August] 7 in the Evening.
Their Numbers 17000 including militia. The Language amongst them before he left the camp That Sullivan had met with a check at R Island—that he had wrote for a Reinformt. in consequence the Congress Regt. was sent.
    John Mackish from Pensylvania of the 9th Pensylvania Regt. Col. Richard Butler—13 months in the Service, was one of those drafted for the L[ight] Infantry Corps—The same story & came in at The same time.
    John McClachlin—Irish—the 9th Pensyla. Regt.—two years in the Service also drafted for the L.I. nearly the same story.
    The Park of Artillery they all agree were 38 pieces including 4 Howitzers.
    2 months pay were given them about 10 days ago.
    The 4 & 8 Pensylvania Regts. were ordered from camp sometime before They left it in order to oppose [Major John] Butler & the Indians.[13]

These accounts show the strength of Washington's army both in terms of manpower and artillery, that a light infantry corps had been formed and detached, that it was commanded by General Scott, where the army was encamped, and what detachments had been made for other areas of operation, namely the frontiers of New York, Pennsylvania, and Rhode Island. This information was recorded and then compared to other sources of information, prin-

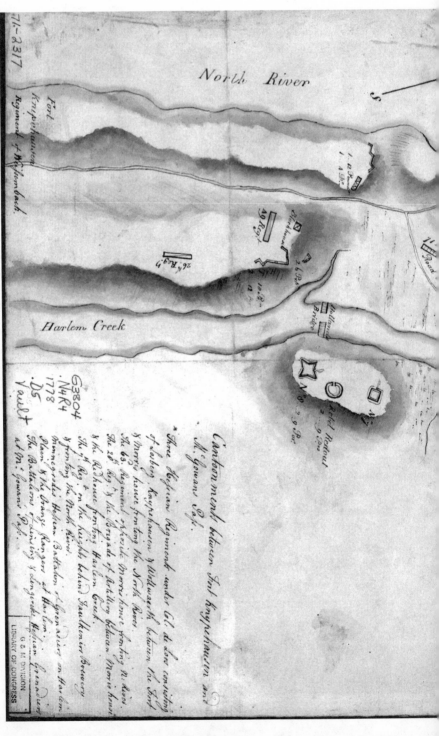

MAP 2. Disposition of British troops, with fortifications north of "Fort Knypehausen" (Fort Washington) to Kingsbridge and Fort Independence, c. 1778. (*Library of Congress*)

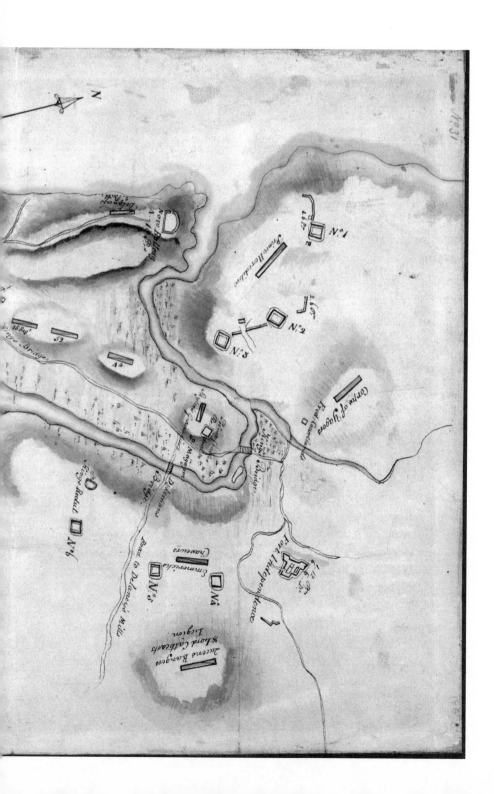

cipally from a reliable spy network the British had established for the Hudson Valley. Of the three principal spies lurking around Washington's camp, two were Provincial soldiers. Emmanuel Ellerbeck of Poughkeepsie was a private in Captain Bernard Kane's company of the New York Volunteers, ostensibly "recruiting at Kingsbridge" while his corps was serving at the time on Long Island.[14] Wynant Williams had served as a sergeant since April 18, 1777, in Thomas Barclay's company of Beverley Robinson's Loyal American Regiment.[15] Like Ellerbeck, Williams was a resident of Dutchess County, residing at Nine Partners when the war broke out. Dispatched to White Plains to "discover the Strength and movements of the American Army, in that neighbourhood" he was discovered and jailed for a dozen days before escaping and making his way back to the British.[16] While these Loyalists may have been useful, having fit men of military age lurking around an army would almost certainly draw suspicion. For this reason, the British employed perhaps their most effective spy of the war, and she soon proved her worth.

At the start of the American Revolution, Ann Bates hardly fit the profile of a spy, being a Philadelphia schoolteacher earning a modest living.[17] She was the wife of Joseph Bates, an armorer in the Civil Branch of the Royal Artillery Regiment, and it is unclear how or why she made the transformation from teacher to spy. But after she arrived at New York following the evacuation of Philadelphia, that is exactly what happened. Recruited at Kingsbridge by Major Nesbit Balfour of the 23rd Regiment of Foot, she was brought to headquarters and introduced to Major Duncan Drummond. Drummond was an artillery officer until becoming an aide-de-camp to Clinton on May 30, 1778.[18] Once he joined the commander in chief's military family, Drummond was entrusted with the purse strings for gathering intelligence. By July 1778, Bates was ready to undertake her first mission, and a complex one it was. Leaving camp on July 29, she was to travel to White Plains and make contact with Captain Stephen Chambers of the 12th Pennsylvania Regiment and inform him that Vice Admiral John Byron was expected any moment. After that she was to ascertain the strength of Washington's army and his intentions for them. On August 5, the spy only referred to in reports as "the woman" returned to be debriefed by Drummond. After informing her handler that Chambers was no longer with the army, she gave a report describing Washington's force as twenty-three-thousand strong, "boys included." [19] She observed that there were no fortifications and that the men were "better cloathed & look better than usual" down to their food (meat, shad fish, and bread). She even spotted the Stockbridges' "9 Indian Tents."[20] The account Bates recorded later when seeking financial compensation for her services corresponds very closely to that written by Drummond, except in more vivid detail and specificity:

> I Proceeded on my journey to the River Crosswicks the Bridge being broke down I waded through up to my armpits, and arrived at the Rebel Camp the 2nd July [August], but the Officer I wanted had (to my great Disappointment) resign'd his Commission so that I could not Execute my design of gaining the position and Strength of the Rebel Army in the manner first propos'd. I then Divided my little Stock [ribbons, thread, needles, combs, knives, etc. previously purchased "to sell in the Rebel Camp"] in Different lots as near as I could form an Idea of their Number of Brigades allowing one lot for Sale in Each Brigade, by which means I had the Opportunity of going through their whole army remarking at the same time the strength & Situation of each Brigade, & the Number of Cannon with their Situation & weight of Ball each Cannon was Charged with[;] going through their Lines I met a Person I was well acquainted with, & by Conversation I found he would suit any purpose and being a freemason gave him what money I made of my Goods that he might attend the Lodge & get acquainted with the Commissaries Clerk who was also a freemason and keep Company with such as would be likely to know the state of affairs. This Succeeded to my Expectation he gave me Information that a Deserter from Captain James's Company of the Legion had come from them & that the whole Company intended likewise the first Opportunity

with their Stores & Accoutrements. I likewise Learn't that 25 Men from each Brigade was drafted with proper Officers to Intercept the English Scouting Parties[;] furnish'd with these Intelligences, I was returning with Expedition to New York but was unluckily taken prisoner by a Rebel party within four miles of White Plaines and was there Confin'd and a woman Strip'd me Naked and Searched every article of my apparel but finding nothing to ground any Suspision after taking from me a pair of Silver Shoe Buckles which cost me two Guineas, a Silver Thimble & a Silk Barcelona Handkerchief with three Dollars in Cash, & a Day & a Night's Confinement I was set at Liberty when I made the best of my way to New York & got there without any further Interruption.[21]

Washington then had no such reliable clandestine service to accurately judge future British intentions and movements. With his generals uneager for offensive operations, the future cooperation of Admiral D'Estaing and the French fleet (then refitting at Boston) uncertain, plus the unknown intentions of the British commander in chief with an army of four thousand men onboard ship, the only logical, safe course of action was to retire into the Hudson Highlands and await events. General Sullivan, then at Providence, was feeding Washington updates on the British fleet in his neighborhood but could give no real intelligence on where they were headed or what their plans were. The best Washington could do was send a few brigades under Major General Horatio Gates to the east. Not willing to be caught short in case of deception, Washington rethought the matter and halted Gates's march within a day of its departure. These men would eventually form the left of the Continental army, anchoring the line at Danbury, Connecticut.[22]

On September 14, a British deserter arrived, informing General Scott that the only British north of Kingsbridge were about two thousand men, "Some red Coats and Greens."[23] Sensing the time was right, Washington issued orders the following day that the army would move north in three columns, with the new headquarters in Fredericksburg, New York. Being located in Fredericksburg, between Fishkill, New York, and Danbury, Connecticut, would enable Washington to draw his force to protect the Hudson or the important supply depots to the east, which had been attacked by the British under General Tryon in April 1777. Covering the pull-back of the army would be Scott and his light corps, to which Washington would add all the cavalry on the east side of the Hudson River. The light troops would take up a new position at Bedford or North Castle, or some other such strong post as Scott saw fit. Still unable to understand British intentions, Washington even optimistically left instructions for what to do if the British evacuated New York, saying one hundred men under an intelligent officer should be sent "with orders to secure on behalf of the U.S. whatever public Stores the enemy may have left—And give imme-diate notice to the Governor of this State [New York] that he may take his measures for the civil Government of the territory aban-doned by the Enemy."[24]

The British would be well informed on all these movements, for on September 11, "the woman" Ann Bates showed up at White Plains. Immediately on her arrival she witnessed the first movement of the army: the removal of the sick, which Washington had ordered to Peekskill and thence to Fishkill, "amounting to 1800 men mostly Flux & Jail Fever."[25] On the sixteenth, Bates marched with one of the columns of troops heading north toward Peekskill, proceeding with the Pennsylvania Continentals until she departed from them at North Castle. Slipping off from the column, she went to a house to meet one of her handlers, a fellow Philadelphia Loyalist named John Craig. Like Bates, Craig had abandoned all his property in Pennsylvania and started a career in the secret service of the British, "always at the hazard of his Life pursuing such steps as were deemed most probable for insuring success."[26] After taking down her information, Craig sent her back to the column, where she was soon after recognized by a deserter from the British 27th Regiment. Not wasting a moment, she again departed and headed toward the British lines, where she fell in with the Continental light infantry. Impersonating a soldier's wife, she met General Scott him-self, who gave her a pass to rejoin her "husband" at White Plains.

Heading in the opposite direction, she ran into the British lines five or six miles below Scott's force, where she was taken under escort to meet General Grant, when "on the road we met the General with his Aid-de-Camp one of whom asked me if I was the Person sent out by Major Drummond, & on my answering in the affirmative he dismist my Guide & Sitting on the Stump of an Old Tree wrote down the Several Informations I had been able to obtain."[27] Bates would again be sent out, but so, too, would the light corps stationed at Kingsbridge, both in search of the Continental army.

Four

A Time for Light Troops

ORDECAI GIST WAS A THIRTY-SIX-YEAR-OLD MARYLANDER who had already distinguished himself in the war. Gist was a fervent patriot whose career path swung from commercial ventures to military training with the approach of war with Great Britain.[1] In 1775, Gist was made captain of the Baltimore Independent Company, a unit "of about sixty Gentlemen of handsome property."[2] When Maryland organized its military for service in the Continental army, Gist was commissioned major in Smallwood's Maryland Regiment, commanding it at the Battle of Brooklyn in August 1776. With the reorganization of the Continental army, this Baltimore soldier, on December 10, 1776, was commissioned colonel of his own corps, the 3rd Maryland Regiment.[3]

On September 16, the day Washington's forces were withdrawing north toward Fredericksburg and Fishkill, Gist was commanding a force of anywhere from 150 to 500 light troops near the house of a widow named Babcock, near a hill bearing the family name along the Hudson River. The position was secured by water on each

flank, which would channel any attacking force directly to their
front, provided no one was able to take a circuitous route and gain
their rear. If that happened, the position would be highly dangerous. The exact composition of Gist's force is unknown. A part of
Scott's light infantry, it included at least a component of riflemen,
some of whom had fired on a British flag of truce on the night of
September 14.[4] The riflemen who had fired, as well as others posted around Gist's position, were acting as pickets, or guards, for the
main body. Pickets were there to protect the main force from enemy
attack and deter deserters from one's own force. They were not
always successful. Through the timely arrival of a deserter from
Gist's camp, the presence of the Continental light force was known
to the British.[5] The commanders of the Crown light corps around
Kingsbridge, led by John Simcoe, quickly saw an opportunity.

The same group of Provincial commanders—Simcoe, Banastre
Tarleton, and Andreas Emmerick—once again developed a plan of
action to advance into Westchester and cut off Gist's detachment.
The key element would be covering all the escape routes, particularly those heading north and east, that might allow retreat to the
safety of the remainder of Scott's command. Early on the morning
of the sixteenth, Simcoe's command, consisting of the Queen's
Rangers, the cavalry of the British Legion, Emmerick's Chasseurs, a
detachment of the 2nd Battalion, DeLancey's Brigade, and some
Jägers, moved out from their encampments around Kingsbridge
and proceeded quietly north into Westchester. In the vanguard was
Lieutenant Colonel Emmerick with the chasseurs, a corps that
included numerous men from Westchester thoroughly familiar with
the roads and byways.[6] It was engagements like this that showed
one of the oddities of the war in America: the Crown forces consisted of men locally raised and familiar with the terrain, and their
Continental foes were in effect foreigners, men recruited in the
Middle Atlantic and unfamiliar with the Hudson Valley.

Below Gist's position, Simcoe divided his force to commence
encircling the enemy camp. The infantry of the Queen's Rangers,
along with those of Emmerick and DeLancey, slipped between two
picket guards to the east and formed a line a mile and a half to the

north, or rear, of Gist's camp. Tarleton, commanding the four or five troops of cavalry present, proceeded east to a position at Valentine's Hill, which would prevent a retreat of Gist's force toward Connecticut. The Jägers were divided into two detachments, one under Major Ernst Carl von Prueschenck, which was to guard the escape route leading northwest over Phillip's Bridge, and a smaller party under Captain Carl August von Wreden, which was to occupy Courtland's Ridge, directly to the south of Gist's camp. If the movements were carried out properly, Gist's command would be encircled.[7]

That British troops were, or were thought to be, on the move to its south was no secret to the Continental army. A report received at White Plains the night of September 13 that five thousand British troops were advancing in two columns to Mile Square threw the camp into alarm, with the troops sleeping on their arms all night.[8] The camp relaxed in the morning as it was reported that the British retired, but the entire episode seems to have been the result of bad intelligence. Gist did, however, discover Simcoe's initial advance on the night of the fifteenth, reporting it to his commander, Charles Scott, who duly informed Washington at seven thirty that evening "that there are a large partie of the enemy, out on the Albany road about a mile below Phillaps's Hous and advancing [and another] Partie was seen Going toward Volentins Hill."[9] Scott reported to Washington the next morning that enemy infantry and cavalry were at Valentine's Hill, and he was prepared to receive them.[10] The commander who apparently was not prepared to meet them, though equally warned, was Mordecai Gist. At six in the morning on September 16, Emmerick's wing advanced to the attack amid a scattered fire from Gist's pickets.[11] Hearing the opening shots of the action, Simcoe moved the Queen's Rangers from their cover and up the slope directly toward Gist's camp. Expecting to see the enemy's escape blocked, the ranger commander was shocked to see Gist's men retreat unimpeded over the unguarded Phillip's Bridge.[12]

At the first fire of their pickets, the men under Gist's command appear to have realized their dire predicament. Seeing the unguarded bridge, Captain John Odell of the Connecticut Militia funneled the fleeing troops to safety over the bridge, retreating northwest toward the Hudson River. Gist himself seems to have gotten off quite hastily, newspaper publisher James Rivington happily reporting in his *Royal Gazette* that "their Colonel in particular, scampered off without his boots or breeches, and, 'tis thought was wounded in his flight." A fanciful nineteenth century account had Gist enamored with the resident of the house on the hill that bore its name, the widow Babcock, claiming "he had barely received his final dismissal from Mrs. Babcock when he was startled with the firing of musketry."[13] With or without his breeches, Gist safely joined his men and led the survivors to safety. But where were Prueschenck and his Jägers?

For reasons known only to Prueschenck, he had decided to join his force to that of Captain Wreden, posted to the south of Babcock's Hill, in effect leaving a wide escape route for Gist and his men. Fellow Jäger captain Ewald was quick to lay blame elsewhere, claiming Emmerick had not extended his men farther to the west and not covered the bridge, but if the Jägers under Prueschenck had maintained their original post, Gist's entire command might have been picked off.[14] As it was, the action was confusing and costly for Gist and his men.

In addition to his initial losses, one of Gist's patrols, unaware of what happened, returned to camp and straight into captivity. Major Benjamin Tallmadge, commanding the 2nd Light Dragoons far to the east of Gist's original position, sent patrols to locate the British and dispatch riders with an officer to find Gist. Four and a half hours after the attack began, Tallmadge was still awaiting official word on what happened: "[A]m much surprised that no acc[oun]ts have been recd of Colo Gist" he wrote Scott.[15] Tallmadge personally rode to within a mile of Babcock's, where he met an officer of Gist's who had just escaped under fire. The officers rode north when they found Gist and the remainder of his corps at Fowlers, presumably the home of one of the members of that large Westchester County family. Gist at that time thought he may have lost twenty or so men, along with a few of the 2nd Light Dragoons who had unfortunately run into Tarleton and his cavalry near

Valentine's Hill.[16] The loss of his dragoons must have irked Tallmadge, who just eight days before lost six of his men to Simcoe, along with two commissaries and twenty-five horses, in a raid above East Chester.[17] Loyalist newspapers in New York variously put Gist's loss at two or three killed along with two or three officers and thirty men taken prisoner, at least some of whom were Marylanders.[18] Two officers taken that day appear to have been Ensign Joseph Briton of the 4th Maryland Regiment and 1st Lieutenant James Simms of the 1st Maryland.[19] The only loss of the Crown forces was one horse killed of Emmerick's.[20] After burning Gist's huts and baggage, Simcoe and the different light corps retired unopposed back to their encampments within the British lines.

General Scott sent out numerous patrols south, detached Major Henry Lee and his legion to New Rochelle, and advanced the rest of his light corps to Chatterton's Hill to secure Gist's retreat. "I believe the enemy must be Gon[e] in and what Can keep Gist I cant conceive," Scott fumed to Washington hours after the attack.[21]

The action at Babcock's in no way impeded or delayed the march of Washington's army from White Plains toward Fredericksburg. There is no evidence to suggest Simcoe's attack was considered by the British as anything more than an opportunity to strike at an advance post. For Scott and his command, it was an unpleasant reminder of the dangers and hardships of being the main army's tripwire. After securing Gist's withdrawal, Scott and the combined corps arrived at White Plains at seven o'clock that night and, without tents, lay on their arms in the rain. The fatigued Scott, surveying the situation, did what he could for his wet, tired men: "Finding them in such a Horrid Condition this morning I Bought as much rum as served each man with One gill. I was obliged to pay the enormous price of Twelve dollars a gallon for it, which I thought better Than letting the men Suffer."[22]

Scott's troops would remain in place for the time being. Despite having no bread for two days, the light corps needed to protect the removal of three hundred barrels of flour from Wright's Mills. Buying provisions from the inhabitants was not an option, as the men composing his corps, drawn from all the units of the army, had not been paid by their parent regiments, who were all with Washington. And of course, there was still the danger of Simcoe and the enemy light corps around Kingsbridge, who were only emboldened now that Washington and his main army were away and out of support range for Scott. Taking advantage of the situation, the British, starting on September 19, again pushed their light troops forward to examine what lay ahead.

The probing force for the latest foray once again consisted of the rangers, chasseurs, and legion, commanded by Simcoe, joined by a small detachment of the 17th Light Dragoons, a British regular cavalry regiment.[23] Not knowing exactly what to expect, the British sent a large force in support, advancing a number of Jägers along the Hudson River, the 71st Highlanders to Valentine's Hill, and the 63rd Regiment to their right.[24] Advancing up Mile Ward's Road, Simcoe, learning of an enemy picket two miles from White Plains, led a detachment fruitlessly in that direction.[25] The remainder of the column turned southwest, crossing the Bronx River probably around Tuckahoe and heading toward Yonkers. At three o'clock in the morning, eight horses were spotted at a house on Mile Square Road. Tarleton, in the lead, ordered a detachment of Emmerick's light dragoons forward, under the command of Lieutenants George Hustis and Benjamin Woolsey Muirson. They captured a patrol of the 2nd Light Dragoons.[26] For Scott, it was yet another minor loss to report to Washington: "A Serjeant and six Dragoons were made prisoners. The Guide escap'd. The Enemy then return'd. I am sorry for the loss of the men, but am in hopes it will be a sufficient warning to others on Duty."[27] Washington took the news stoically, by this point in the war more accustomed to minor reverses, and, through an aide, he asked Scott "to remind the Officers under your command, that our losses upon the lines have chiefly arisen from being surprised or inadvertently led into ambuscades, and he [Washington] hopes that the damage which they have sustained will be a warning in future."[28]

While each army's light corps jabbed and sparred in Westchester, the commanders of those armies attempted to grapple with much weightier issues among their own forces, and sometimes with each other. Washington wrote two letters on September 16 to his British counterpart, Clinton. One letter was simply forwarding a resolution of Congress to the Carlisle Peace Commission, of which Clinton was a member. The second of Washington's letters was more embarrassing, offering regret, if not an apology for Gist's riflemen firing on the British flag of truce; it was written while Gist's command was unknowingly under attack: "I was much concerned to hear, that one of our patroles fired on a Flag coming from your lines on monday Evening. I shall do every thing in my power to prevent the like mistake on any future occasion."[29]

Washington's issues with the British commander in chief were secondary compared to the state of disarray his own senior command was then in. It was a blessing that the British had made no serious push at Washington late that summer, as no fewer than four of his major generals were either being tried by a court-martial or were under a cloud of suspicion. Arthur St. Clair and Philip Schuyler were being tried over the loss of Fort Ticonderoga to Lieutenant General John Burgoyne's troops in July 1777. Before their trials came the trial of Charles Lee, whose apparent lack of zeal at the Battle of Monmouth in June had caused Washington to place him under arrest. The exact charges against Lee were "disobedience of orders in not attacking the Enemy on the 28th of June agreeable to repeated Instructions; For misbehaviour before the Enemy on the same day, by making an unnecessary, disorderly & shameful Retreat [and] For disrespect to the commander in chief in two Letters dated the 1st of July & the 28th of June." Lee was found guilty on August 12, 1778, and sentenced to be suspended from any command in the army for one year.[30] That sentence, however, needed confirmation by Congress, which did not come until four months after the trial, leaving Lee awkwardly in camp with the army in Westchester. On September 15, the day before the army marched from White Plains, Lee requested that Washington allow him to go to Philadelphia to await his fate, which indulgence was granted.[31]

Duels fought in December 1778 were still in the future when Washington was at White Plains. His staff had already survived a

similar incident involving yet another major general, Horatio
Gates, the man hailed as the victor of Saratoga. Gates and
Washington were by no means on good terms at this point, the lat-
ter having learned of the former's aspirations to replace him in what
came to be known the previous winter as the "Conway Cabal."
This ill-fated attempt to oust Washington was the brainchild of
Thomas Conway, an Irish adventurer and French officer turned
Continental army major general. After much flattery and insinua-
tion thrown Gates's way by Conway, the former's aide-de-camp,
Lieutenant Colonel James Wilkinson, a man of considerable noto-
riety himself, exposed the machinations secretly to General
Alexander, who promptly alerted Washington to them. Gates in
turn wrote to Washington, blaming Wilkinson. The would-be coup
dissolved under the weight of public exposure, and in February
1778, Gates and Wilkinson met to settle their differences like gentlemen: with pistols. Meeting behind the Episcopal Church of York,
Pennsylvania, at 8:00 AM, February 24, 1778, Wilkinson and Gates,
with their seconds (referred to as "friends" during the period) prepared to face off with each other but were dissuaded by the others
gathered for the occasion.[32] The matter seemingly at an end, the
would-be combatants parted, and there the matter lay.

By early September 1778, Gates was in Westchester. With plans
for an intended expedition against the Seneca tribe having been
scrapped, the former conspirator was awaiting his move east
toward Connecticut when his old antagonist Wilkinson once again
appeared on the scene, seeking to redress their past differences. On
the evening of September 4, 1778, the two met, once again accompanied by seconds, Colonel Thaddeus Kosciuszko for Gates and a
John Carter for Wilkinson. The two were ordered to fire three
times: twice Gates's pistol flashed in the pan, and once he refused
to aim; Wilkinson fired once in the air and twice at Gates, but
missed.[33] At that point, Kosciuszko and Carter intervened, and the
matter was deemed over once and for all.[34] On September 6,
Continental army hospital surgeon's mate James Thacher noted in
his journal:

A duel was fought a few days since between General G. and
Colonel W. Two shots were exchanged without bloodshed, and
a reconciliation was effected. The gentlemen, it is said, displayed
a firmness and bravery becoming their rank and character, and
have established their claim to the title of gentlemen of honor. As
their courage has never been called in question, the present ren-
contre was unneccessary, unless it be to evince that they possess
malice enough in their hearts to commit a murderous deed. The
example of superior officers will have great influence with those
of inferior rank, whether contending with the dogs of war, or in
adjusting the minor points of honor.[35]

While matters of high-ranking officers were certainly of consequence, Washington also had the stress of dealing with junior officers, Congress, and sometimes the effects of one on the other. Of
imminent concern were the amalgamation of regiments and the
ranking of officers, as related in a letter from Gist to his wife:

A Committee of Congress have been here some time endeavour-
ing to regulate the Army upon the new establishment in consequence of an arrangement in the Virginia line. The whole Corps
of Officers waited upon his Excellency with their Commissions
to resign. The Complaint was a little palliated, and they have
since returned to their duty. Never were Officers of an army so
universally dissatisfied, and if their Complaints are not redress'd,
I expect but few Gentlemen will serve longer than this
Campaign, & of course my Companions next year will not be
very agreeable.[36]

That at least could wait until the winter. Washington needed the
army to get through autumn first.

Washington's situation might have been challenging, but
Clinton's days must have seemed excruciatingly long and singular-
ly unpleasant. In order to carry out the king's instructions, a complete review of the strength of the army and each individual regiment would need to be done. This meant long hours for the adju-

tant general's office. Once the regiments to make up the different expeditions had been identified, their commanding officers needed to be notified so they would have an opportunity to purchase summer- or winter-weight clothing, depending on their destination. The ten British regiments heading to the West Indies under General Grant needed to be brought up to strength, at least as far as circumstances allowed. While prisoner exchanges that had been going on since July returned some men to their corps, hundreds more were needed. To fill the ranks of these corps, Clinton ordered the three weakest-strength regiments in the army, the 10th, 45th, and 52nd, to be drafted, that is, their effective private soldiers distributed to the ten corps under Grant. The officers, noncommissioned officers, and drummers of the three drafted regiments would return to England and recruit their regiments anew.[37]

British regiments were not the only ones that needed consolidation. No less than eight Provincial battalions were intended to leave New York: the King's Orange Rangers to Nova Scotia; the Pennsylvania and Maryland Loyalists to West Florida; and the 1st and 3rd Battalions of the New Jersey Volunteers, the New York Volunteers, and 1st and 2nd Battalions of DeLancey's Brigade for the Georgia expedition.[38] Several recently raised Provincial units were prime candidates for drafting. The West Jersey Volunteers, raised at Philadelphia in January 1778, had fallen to a strength of less than 175 officers and men after having suffered numerous desertions on the march across New Jersey the previous June, many of the men having enlisted under the (mistaken) belief that they were not to serve away from their home area. Drafts from this corps went to the Pennsylvania Loyalists, British Legion, and 1st and 3rd New Jersey Volunteers. The Royal American Reformees was a corps raised at New York earlier in 1778, commanded by Lieutenant Colonel Rudolphus Ritzema, formerly the colonel of the Continental army's 3rd New York Regiment. Ritzema's idea of a Provincial unit consisting only of deserters from Washington's army was not a bad one, but raising it at New York at a time when Washington's army was at Valley Forge, Pennsylvania, was probably not the best timing. The four companies that made up this corps were drafted into the British Legion and the 3rd Battalion of DeLancey's Brigade.

Perhaps no unit qualified better for being broken up than the Roman Catholic Volunteers. They were recruited at Philadelphia from Catholic Loyalists in the Maryland-Pennsylvania area, and they sorely lacked discipline, including the officers. This could not be better exemplified than by two of the captains of the regiment, Martin McEvoy and John McKinnon, the former court-martialed and cashiered for plundering on the march across New Jersey and for kicking a fellow officer while on the parade, and the latter for likewise plundering and allowing himself to be kicked on the parade and not properly resenting it.[39] Their men were distributed to the 1st Battalion of DeLancey's Brigade, 2nd Battalion of New Jersey Volunteers, and Volunteers of Ireland.

The King's Orange Rangers did not receive any drafts, despite an alarming rate of desertion from the corps. Of 427 enlisted by July 1778, 121 had deserted, and the rate was only increasing.[40] The soldiers of the corps, despite "mutinies and desertions among the men," still earned some respect, as reflected by the Provincials' muster master, Edward Winslow: "I am sensible that on days of public parade, such as Inspections and Musters, there is not a Provincial Corps in his Majesty's service more capable of distinguishing itself by a performance of military exercise & maneuvers, than this, nor is there a better body of men."[41] Winslow mused about something wanting among the officers but could not put his finger on it. For unrelated reasons, it needed a new commander, at least temporarily, as its lieutenant colonel, John Bayard, was under a sentence of being cashiered for the murder of one of his own lieutenants, William Bird.[42] Bayard was, on paper, temporarily replaced by Lieutenant Colonel George Campbell of the King's American Regiment, who would be promptly captured at sea en route to join the regiment in Nova Scotia.

Another consideration for the Provincials concerned the regular British army units that would be embarking, as some of those had officers who were serving in Provincial units, most notably John Graves Simcoe, commander of the Queen's Rangers but also cap-

tain in the 40th Regiment. The British War Office recognized that
officers holding two commissions could only physically be with one
at a time, to the detriment of the other, and had requested that any
officers under this predicament choose which they wished to abide
by and resign the other. Clinton simply could not afford to lose his
best partisan officer, and therefore unilaterally issued orders
exempting the head ranger: "The Commander in Chief in
Consideration of the Services Performed by Lt. Colo. Simcoe at the
Head of a Corps which has much Distinguished itself, is Pleased to
Exempt him from this Alternative, and Allows him to Remain in
the Command of the Queens Rangers, Still holding his Company in
the 40th Regt."[43] Had one British officer had his way, Clinton
would have not only been deprived of Simcoe but the entire corps
of Queen's Rangers. General Grant, stationed in the Kingsbridge
area, had an excellent position to watch the exploits of Simcoe and
his corps, and asked the ranger commander if he and his corps
would consent to being a part of his impending expedition. This
was a breach of the unwritten assurances given to those serving in
Provincial units that they would never be sent to serve in the West
Indies, which was considered, for good reason, a most unhealthy
and lethal place to soldier in. Simcoe politely declined:

> General Grant, being to embark for the West-Indies, was so well
> satisfied with the Queen's Rangers, that he told Lt. Col. Simcoe
> if he could get Sir Henry Clinton's permission, he would readily
> take him, and his corps, among the number of chosen troops
> destined for that service. This kind and generous offer, could not
> but be highly agreeable to him, and to the officers of the Queen's
> Rangers, and nothing could have made them decline it, but a
> conviction that it would not be just in them to the many very
> valuable native Americans who were among their non-commis-
> sioned officers, and soldiers; Lieut. Col. Simcoe, therefore,
> respectfully declined this very advantageous offer, and the cer-
> tainty of British rank which must have resulted from it. Major
> Ross went upon the expedition as Brigade-Major and Lt. Col.
> Simcoe was deprived of the assistance of his valuable friend, as

his country was, too soon, of the services of this gallant officer, he being unfortunately killed at St. Christopher's. Captain [Richard] Armstrong was appointed Major in his room. Lieut. Col. Simcoe, Captain in the 40th which regiment went with General Grant, was permitted to remain in the Rangers, by a very honourable distinction which the Commander in Chief was pleased to make, in public orders.[44]

The logistical challenges facing Clinton were formidable to say the least. He needed to tend to everything from budgeting cash to send with each force to filling out blank court-martial warrants so that those forces could administer military justice when necessary. Aside from all the minutiae attendant upon an army, two significant needs had to be filled: shipping needed to be contracted to move the regiments to their destinations, and provisions for humans and horses sufficient to last weeks at sea needed to be on hand when the ships were ready to sail. It is staggering to try to conceive the planning and material support needed to keep the British military, its animals, and the population under its governance all fed. On a daily basis, at the end of July 1778, for the army at Rhode Island and New York, the British fed 39,775 men, 4,032 women, 2,934 children, 162 wagoners, and about 300 general officers and refugees.[45] And that number was increasing every day thanks to prisoner exchanges, Provincial recruits, and refugees flooding in from the countryside. The number does not take into account the thousands of sailors with the Royal Navy, the merchant shipping, privateers, and especially the thousands of inhabitants. All that food and forage had to be either sent from Europe, grown locally, or even captured at sea and sold at the markets. Calculations had to be taken on what was in stores, when to order from Europe, and how long the food would take to come to America. The time to worry for the British was generally when stocks were down to a four-to-six-week supply.

The weekly allowance of food issued to each man was 7 pounds of bread or flour, 7 pounds of beef or 4 pounds of pork, 6 ounces of butter, 3 pints of peas or 1 1/2 pints of oatmeal, and one-half pint of rice, to which was added daily 1 1/3 gill of rum.[46] This was supplemented by fresh vegetables grown by the military on garrison and regimental levels. This local produce could not supply the needs of all the troops but was of sufficient value for the use of the sick in hospitals, where the value of a healthy diet was recognized. The growing of vegetable gardens in a garrison as large as New York was bound to be attended by problems, not the least of which was the expense of gardeners, whose wages alone for 1777 and 1778 amounted to nearly 1,400 pounds New York currency. Worse, the 1778 crop from Governor's Island off Manhattan's southern tip was severely damaged by the Royal Navy when Rear Admiral James Gambier ordered "his Sheep, Cows & Hoggs into it."[47] Spruce beer became a regular part of the soldiers' rations, with breweries at New York City devoted entirely to its production. One brewery was operated by the commissary general's department, with eleven men turning out 4,233 gallons every two days.[48] The beer was issued in casks at the brewery, which the regiments were responsible for returning in order to receive further issues.[49]

In doing their calculations, Clinton's commissaries looked at their present garrison as well as how much food they would have on hand by type, subtracting for the ten thousand men being shipped off. The quantities, for whatever reason, did not break down evenly. By September 14, 1778, the garrison at New York was down to 50 days' worth of bread, flour or rice, 74 days of beef and pork, 62 days of butter, but a whopping 167 days of oatmeal and peas. Calculating the rum to be sent with the departing troops and those left at New York, there was 52 days' worth of that beverage, or 38,769 gallons.[50] The supply situation would have been much worse had not six provision (or victualing) ships arriving from Cork, Ireland, learned by chance of the evacuation of Philadelphia while they were headed up the Delaware River. Writing to Lord Germain on September 15, Clinton pleaded, "With great deference I submit to your Lordship the consequence, if by any accident, we should happen to fall Short of Provisions, and whether in these precarious times, it is not absolutely necessary for the safety of this Army, that there should be a large Supply in Store."[51]

The horses an army kept were as valuable a resource as ammunition, arms, or uniforms. Horses were indispensable in mounting cavalry and officers, as well as drawing the hundreds of wagons in the service. Without the wagons, no provisions, ammunition, or baggage could be drawn, to say nothing of transporting artillery. In New York in December 1777, with but a small garrison and no cavalry to speak of, 907 horses were drawing rations daily.[52] With each horse drawing about fourteen pounds of hay (or forage) daily, that added up to over six tons of hay every day. With the army's return from Philadelphia, and around a thousand cavalry horses, that number skyrocketed. A return made out on August 30 by Deputy Commissary George Brinley showed there was 748 tons of hay on hand, an additional 1,750 tons yet to be harvested within the lines, and more within reach in Westchester. "A very Considerable quantity of Salt Hay might be had at Long Island, and Staten Island, provided the Farmers could be assured of a price that would pay them for cutting it," Brinley advised Clinton.[53] Great Britain's commander in chief in America definitely had the acquisition of more forage on his mind, with the expedition of General Tryon to the east end of Long Island conducted for that purpose. There was, however, a much greater source of forage nearby, one that Brinley did not take into account. Clinton was poised to invade Bergen County, New Jersey.

Five

Food and Forage

O N THE NIGHT OF SEPTEMBER 22, 1778, CLINTON MIGHT HAVE been excused if he showed his frustration at this particular point in his military career. The bulk of his offensive power was being stripped away and there was little prospect, as he saw it, of putting an end to the rebellion with the residual force left behind. Clinton longed for a real opportunity to put a significant victory under his belt before he was forced by London to deal away his best cards. In Clinton's mind, the relief of Rhode Island that August had been his chance. Contrary winds delaying his fleet and a precipitate retreat by the Continental army under General Sullivan prevented Clinton from any possibility of striking:

> [M]y arrangements and plans for intercepting the enemy's retreat (by running up the Narragansett Passage to the Bristol Neck, where I proposed to land and seize their batteries, boats, stores, etc.), I had reason to hope that with the assistance of the frigates and galleys in the passage of Hoogland's Ferry, and the cooperation of General Pigot's army acting in his rear, matters might be

so managed that very few of Sullivan's troops could have found means of escaping, had we been but fortunate enough to have had only a common passage.[1]

Rather than being pleased with the aggressive spirit shown by Rhode Island's commander, General Pigot, Clinton seethed, not so privately, thinking his subordinate had acted rashly in driving Sullivan's force from the island instead of awaiting the arrival of reinforcements. In truth, Pigot probably acted no differently than Clinton would have a year earlier when he was a garrison commander with limited forces and acting at a distance from his commander, General Howe, who was then off conquering Philadelphia. Regardless, word of Clinton's displeasure quickly spread through the staff officers and no doubt to Pigot. One of those officers, Captain Frederick Mackenzie of the Adjutant General's Department, confided in his diary, shortly after Clinton's arrival off Newport:

> Sir Henry Clinton was not a little disappointed on his arrival here to find that the Rebel army had entirely quitted the Island. He and the Officers about him were in hopes to have had the Credit of driving the Enemy off, and raising the Siege, and they were so much chagrined that they found great fault with Genl. Pigots latter operations, blamed him for Marching out after the Enemy, and for not returning within the lines the same night, by which they said he risqued the loss of the Island, which the Rebels might have possessed again, had they attacked us on Quaker-hill that night. They said he should not, on any account, have pursued them, as he knew Sir Henry Clinton was hourly expected with a Reinforcement. In short as they did not come in for any share of the Credit, and the affair was finished before their arrival, they thought proper to find fault with every thing, and went off in a very ill humour.[2]

Clinton's arrival at Rhode Island was, by his own admission, delayed by contrary winds so it was reasonable for Pigot to have acted in a manner he saw fit, not knowing when or even if reinforcements would arrive in time to be of any use. Still looking to achieve some success before returning to New York, Clinton sought to follow Germain's wishes in making descents on the coast, particularly in attacking enemy ports. The overwhelming advantage of Great Britain in the early years of the war had clearly been the Royal Navy, against which the new United States had nothing approaching a fleet to oppose it. The states knew they could not beat the Royal Navy in a traditional fleet action, so the chief maritime warfare they conducted was through the issuing of letters of marque and retaliation, that is, the use of privateers. Privateers were legally commissioned private vessels of war granted a license to attack and seize vessels of a belligerent nation specifically mentioned in the terms of their commission. Privateers were generally small schooners, sloops, and brigs, lightly armed but fast. They were not intended to battle warships but rather board and capture enemy merchant ships. The "prize" ship was then manned and sailed to a friendly port, where the ship and its contents were sold at auction for the benefit of the owners of the privateer and its crew. The number of shares each man received was based on his rank on the ship. The more prizes captured, the more profitable a voyage. By 1778, privateers operating out of New England and the Middle Atlantic states were taking their toll on British and Loyalist merchant ships coming and going between England and New York, and elsewhere. The downside to privateering was the chance of actually meeting up with a Royal Navy warship at sea. If captured, privateersmen were at the bottom of the barrel as far as exchanges were concerned, condemned to a prison ship until an opportunity presented itself for liberation. As American sailors always outnumbered British sailors in captivity, and Congress refused to exchange sailors for soldiers, the length of time in captivity could be substantial.

With no opportunity presenting itself at Rhode Island, Clinton turned to Connecticut. New London, just over the border in eastern Connecticut, was close enough to Rhode Island that the fleet could arrive before any reinforcements could march from Providence, where General Sullivan had retired to after evacuating the island. Despite a belief that Sullivan could not reinforce the place from Providence in less than four days, nor from White Plains in less than eight, Clinton felt that no more than twenty-four to forty-eight hours at New London was safe or prudent, "great numbers [of militia] such as they are may be assembled in that time."[3] Once again the wind was against Clinton, and the transports stalled before reaching New London's Thames River. After a full day's delay, given the safety time Clinton thought necessary, the expedition was given up. Clinton had had enough of waterborne operations; sending the troops under General Grey back toward Rhode Island and Massachusetts, the British commander in chief returned to New York.[4]

Grey was an ideal choice to engage in the sort of predatory warfare suggested by London. Aggressive by nature, he had made a name for himself (good or bad, depending on whose side you were on) with an early morning attack on General Wayne's troops at Paoli, Pennsylvania, on September 21, 1777. For the loss of a dozen of his men killed or wounded, Grey killed, wounded, or captured over four hundred men of Wayne's command, with the British relying solely on the bayonet for their attack.[5] Grey and his transports full of troops left Clinton and sailed east, past Newport and into Buzzards Bay. Debarking some of his troops, they advanced up the Acushnet River to Fair Haven and Bedford, Massachusetts, destroying shipping, barracks, a magazine, and a fort with eleven pieces of artillery, at the cost of just one man killed, four men wounded, and sixteen missing.[6] Grey promptly took sixteen of Bedford's residents to try to use in exchange for his missing troops.[7]

After the business around Bedford was done, Grey's fleet sailed back west, out of Buzzards Bay, then southeast to the island of Martha's Vineyard. Arriving in Holmes Hole Harbor, by Tisbury, the fleet was unexpectedly met by a delegation of the principal inhabitants of the island "to ask my intentions," as Grey put it.[8] Rather than risk a needless battle and the desolation of their homes, the islanders agreed to supply the British with "The Arms of the Militia, the public money, 300 Oxen and 10,000 Sheep." On September 12, a fleet from Rhode Island arrived to take off 6,000 sheep and 130 oxen, and by the fourteenth, Grey had embarked the remainder.[9] The arms turned in were probably only a fraction of those actually on the island, and those probably old or otherwise unserviceable. A total of 388 muskets were turned in, nine of which were returned to their owners for whatever reasons. Four pistols and a drum were among the other warlike stores turned in.[10] Heeding the advice of Admiral Howe, who suggested Grey return to a friendly port "with all convenient dispatch," Grey left Martha's Vineyard with the fleet and arrived safe off Whitestone, Queens County, Long Island, on September 17, 1778.[11] After receiving Grey's report, Clinton could now reflect on the past few weeks' activity. "I hope it will serve to convince these poor deluded people," Clinton wrote to General Benjamin Carpenter back in England, "that that sort of war, carried to a greater extent and with more devastation, will sooner or later reduce them."[12] Clinton at that very moment was assembling a force of six thousand men to bring "that sort of war" to New Jersey.

Bergen County, New Jersey, is nestled in the northeastern corner of the state, with New York bordering to the north and the Hudson River on its east, opposite Manhattan Island. The county has the major Hackensack River running north to south through it, effectively making a substantial part of its southeast a neck of land between it and the Hudson River. The Passaic River runs to its west, bordering Essex County. Ridgelines and valleys facilitated traveling north and south. The Bergen County of 1778 was much larger than it is today, having had the counties of Hudson and Passaic carved whole or in part from it in the first half of the nineteenth century. Divided into six townships, the county was a melting pot of different cultures. Although commonly referred to as "the Jersey Dutch," many nationalities made up that population, including French Huguenots, German Palatines, Danes, Poles, Swiss, Irish, Scots, English, and, of course, a good amount of Dutch. There was a sizable black population, some free but mostly slaves. Economically, the county was relatively prosperous, with large farms, mills, and water carriage to bring produce to New York City, or even the West Indies. Politically, the inhabitants were rather conservative, and as a consequence, primarily Loyalist.[13]

When the war came to Bergen County in 1776, there was little evidence of the patriotic fervor that infected other areas of the state. When the provincial assembly authorized five battalions of state troops to assist in defending New York City from British attack, only three companies were to be provided by Bergen County, of which only two were raised, and each of them had less than twenty enlisted men.[14] Perhaps only one man from Bergen County enlisted in the Continental army in 1776.[15] While the county's response to the war effort may have initially been lackluster, its strategic importance was fully recognized by both sides early on. After Royal Navy warships were able to pass up the Hudson River with minimal damage in July 1776, efforts were made to close the river. Fortifications were thrown up at Bergen Point, modern-day Bayonne, to defend against attacks from British-held Staten Island. A strong fort was raised at Paulus Hook (now Jersey City), directly across from lower Manhattan. These positions were manned by troops of the Flying Camp and other state regiments but proved of limited use. Paulus Hook was captured in September 1776 by British troops under Lieutenant General Hugh, Lord Percy, without a shot fired.[16]

Realizing even months before Paulus Hook's loss that more-robust works would be necessary to close the Hudson, two were started diagonally across from each other, one at the northern tip of Manhattan known as Fort Washington and the other across the river to the south, named Fort Constitution, later Fort Lee. Mounting heavy guns and mortars sitting atop the Palisades and Mount Washington, the posts were further strengthened by a sunken warship and *chevaux de frise* (long heavy poles tipped with iron) meant to stop or even sink any warships attempting to sail past. The plan was a good one, but it was undone when a Loyalist ferryman working at the base of the Palisades by Fort Lee took minute notice of a channel left open for friendly craft and duly got word to the British as to its location.[17] It mattered little. By the middle of November 1776, Fort Washington was taken by storm, with the loss of nearly three thousand of General Washington's troops. Fort Lee fell four days later, the garrison escaping only by gaining the crossing at New Bridge before its route could be cut off by five thousand troops under General Cornwallis.[18]

Since that time, large-scale operations had mostly avoided the county. Loyalist troops had been raised by the hundreds, primarily by Teaneck's Abraham Van Buskirk, a prominent "Practitioner of Physick" settled on an estate at New Bridge.[19] As a lieutenant colonel of Provincial forces, Van Buskirk, in conjunction with his newly appointed officers, was able to recruit ten companies of men to form the 4th Battalion, New Jersey Volunteers, a part of Brigadier General Cortland Skinner's brigade.[20] Van Buskirk and his men spent much of the first half of 1777 posted at Bergen Point and conducting raids into the Bergen County countryside but after that had been with most of the other battalions of the brigade on Staten Island. The situation and political leanings of the county had not escaped the notice of William Livingston, the first governor of the state of New Jersey. After suppressing Loyalists in the state's northwestern Sussex County, Livingston turned his attention to Bergen, informing George Washington on July 11, 1777, "The Council of Safety has pretty well suppressed the Spirit of Disaffection in this County; & I hope by the vigorous measures lately adopted, we shall soon reduce that almost totally revolted County of Bergen to the obedience of the States."[21] Livingston sent about 150 militia into the county, and a couple dozen Loyalist civilians were rounded up and sent to prison; one was shot while trying to escape.[22] While overt loyalism to the British may have been dampened, it would still be prominent for the remainder of the war.

Clinton was familiar with Bergen County and what it had to offer. While not a part of the original 1776 invasion (Clinton was at the time leading the expedition to capture Rhode Island), he nevertheless had his opportunity while in command at New York City. In charge of a highly diminished garrison of about seven thousand five hundred men while General Howe was involved in the Philadelphia Campaign, Clinton was at his active best, using the forces at his disposal to attempt to draw off Continental troops and militia from opposing either Howe in Pennsylvania or General Burgoyne's expedition from Canada. Clinton initially made his

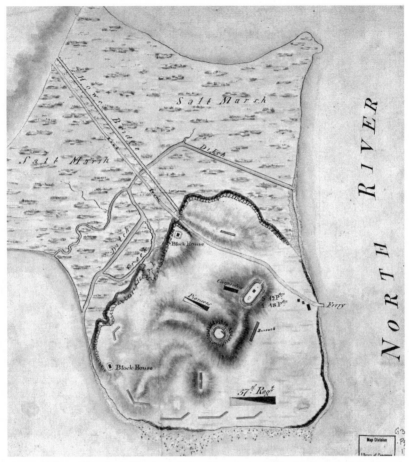

MAP 3. Plan of Paulus's Hook and Fortifications, 1778. (*Library of Congress*)

move on New Jersey, spending September 12 to 16 invading Essex and Bergen counties simultaneously, advancing from four different routes, north to south. As he explained to General Howe:

> My principal Motive was, if possible, to attempt a Stroke against any detached Corps of the Enemy, if one offered, or if not, to collect a considerable Number of Cattle, which would at the same Time prove a seasonable Refreshment to the Troops, and deprive

the Enemy of Resources which I understood they much depended upon, and finally to retire, with our Booty, by the only Road
practicable with those Embarrassments, to reembark, return to
our Camp, or proceed to some other Expedition if anything presented itself.[23]

The expedition proved of some success, bringing in four hundred cattle, four hundred sheep, and some horses within the British
lines. The cost of this acquisition to the British was forty-one men
killed, wounded, missing, and taken prisoner, mostly centered on a
battle at Acquackanonk and the surprise of a small picket of the
52nd Regiment at New Bridge by Lieutenant Colonel Aaron Burr,
second in command of Malcom's Additional Continental
Regiment.[24] Commodore William Hotham, Clinton's Royal Navy
partner in the operation, reported to Admiral Howe that "the
Acquisition of Cattle derived from this Incursion has been as considerable, as I hope it will be found beneficial to the Troops and
Seamen, added to the End it seems to have had of throwing the
Enemy into a general Alarm."[25] Clinton was pleased, in general,
with the expedition, although he doubted it much helped either
Generals Burgoyne or Howe. "I had the satisfaction to see most of
its other objects accomplished" he allowed himself, "without
affront or material loss."[26]

While Clinton may have had in mind a similar move into Bergen
County that night in September 1778, Washington had actually
beaten him to the punch, albeit in a more modest manner.
Following the Battle of Monmouth, Washington and his army had
wound their way north through New Jersey and into New York, via
Bergen County. Being aware of its strategic position, Washington
on July 16, 1778, ordered Captain David Hopkins and a detachment of the 4th Light Dragoons from the army at Haverstraw to
Closter in Bergen County, about four miles south of the state border. There Hopkins was instructed:

You are to keep Scouts down towards the English
Neighbourhood, with orders to watch the River, and if they per-

ceive any Ships or Vessels moving up to give you immediate notice. If these Vessels are of any considerable number you are to send an Express to the commanding Officer at King's Ferry, desiring him to forward the intelligence to His Excellency [Washington] where ever he may be; but if only a single Vessel or a few Boats go up, you are to take it for granted that they are after Supplies of some kind, and are therefore to send a party to keep pace with them and prevent their landing upon this Shore.[27]

Washington's concern clearly was the ability of the British to project their forces rapidly by water. While the Continental army was locked in its struggle to defend Philadelphia in 1777, Clinton, with as much of his small New York garrison as he could muster, rapidly advanced by water up the Hudson, storming and capturing Forts Clinton and Montgomery, sailing past the defenses of Constitution Island, and then burning New York's capital, Kingston. New and improved defenses at West Point would prevent a repeat of that sort of expedition, but the Royal Navy, Washington knew, could still place Clinton's army on either side of the Hudson pretty much anywhere below that.

Having cavalry in Bergen County also gave Washington an opportunity that he wished to take advantage of. Knowing that the proximity to the British lines led many of the inhabitants to sell their cattle and produce to the king's troops, the Continental army's commander in chief sought to curtail that and provide supplies for his own troops at the same time. Having some of the 4th Light Dragoons, commanded by Colonel Stephen Moylan, already in the county made this desire a possibility. In addition to the detachment at Closter, Moylan commanded three of the army's four cavalry regiments at Tappan, New York, right on the border with Bergen County. These he wanted to move down to the village of English Neighbourhood, near where Fort Lee was located, but Washington had other ideas.[28] Thinking English Neighbourhood perhaps too exposed, Washington told Moylan his cavalry should be prepared to follow the army across the Hudson to White Plains, but until then New Bridge and Hackensack would be a more advantageous location, allowing him to sweep the county between the Hackensack and Hudson rivers, and the Hackensack and Passaic rivers.[29] Arriving at New Bridge on July 27 and then proceeding south to Hackensack, Moylan realized he was not in the friendliest country to the Patriot cause. That being the case, it should have been an easy matter to collect cattle and forage from undefended Loyalist inhabitants, particularly those closest to the British lines in Bergen Township. He was perhaps not ready for the reception he received:

> [O]n my arrival I reconoitred the country and found a great majority disaffected, and taking every opportunity of Supplying the enemy. Yesterday [July 28] I Sent a party of 80 horse to Bergen with orders to drive up what Cattle they Coud Collect, from that town, to the point, which they have effected by bringing with them near 300 head of horned Cattle, 60 sheep, Some horses mares & Colts, many of the first are milck Cows, and tho its certain that the milck & butter is for the chief part Sent to New York from that Quarter, there appears a great degree of cruelty in taking from a number of famillys, perhaps their only Support. I am teased by the women, and with difficulty can prevail on my feelings, to suspend my giving to them their cows, until I have your Excellencys opinion and orders on this Subject.[30]

On July 30, Washington relieved Moylan of any further teasing by Bergen's women, leaving him discretion to return such milk cows as he thought proper and to take his cavalry and join the army at White Plains, an officer and twenty-four men excepted, "to keep a good look out from Fort Lee and if he perceives any extraordinary movement to make report to me."[31] These men were soon replaced, or joined, by a much larger force. In that force was Major Alexander Clough of the 3rd Light Dragoons. For an all too brief time, he was Washington's best procurer of intelligence. Stationed at Hackensack, Clough was in a good position to observe British movements from Manhattan and to utilize the frequent intercourse between Bergen's residents and the New York City markets. Washington urged Clough to send several people into New York City so that different accounts could be compared and perhaps the truth ascertained. Clough was also urged to take advantage of the "London Trading" between the inhabitants and the British: "If the person, who goes in, cannot make an excuse of Business, he must be allowed to carry a small matter of provision in; and bring something out, by way of pretext."[32] Acting immediately on his commander's instructions, Clough sent people into the city on August 26 and rode to the banks of the Hudson River to see what he could. If Clough was hoping for immediate fruits, he was mistaken. The best information he got came randomly from three British sailors who deserted, and they could inform him of little more than he could see with his own eyes. The most valuable information was that the British transport ships were supplied with wood and water for a voyage of six months[33]

After several more days of fragmentary and incomplete accounts, Clough finally got what Washington had been looking for, and what Charles Scott and his operatives out of Westchester could not learn: specific accounts about regiments, or at least *a* regiment and the transports. On September 4, 1778, Clough was able to tell Washington: "I am informed by a person from New York, that the 27th Regt. have sent thayr Baggage on board the Britania transport, three companys of artillery are orderd on board the Howe, the Officers Baggage is sent on board. Another informs me thayr waggons are repair'd, and the horses are shoeing in every part of the town. Major Tenpeny is orderd to raise a Corps of horse."[34]

The 27th Regiment was indeed one of the regiments destined for the West Indies expedition under General Grant, along with three companies of artillery. Sending the baggage (tents, spare clothing and arms, wagons, etc.) onboard was an indication that a regiment was leaving for an extended period, if not permanently. Washington now knew for certain that troops were leaving, but there was still much to learn.

Clough was not alone in Hackensack. With him was his regiment, the 3rd Light Dragoons, under the command of Colonel

George Baylor. The corps went under many unofficial names, including General Washington's Life Guard or simply by the name of its commander, as Baylor's Dragoons.[35] The corps had served well the past year, fighting last at Monmouth in June. Proceeding to Hackensack after the battle, ostensibly to cover the country, the 120 or so dragoons soon found themselves, or more correctly their horses, in competition for forage with the baggage horses stationed nearby at Pompton, Acquackanonk, and elsewhere. Trying to supply his wagon horses at Morristown, New Jersey, Deputy Quartermaster General Moore Furman complained bitterly to Commissary General of Forage Clement Biddle from Acquackanonk on August 26, 1778:

> I sent up for McKinnan, he is with me, & Says no long Forage or Short can be procured at Pompton so that all the Teams Employ'd between Morris Town & Kings Ferry must be Supplied at Morris Town. McKinnan says that the Light Horse have taken so much Lately that the People, except a very few, that will not thrash out have none to spare, and there is no Law now in force in this State that enables the Forager to Call out what is to Spare. Another thing he Complains of that some of the Foragers from Camp go and send about in Bergen County and give 20/ [20 shillings] for Wheat &ca which prevents his geting it for Less if to be had, when Corn & B[uck] Wheat Comes in he thinks he can get some, but untill then he cannot Collect any of Consequence at Pompton or any where in B. County. . . . Agreeable to your desire I waited on our Governour, I believe that County [Salem] to be very short, but not more so then Hunterdon nor have they Occasion to make such an Application as no man in it have had a Grain taken from them without their Consent, unless by the [Light] Horse who is under no restraint, which I think very extraordinary Indeed when every other part of the Army is, they are so far just that they take without respect of Persons, whatever they please and in what Quantities they please, but Suppose the Commissioners now Sitting will think of them in turn and put them under some Orders.[36]

Furman closed his letter with even more bad news, this caused by nature rather than cavalry, lamenting, "The last long Rains destroy'd a great Quantity of Hay in this State, some Farmers lost from 10 to 20 Tons. Corn & Buckwheat looks well, we may come in for some of that by & by but that will be some months first."[37]

Cavalry doing as it pleased in the fields of Bergen's Patriot farmers was not what the county's residents considered a just reward for standing forth in the cause of their country. The dragoons, mostly from Virginia with a smattering of New Englanders, do not appear to have been concerned about the feelings of Jersey Dutch farmers, most of whom they considered Loyalists and therefore enemies, as Colonel Moylan had done with those whose cows he made off with the previous July. Peter Dey, a sergeant in the Bergen County Militia and son of the regiment's commander, Colonel Theunis Dey, many years later recalled the animosity that existed that September: "There was some ill will existing between Baylor's Corps and our militia on account of Deponent's father being called upon to aid with his regiment the Sheriff of Bergen to serve civil process on Baylor's quarter master & other officers for having taken Citizen's Cattle by force, at the home of one Aaron Schuyler."[38] Young David Ritzema Bogert, a militiaman of Hackensack, added, "The Quarter Master of [Baylor's] Regt. pressed a quantity of grain at the house of a farmer named Berry for the use of the Regt. & Berry took out a writ for the Qr. Master & Clough refused leave to the Sheriff to execute the writ, the Sheriff called out the Posse when the Regt. of Militia assembled and our Company were also assembled to assist the Sheriff."

The posse of militiamen assembled at Hackensack under Colonel Dey on the night of September 22, 1778, determined to confront Baylor's men. Clinton would change their minds.

Six

Bergen County
in the Crosshairs

A T 3 O'CLOCK IN THE MORNING ON SEPTEMBER 22, 1778, Captain John Peebles of the 42nd or Royal Highland Regiment's grenadier company was standing on the parade along with over one thousand two hundred other officers and men serving in the 1st and 2nd Battalions of British Grenadiers. The grenadiers were one of the ten companies that made up a standard British regiment. They, along with the one light infantry company that each regiment possessed (also collectively known as the flank companies from their placement in the line), were generally brigaded together to form unique battalions of grenadiers and light infantry. These were considered elite formations, renowned for bravery and quick movement. Within the hour, Peebles and his men would be embarking at Red Hook, Brooklyn, on transport ships and flat-bottomed boats, crossing in the wee morning hours to Paulus Hook, New Jersey. Clinton's Grand Forage had begun.[1]

The movement of troops to Paulus Hook was an immense operation, drawing regiments from Long Island, New York City, and Staten Island. The garrison of Paulus Hook itself was but one regiment, some four hundred men of the 57th Regiment. On the morning of the twenty-second, those troops were joined by a force of over six thousand men, including some of the best corps in the army: the 1st and 2nd Battalions of Grenadiers, the 1st and 2nd Battalions of Light Infantry, the Brigade of Guards, the eight regiments of the 3rd and 4th Brigades, the Volunteers of Ireland, the British Legion infantry, the 4th Battalion New Jersey Volunteers, and the Guides & Pioneers, along with two hundred men drawn from the 16th and 17th Light Dragoons and a detachment of Royal Artillery, all under the command of General Cornwallis.[2] The landings at Paulus Hook went on for hours, with the bulk of the troops advancing just three miles to the heights of the town of Bergen, no doubt to consolidate their forces before proceeding farther.[3] In order to keep the landing a secret and to prevent being surprised themselves, the British Light Infantry, which included a mounted troop, was advanced northward up Bergen Neck.[4]

Despite the apparent presence of intelligence agents working for Major Clough and the bulk of the water crossings being done in broad daylight, the British troop movements seem to have gone completely unnoticed by anyone in Bergen County until late in the afternoon. A series of misstatements and misassumptions delayed a realization in Washington's headquarters at Fredericksburg as to what was happening. The information of course came to Washington via Charles Scott, still trying his best to decipher what the British were up to at New York City. Writing to Washington on September 23 from his post at King Street, Scott appears to have somehow confused what his informant said to mean September 21, when he meant the next day, September 22. The account he sent Washington read:

> Some time in the day Yesterday [September 22, 1778] a Country man was seen on the North river who told that a large Body of the enemy had Crossed the North River into the Jerseys the day before. About the time he says they Crossed my Patrolls inform me they heard a Smart Firing of Small arms on the other Side of the river, as they thought. I immediately on hearing this Sent

Colo. Grayham to Dobb's Ferry with orders to provide a Propper person, and Send over the river to make what Discoverys he Could. He is not Yet returned neither have I heard from him. There are ten deserters from York Island Yesterday who knows nothing of Such a movement. They Say that about the time it is said that they (the Body of troops) Crossed over The river Four Regiments imbarked for the west Indeas, and are now Lying off New York in the North River in Readiness to Sail. By the last Accounts From York the Transports are preparing to receive the Cavelry and they are accordingly ordered to hold themselves In readiness to embark on the Shortest notice. However I hourly expect a very good man out, who will give me a more particular acct. of things in Gen[era]l.[5]

Washington, through his aide Tench Tilghman, initially dismissed Scott's report outright, telling him, "It is not possible that any troops could have passed over into Jersey the 21st, had that been the case we must have had intelligence of it before this time from Colo. Baylor who is at Hackensack."[6] From Washington's perspective, the point was valid: three days would not have passed before Baylor would have notified his commanding officer of a British invasion. The mistake of Scott's informant reporting the British incursion as being on the twenty-first instead of the twenty-second certainly was part of the problem. On the New Jersey side of the Hudson, Baylor himself seemed slow to realize the danger of Clinton's plans and the immediate threat they posed to his troops.

Indeed, the British incursion actually solved one of Baylor's immediate problems, that of the farmers and the writ against his men. "A Regiment of Militia which were here last evening to assist the sherrif in taking two of my men Prisoners deserted us, as soon as this news was heard, the Colo. himself could not be prevailed on to stay," Baylor wrote to Washington from Hackensack on September 23.[7] He went on to inform the commander in chief that the British had crossed over only late in the afternoon, which was discovered by a party of militia. The militia estimated the force at five thousand men, extending five miles north of Paulus Hook. It is unknown exactly what militia made the discovery. It is unlikely anyone with Colonel Dey, Sheriff Adam Boyd, or those come to serve the writ in Hackensack were patrolling down Bergen Neck. The most likely source of the patrols was a standing force at Hackensack, commanded by Major Peter Fell. Fell had only recently arrived at Hackensack. As a part of Morris Graham's battalion of New York State troops, Fell had been serving under Charles Scott with the light infantry in Westchester. Fell brought with him but one company from Graham's corps, that commanded by Captain John Bell. Raised the preceding April in neighboring Orange County, the company consisted of about three officers and sixty enlisted men.[8] They may have been joined by Captain John Barnes of the same corps, even though with a major, captain, and two lieutenants there were more than enough officers to command the number of men present. These troops were stationed at New Bridge, guarding the vital span across the Hackensack.[9]

The advanced post of the small force in Bergen County, which was apparently unaware of the massive British force arrived in the county, was that of Captain Elias Romaine. It consisted of about sixty Bergen County militia stationed at Liberty Pole. Liberty Pole lay about halfway between what had been Fort Lee and New Bridge. The road to the north led to Tappan, just over the border in New York, while that leading west went over the Hackensack River at the bridge. A second major north-south road between Liberty Pole and New Bridge ran through Schraalenburgh and Haring Town to Tappan. Occupying Liberty Pole controlled much of the traffic passing through the northern villages to the area of English Neighbourhood and Teaneck, all of which made up what was known officially as Hackensack Township.[10] The force under Captain Romaine was not exclusively from his company but rather consisted of drafts from companies across the county. A number of the militia under his command were in their teens, no fewer than five of them only sixteen. Peter S. Van Orden of Schraalenburgh had not even turned sixteen yet, nor had Romaine's brother, Benjamin. Benjamin Romaine and his family had fled New York City in 1776 as Fort Washington was being stormed and captured by the British. In 1777, at age fourteen, he sought to take advantage of the war by engaging in youthful pursuits other than school, as attending the latter might prove dangerous in the exposed Bergen County countryside. His family thought otherwise:

> I had pleaded excuse from going to school, as my Father had requested, (we then lived on the lines where both the belligerant parties had alternate possession). One evening my Father came into the house with a large english musket, and its appendages, with a catouch box filled with 24 rounds of ball catriges. He sat the musket in the closet; mother asked his meaning, he answered not. In the early morning he bid me rise, and buckled on me the armour, and said, "you have refused to make effort with me to perfect your education, now go to your Brother and defend your country!"[11]

On September 23, 1778, the day before his sixteenth birthday, Romaine learned the difference between school and battle.

The day following their landing, the British forces encamped around Paulus Hook stirred through the early morning rain. The day would feature constant rain and wind. Undeterred, Cornwallis and his troops set off at 5 AM, at or near daybreak, marching north through Bergen Township. On reaching the ground of Fort Lee, the army struck northwest, replicating the march the Continental army had taken two years earlier when it abandoned the fort to Cornwallis's troops during the British invasion. This time the only force between Cornwallis and New Bridge was Romaine's picket at Liberty Pole. Moving ahead of Cornwallis's main body was the light infantry, preceded by the cavalry of the 16th and 17th Light Dragoons. Early that morning, the cavalry surprised and struck Romaine's picket.

"Suddenly at day break aroused by a Number of British Light Horse," recalled eighteen-year-old militiaman Peter I. Sisco of Bloomingdale.[12] Captain Francis Needham of the 17th Light Dragoons, leading on the British cavalry, found the militia by a clearing near the woods and commenced an immediate charge. To their credit, the militia initially stood their ground, killing one and wounding perhaps one or more.[13] Numbers and discipline soon took their toll, however, and the militia broke. Robert Gould, a six-teen-year-old militiaman from Bloomingdale in his first action, recalled "we were over powered and forced to Retreat with the Loss of a number of our men Taken prisoners."[14] Abraham Cisco, twenty, of Pompton, was cut "over his hat with the broad sword of a Lt. Horseman without being wounded." His brother Peter, how-ever, was rounded up and sent off a prisoner.[15] Young Benjamin Romaine referred to the action as "a very severe affair of arms" in which his company lost a "considerable number" of killed, wound-ed, and prisoners. Samuel Vervalen of Harrington Township was sabered in the head and taken prisoner.[16] First Lieutenant John D. Haring no doubt had Vervalen and others in mind when he wrote "several of our men were wounded and severely cut to pieces by their Light Horse."[17] That the British cavalry might have included dismounted troopers as well as mounted men may account for one of the militiamen, Elias White, being bayoneted.[18]

After the militia line had broken, for the British cavalry it was simply a matter of rounding up as many fugitives from the battle as possible before the defeated militiamen drifted away into the coun-tryside. The number of prisoners taken by the British was various-ly reported by both sides as anywhere between twenty-three and thirty.[19] The prisoners were sent to New York, where they remained anywhere from five to fourteen weeks, being exchanged piecemeal over that time. For sixteen-year-old Benjamin Woodruff of Franklin Township, the experience was understandably horrific: "he with about thirty others of the Militia were taken prisoners by the British, marched to the city of New York and imprisoned in the old Sugar house where the[y] Suffered every privation on Short allowance for Seven or eight weeks, until an exchange of prisoners took place and he got home to New Milford Some time late in December of that year in a Sickly condition."[20]

One of the prisoners was actually a Continental officer, First Lieutenant William Rogers of the 8th (later 4th) Virginia Regiment.[21] Several militiamen noted decades after the battle that there were Continental troops there, under a Lieutenant Hays or Barnes. While Barnes appears to have been from Graham's state troops, no Lieutenant Hays appears anywhere there, nor any other Continentals other than Rogers.[22] Interestingly, no militia pensioners named any of their dead, although most recalled that they had lost men killed. While the British simply mentioned in passing "a few" were killed, most of the militia veterans only recalled "some" were killed; the exception was John G. Ryerson of Pompton, another of the sixteen-year-olds, who stated the British had killed fourteen of his comrades.[23] Samuel Helm of Closter, also sixteen, recalled "seven or eight" wounded.[24] Regardless of the actual count, the Bergen County Militia had just suffered its bloodiest defeat so far in the war.

Once the militia had dispersed, there appears to have been no effort to rally or reassemble them, with the survivors making the best of their way to their respective homes. Someone at least had the sense to alert Colonel Baylor in Hackensack and Major Fell at New Bridge. Baylor and the dragoons still remained at Hackensack on the twenty-third, although the colonel had written to George Washington the day before to say he was on the verge of moving northwest to Paramus, "where the Regiment can be quartered together, which is necessary both for our safety and the keeping of good order."[25] For their part, the British continued their advance unopposed, the light infantry, cavalry, and Volunteers of Ireland securing the New Bridge intact along with the surrounding area.[26] The advance may have been slowed, even though it covered twelve miles, because of the weather, marching "thro bad Roads & an excessive rainy day that wet us all to the Skin."[27] The weather certainly added to Cornwallis's stress. While tactically all had gone well, a logistics foul up had delayed the camp equipage from arriving, which, given the rain, would make for an uncomfortable night's sleep. Setting up his headquarters for the night in English Neighbourhood, he submitted his first report to Clinton:

> The very severe rain almost frightens me about the provisions from Paulus Hook. If a provision sloop could be sent tomorrow

to Fort Lee, besides all the other precautions it would make us more secure, I think it so essential a point, in the present situation of the troops, that we cannot use too many means to put it out of the Power of chance to disappoint us. The mistake about the craft yesterday has distress'd us beyond expressions. No Officer has or is likely to have any change of cloaths or linen or any thing to eat or drink. I hear none of the horses of the regimental waggons are yet landed. Excuse my troubling you, but I know you are full as anxious as myself about this business.[28]

While the regimental wagon horses may not have been landed, some of the corps apparently took matters into their own hands to alleviate the situation, much to Cornwallis's disapproval:

"Ld. Cornwallis is Much Surprisd. to find that Notwithstanding his Positive orders to the Contrary Many horses have been taken from the inhabitants. he Expects that Commg. offrs. will See them Restored and Prevent the like practice in future, if it necessary to press any horses for the Regl. Waggons, the Comm offrs. will give Receipts for them & Report to the Commandg. offr. of the Brigade."[29]

For many Loyalists whose horses and wagons were pressed, it would take nearly five years before the receipts issued them would be honored for gold.

The 3rd Light Dragoons at Hackensack were well known to the British, despite Baylor perhaps thinking otherwise. Five days before the arrival of the British, one of the 3rd Dragoons, an Irishman named William Cunningham, deserted from his picket post at Little Ferry, perhaps two miles below Hackensack. He informed the British of Baylor's presence in the town, and the picket post, so there is little doubt that the British were aware of their enemy's disposition.[30] With the British occupying both sides of New Bridge, Baylor probably made his way out of Hackensack on the road leading northwest to Zabriskie's Mills and from there north to Paramus, where he reported to Washington early in the morning of September 24:

MAP 4. "Sketch of the Road from Paulus Hook and Hobocken to New Bridge," 1778. (*Library of Congress*)

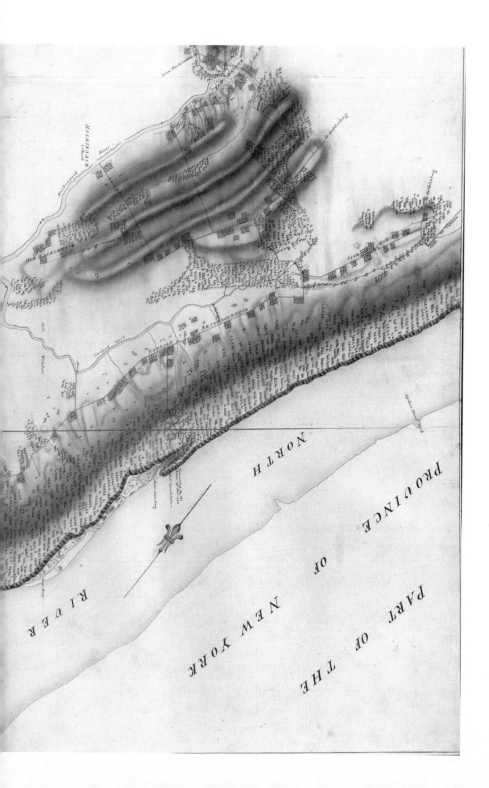

The Enemy left Bergen wood early yesterday morning and marched through the inglish neighbourhood, they pas'd by the new bridge two miles without taking the smallest notice of us. I thought it advisable from these circumstances to order Major Fell with his party which consists of one hundred and twenty to the old bridge, he moved there and from thence joined me in this place. The Enemy encamp'd last night on the east side of the Hackingsack River above and below the new bridge. I every moment expect the return of Major Clough whom I sent out last night for intelligence of their numbers and movement.[31]

Clough failed to return before Baylor dispatched his letter to Washington at Fredericksburg. In Clough's travels, if he had approached the area around New Bridge, he would have seen it then in the possession of the 2nd Battalion of the British Light Infantry. If he had patrolled three miles to the south, to his old quarters in Hackensack, he would have found it being patrolled by five more companies of light infantry.[32] The British never occupied Hackensack during the time they spent in Bergen County. That does not mean the town had no visitors. One former resident who accompanied the British on the expedition was Daniel Isaac Browne, whose home stood near the county courthouse in Hackensack. When the war broke out, Browne was clerk of the court and keeper of the records for the county, surrogate judge of the eastern division of the province of New Jersey, and had his practice as an attorney.[33] Upon the British first entering the county in 1776, Browne recruited men and joined Abraham Van Buskirk as a major in the 4th Battalion, New Jersey Volunteers. Upon a consolidation of the brigade in April 1778, Browne was placed on half pay and involuntarily retired as a surplus officer.[34] His purpose in coming along on the expedition in 1778 is unclear, but it would not be unreasonable to assume he wanted to recover some of the property he had left at home when he joined the army. What he found instead was an advertisement for the auctioning off of his estate by the state of New Jersey.[35] The following April, his house and belongings were sold, the home being bought by Adam Boyd, the sheriff who had attempted to serve the writ on Baylor's officers.[36]

By September 24, word was spreading far and wide that thousands of British troops were pouring into Bergen County. Washington had been informed of the British arrival the previous day and duly informed Congress, "I was also informed by Colo. Baylor, that a considerable body of the Enemy landed at Powles Hook, in the Evening of the 22nd and encamped that night in the wood, between four & five miles from the Town of Bergen. He had not learnt their object, but it is likely they are after forage."[37] Before Washington had any time to seriously consider what aid could be given to Bergen County, more couriers were making their way to Fredericksburg. Major General Israel Putnam, stationed at Peekskill, sent what intelligence he had been informed of by Colonel Ann Hawkes Hay of the Orange County Militia: "the Enemy had got as far as Scrolingbour Church and was incamped thare and it was said thay war waiting for a wind to bring up the ships: the Enimy are Colecting all the catel Sheap & hogs thay can." Wishing to learn more, Putnam rode down to King's Ferry, where he indeed did learn more, but not what he was expecting, as "on my way met 4 men with their horses loded with bagig going back into the contry which said thay Cam from within 2 milds of tarytown who said the Enimy had com out of New york in 3 larg colloms won by the way of maranack and won by taritown and won had on into the Jarsys."[38] Putnam's report confirmed a report just earlier received from Charles Scott:

This day proving so exceeding bad I had Concluded to wait untill the weather was better before I posted the Horsemen, but a deserter, the Serjant Majr. of the 2nd Betallion of Hylanders coming out with the following intelligence I thought proppor to forward it immediately. He says that the 1st & 2nd Battallions of hylanders with Some other British regiments, Some of the Greens & about one hundred horse In the whole about 3000 Marched this morning with three days Provision Cooked, he left them four mile this side of kings bridg. They brought with them Several Field peaces and a Number of wagons. The day has been so very bad that I dont think they have been able to proceed or

I should have heard something of By my Hors patrols before this. . . . He says that he heard Some of the Soldiers who was from the City say that 7000 men had gon into the Jerseys about two days ago, which agrees with the accounts I have had. He also Says that a Considerable number of Flat bottom boats was Brought up the North River Yesterday, opposite Kings bridg.[39]

A Poughkeepsie newspaper of September 23 had published the highlights of the intelligence gathered from the sergeant major, which properly identified him as coming from the 71st Regiment: "He reported that 3000 of the enemy with 6 field pieces, and a considerable number of waggons, &c. were at Valentine's, about two miles from King's-Bridge, and on their way to the White Plains."[40]

The second phase of Clinton's plan was starting to unfold. On September 23, 1778, the light corps that had so chastised Scott's light corps—the Queen's Rangers, the British Legion cavalry, and Emmerick's Chasseurs—were pushed forward to Hunt's Bridge; following them, the Hessian Jägers moved to Philipse's House, a ground they were now familiar with. Moving to Valentine's Hill, the former battleground, was the 71st Highlanders, now under the command of their talented lieutenant colonel, Archibald Campbell.[41] The Hessian Grenadiers and the brigade of Major General Johann Daniel Stirn marched on to Van Cortland's House, the entire force under the command of Lieutenant General Wilhelm von Knyphausen. The following day, September 24, these troops advanced farther into Westchester, joined by six British regiments and the Hessian brigade of Colonel Carl Wilhelm von Hachenberg, the new arrivals being posted at Philipse's House, which was then established as headquarters. Facing north, the left of the line was anchored on the Hudson River by HMS *Phoenix*, a 44-gun frigate capable of closing the river to any traffic within range of its guns or any movement of troops attempting to advance along the shoreline. On land, the line from west to east, starting at the 20 Mile Stone on the road to Dobb's Ferry, consisted of the Hessian regiments of Donop, Leib, Erb Prinz, and Wissenbach, followed by the Hessian Grenadier battalions of Köhler, Minnegerode, Lengerke, and

Linsing. To the right of the Hessians lay the British 7th, 26th, 49th, 63rd, 71st, and 4th Regiments of Foot. Two companies of foot Jägers under Captain von Wreden were covering the center of the front at Saw Mill Creek while the light corps under Simcoe covered the right at the Bronx River.[42]

By the end of the day September 24, 1778, Clinton had taken the field with the Brigade of Guards, four battalions of British Grenadiers and Light Infantry, 17 battalions of British infantry, two hundred British cavalry, a large detachment of artillery, twelve battalions of Hessians including all their grenadiers, a large detachment of Jägers, and six battalions of Provincial infantry and cavalry. The total strength, both sides of the river included, was probably somewhere between ten thousand and eleven thousand men under two of the most able Crown officers available, Cornwallis and Knyphausen. Although he had no way of knowing it then, this was the last time Clinton would field a force this large in the northern provinces of America. It was now left to Washington to figure out what Clinton's plans were.

Seven

The Fog of War

WITH BRITISH FORCES ON THE MOVE ON ALL FRONTS, THE calls for help went in many directions. On September 24, Governor Livingston of New Jersey and his privy council ordered out all the militia of Bergen, Essex, Morris, Middlesex, Somerset, and Hunterdon counties, complete with three days provisions, to march to Brigadier General William Maxwell at Elizabethtown "with the utmost dispatch."[1] Colonel Gilbert Cooper of the Orange County Militia, along with John Haring of Harrington Township, Bergen County, wrote to the government in New York State seeking support, stating, with some exaggeration, that the British were adding troops every day, assaulting women and children, and burning down all before them. They also related that a woman who had been at Liberty Pole had counted seventeen pieces of British artillery there.[2]

On the Westchester side, General Scott also tried making sense of what was happening before him, informing Washington he had sent Major Lee and his legion forward to reconnoiter while he himself had his men tend to removing quantities of rum and onions that could fall into British hands. Of particular concern to Scott, and correctly so, was the traffic on the Hudson River: "The flat Bottom boats being moved up to King bridg Leads me to believe they Ither intend to Turn my Right, whilst they amuse me in Front or that they intend passing Some Troops over the river under Cover of this Partie."[3] The boats in the Hudson were not there by accident; they were part of Clinton's hope that Washington might offer him battle on either side of the river, and he would be in a position to draw together a superior or at least equal force in short order:

> [T]he army was placed in a situation to be assembled on either side the North [Hudson] River in twenty-hours, a number of flatboats being held in constant readiness for that purpose; and, as we had the command of it by means of our galleys and other armed vessels as far as the Highlands, Mr. Washington could not draw his together under ten days. And, should he be tempted to quit his mountains to interrupt our foraging in the Jersies or support any detachments sent thither for that purpose, I had a good chance of having a fair stroke at him, the probability being very great that by such a move he must have risked a general action.[4]

While Clinton's army began its forage in Bergen County, to appearances it would have been understandable if its intentions were misinterpreted. About one-half mile to the northwest of New Bridge, starting on September 25, two hundred of the British Grenadiers, joined by the 15th Regiment of Foot, started working on two forts, in a line to the north, in the area known as Brower's Hill. Captain Peebles of the 42nd Regiment examined the ground nearby: "A fine day, took a walk to Newbridge 3 miles by the road but less in a line. A pretty little Village with a Bridge over the Sacking [Hackensack] River to which the tide comes, & is navigable for small craft; 2 miles down on the N: W side is Hackinsack a larger Village."[5] While Captain Archibald Robertson of the Engineers, someone whose job was planning and designing fortifications, blandly noted in his journal on the 25th that the British started two square redoubts "on a Rising Ground West side of New

Bridge to secure our left Flank,"[6] Captain Lieutenant Peter Russell provided a much more comprehensive view of the British position:

> The 15th Regt. sent to cover a working Party employed in throwing up two Square Redoubts on the Heights on the other Side of the Bridge. The army are now posted in the following order, One Regiment in the Redoubts across the Hackinsack on the left an advanced Guard from the light Infantry below them & at the Bridge, a large Picquet of Cavalry on this Side the Bridge. The Volrs. of Ireld. next, the 2nd Battalion light Infantry on the Heights. The 2nd Battalion of Grenadiers covering head Qrs. a mile on this Side—the 3rd & 4 Brigade with the Guns lining the Road—The Guards to their Right, the other Battalions of Grenadiers & Light Infantry to the right of them—and on their Right the American [British] Legion with Part of the 57th preserving the communication to Paulus Hook—The whole amountg. to 6000 men forming a cordon of 10 miles from the Hackinsack to the North River. This army seems to be intended to cover a Grand Forage.[7]

On a line from New Bridge in the west to the Hudson River in the east, the British army presented the following front: the 15th Regiment at the two forts under construction by Brower's Hill on the west side of the Hackensack River, the British Light Infantry at New Bridge, the Volunteers of Ireland along New Bridge Road up to southern Schraalenburgh, the British Grenadiers on either side of Schraalenburgh Road leading south into Teaneck, then along the road from Teaneck to Liberty Pole the 37th and 64th Regiments, and from Liberty Pole southeast toward Fort Lee the 46th, 33rd, 44th, and 42nd Regiments, followed by the Brigade of Guards.[8] The right of the line, anchored to the Hudson, was occupied by the 17th Regiment of Foot, which on September 26 occupied the grounds of Fort Lee.[9] No mention was made of where the remainder of the Provincials or the cavalry were located, although there is some evidence to suggest the latter were broken up into detachments and distributed along the lines.

Colonel Baylor did his best to keep Washington informed of what was happening in Bergen. Indeed, with Major Clough and 120 horsemen under his command, Baylor was in an excellent position to perform the chief duty of light cavalry, to scout and reconnoiter the British. Of most importance, Baylor correctly observed that the British were collecting more forage than was necessary for the daily consumption of the horses on the expedition. If the British were collecting additional forage, it was either for a magazine for the coming winter, or to go onboard ship for an expedition or evacuation. Baylor also explained British positions as best he could: "They are encamped from the new bridge on the Hackingsack river, to the foot of the hill opposite to Fort Lee, in bush huts. They are fortifying a very commanding Hill a little on this side of the new Bridge, which appears to be extensive."[10]

In addition to the two redoubts on Brower's Hill, Baylor also noted that small entrenchments were set up across the two main roads: one leading from Tappan to Liberty Pole in English Neighbourhood and the other about two and a half miles northeast of New Bridge, across Schraalenburgh Road, near a church.[11] Baylor closed his report by enclosing an account of the first deserter who had come in, Private Hantras Hysonec of the 15th Regiment of Foot. Hysonec provided little new information.[12] One anonymous New Jersey Militia officer, part of the force then starting to collect at Acquackanonk, well summed up the situation:

> This irruption into our State has been conducted with the utmost degree of prudence and circumspection;—with a force sufficient, had it been managed with dexterity and spirit, (in the interval of assembling our militia) they might have harrassed a considerable extent of country and perhaps secured a large number of cattle. 'Tis true in attempting this they must have exposed their retreat to the sagacity of a commander, who from his vicinity to Jersey, had it in his power to cut them off. Instead of penetrating into the state, they confined themselves to a small portion of country, between two navigable rivers, exposing only a small front, impenetrable by its situation, and by works thrown up for its

further security. Here they lay foraging, chiefly among their friends the tories, in the neighbourhood of Hackinsack.[13]

And forage the British did. Small private vessels of every sort, in the employ of the Commissary General's Department, went up and down the Hackensack River, taking cattle, crops, and forage. The militia officer who wrote that they were foraging among "their friends the tories" was right to some degree, given the large number of Loyalist families located in the central and southern part of Bergen County. An example of how the relationship worked between the Loyalists and the British is shown by Abraham Ely of Hackensack. Ely was requested to supply a wagon, driver, and two-horse team for the use of a detachment of the British cavalry under Major F. E. Gwynn at New Bridge. Ely's wagon, driver, and team would eventually be used for twenty-one days, September 23 to October 13, 1778. For each day employed in the service, Ely would be paid twelve shillings hard currency. In addition, Ely provided two days' worth of forage to the cavalry detachment, amounting to 1,680 pounds, resulting in a payment of 4 pounds, 4 shillings, to which would be added 12 pounds, 12 shillings for the wagon hire.[14] Unfortunately for Ely and many other Loyalists, it would take four and a half years to receive their payment, when their receipts were presented to a board of officers appointed by the British to examine unpaid goods and services before the final evacuation of New York.

Information on British activities also came from one other location, in what might be considered the southern flank of Cornwallis's army. General Maxwell, senior officer of the four New Jersey regiments of the Continental line, was commanding at Elizabethtown, directly across from British-held Staten Island. Maxwell was in the unenviable position of having a trained military force under his command but being unable to march them anywhere due to their being anchored to the defense of the town, as he noted to Washington on September 27:

They [the British] have threatned us every night for some time past only last night. I am told that the Enemy does not advance beyond Hackensack River & I am told there is no attacking them below it. General [William] Winds, Coln. Dye [Dey] and some others is there. If the Enemy was in such a position that I could attack them with any prospect of success I should be glad & leave General [Nathaniel] Heard here but it is the opinion of most that there can be nothing more done, than keep them within the Bounds of Hackensack River, and that it is likely the Enemy would make a stroke here & Sweep from this to Amboy at least if we should go.[15]

While there is no evidence to suggest that the British had plans to make a move into New Jersey from Staten Island, the possibility alone kept Continental troops tied down for the duration of the British expedition in Bergen County. Washington would need to send support from the main army in the highlands, Westchester, and elsewhere, besides nudging Maxwell to move some of his troops despite his fears. The only question was, would Clinton's troops act before Washington was in a position to consolidate some force to counter him?

First, to bolster the militia assembling under Brigadier Generals Winds and Heard at Acquackanonk, Washington ordered Maxwell to leave Elizabethtown and "immediately march to the high grounds, west of Acquakenonck with your Brigade, in order the better to cover the Country, the public Stores at Morristown, give confidence to the militia, and promote the driving off the cattle &ca."[16] Second, on September 27, Washington ordered General Putnam to send from the highlands the Virginia brigade of Brigadier General William Woodford to the area around Clarkstown, Orange County, near Tappan, "for the purpose of hindering the Enemy from advancing parties from their main body about Hackensack Bridge, to carry off the Stock which has been drove out of the Necks."[17] Perhaps most importantly, recognizing the exposed position of the 3rd Light Dragoons, Washington sent orders to Colonel Baylor at Paramus, informing him of Woodford's taking position at Clarkstown and directing him to "join his Brigade with the Cavalry under your command and act with it till further orders."[18]

Cornwallis awoke on the morning of September 25 to find the weather cleared. "This fine weather has made us forget all grievances," he wrote to Clinton, before continuing:

The provision is not yet come but we can make a shift today without it. I have not heard of the Sloop at the creek, or the victualler at Fort Lee, I have sent to enquire about them. I am convinced that Fort Lee will be the best & safest manner of our subsisting. I have sent out people to enquire about Militia, Cattle &c, & will do the best I can to get at one or the other. There are certainly not above 200 men of the Continental Army in this part of the Country. You had better bring up the dragoons from Paulus Hook as an escort, for fear of small party's crossing the Hackensac river, tho' there cannot be much danger as I have order'd posts from the 57th Regt. at Brown's, Schuyler's, & the Little Ferry.[19]

Clinton arrived in camp shortly after this letter was written. After taking a tour of Hackensack, he established his headquarters at New Bridge, where he consulted with Cornwallis. Later events would show the two were planning on immediate moves against whatever corps were within reach, those they could "get at" to use Cornwallis's phrase. To all outward appearances, though, the army was going about the business of foraging, one hundred wagons making their way to camp on the twenty-sixth, while other troops continued working on the forts at Brower's Hill. Clinton would only stay until the early morning of September 27, needing to cross the Hudson and make his way to Westchester and Kingsbridge to meet with his other commanders. "He flies about like an apporition" Captain Peebles of the 42nd Regiment noted of his commander.[20]

Since Knyphausen's troops had advanced into Westchester and taken up their ground, little had been done in the way of action or movement. As in Bergen, troops collected cattle and forage, although the availability of both was not nearly what it was in New Jersey. Once again it was left to General Scott and his light corps to screen the countryside and determine British intentions. He wrote to Washington on the twenty-fifth, "The enemy that came out Last Wednesday having taken post on Gil Volentins Hill & Within Striking distance of my Camp I thought Prudence Dictated a move of my Corps, which was don This morning at 3 oClock, Leaving the picquets and Some Horse to watch their motions until we could reach our new position." The new position was presumably where the letter was dated from, "Lyon's house on the Bedford Road."[21] Scott's position was flanked on either side by "impassable" terrain. If the British wanted to surprise him, he would not make it easy for them.

Despite his assurances of safety, on the twenty-sixth Washington ordered Scott's withdrawal northwest to North Castle on the approach of British troops who proved to be nothing more than a foraging party.[22] Washington implored Scott to continue sending officers and spies to gather intelligence. "I hope for information that will unfold the real designs of the Enemy," Washington wrote, revealing that Clinton's moves were still unclear to him.[23] Things were only made more confusing when it was reported that a British embarkation had taken place and proceeded to Sandy Hook, where British shipping generally gathered before heading out to sea, "But their Destination I am as Yet a Stranger to and also of the number," Scott admitted.[24] That embarkation would make itself known eventually, but more local events would occupy Washington's attention.

Despite some skirmishing between the cavalry of each side, Scott was able to withdraw in safety, losing only a cavalryman of Lee's legion and another of the 2nd Light Dragoons taken prisoner. Of distress to him was the British position that formed a chain from the Hudson to the Bronx, cutting off all of Scott's spies. Because Scott was forced to rely on civilians who had been near the British, the intelligence gathered in this manner was less than accurate. One woman confidently assured him that a Royal Navy officer asserted to her that they were sending an embarkation to New London to attack the privateers. While no such raid manifested itself, the foraging of the British more than held Scott's attention, as he reported to Washington from North Castle Church on September 27:

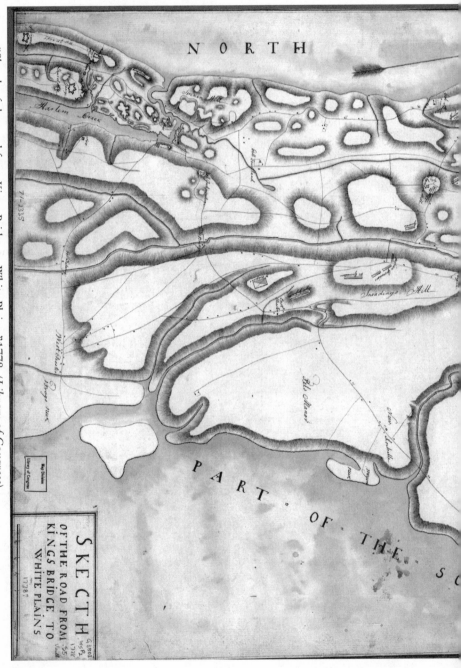

MAP 5. "Skecth of the road from Kings Bridge to White Plains," 1778. (Library of Congress)

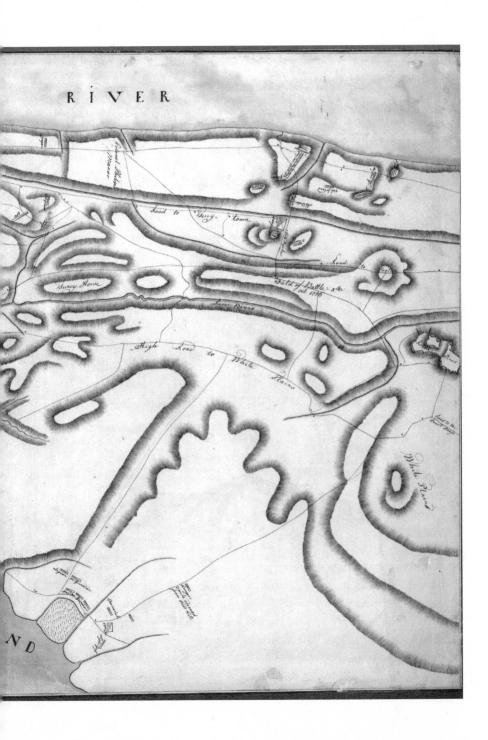

"They have taken off large Quantitys of wheat in the Straw and all the hay that is in that Country which is carryed Immediately on Board of vessels lying off Phillaps's Hous. They have Robed and plunder'd the Inhabitance In a most Cruel manner Striped the Cloths of the Children of many Famalys and havnt left them an attams worth of any thing to subsist on. Ther is no distintion made between whig and Tory."[25]

The distractions made by the British troops in Westchester made no impact on the disposition of Washington's main army, somewhat to Clinton's disappointment. "Mr. Washington . . . would not be moved from North Castle, where he continued in perfect security," Clinton lamented, but only for a moment.[26] The British commander in chief was not on the east side of the Hudson to lead an attack on Washington but to set in motion operations on the New Jersey side of the river. And they began that night.

At midnight, as September 27 turned to September 28, Cornwallis moved off from the picket line at Liberty Pole and headed north on the road to Tappan.[27] Cornwallis had under his command the 1st Battalion Grenadiers, Brigade of Guards, 37th Regiment of Foot, and 42nd Highlanders, some of the best troops in the British army.[28] Three-and-a-half-hours march to their front lay 350 to 400 Orange County Militia, commanded by Colonel Cooper, there to keep an eye on British movements and bring away as much livestock as possible to keep it out of British hands.[29] Cooper had been extremely frustrated by a lack of support, particularly from the Continental army. He vented that frustration on General Putnam on September 26:

I have dispatched Several Accts. to You of Our distressed Situation in this part of the Country and as yet Cant learn That we are likely to get any assistance. I am hereby importuned by the Militia, and Inhabitants in general, to press for help to repel these british Invaders. The Men under my Command begin to be much disheartened that no Continental troops Comes to their Assistance. The Enemy Continue with their main body at the New Bridge and so Across to the liberty Poal, at which place they have Thrown up a Breast work. by the best Accts. we can Obtain They sweep The Country Clean and Commit many outrageous Cruelties—by a deserter just Come in & who is an American That was Compelled to inlist Among them, we are informed That The Numbers are about Six Thousand. That they are alltogether British Soldiers. That they were possessed of eight pieces of Artillery, and how many more he Could not Say. That They were Commanded by Lord Cornwallis. The Said diserter is on his way to your Quarters. we hourly expect They will ravage This part of the Country, which may be prevented if your honour Sends Speedy relief. As we Make no doubt you must be Sensible, that three or four hundred Militia Cannot Stop the progress of Such an Enemy, we Therefore beg if you have any regard for the Sons of liberty in this Quarter, to Send us relief as quick as possible, and prevent This plentifull Country from being dispoild, which will Oblige many hearty friends to their Country.[30]

To cut off the retreat of Cooper's men, Clinton had tasked Lieutenant Colonel Campbell—with one thousand men of the 71st Highlanders, Queen's Rangers, and possibly Emmerick's Chasseurs—to embark from Philipse's House in Westchester and land above Tappan to prevent any escape to the north. Between Cornwallis's column and Cooper's force lay at least one picket of Bergen County Militia. At Closter, just south of Tappan, Sergeant James Riker, a seventeen-year-old militiaman from Harrington Township, was the first to encounter British soldiers approaching. Rather than an overwhelming column of British troops bent on destruction, it was but two men, Francis McCarny and George Motisher, deserters from the 37th Regiment, one of the regiments advancing on the road through Closter to attack Tappan. Riker later recalled:

That he was on a picket guard at Closter, under Captain [Thomas] Blanch, when two Soldiers, deserters, said that the British were coming that night to surround the American militia

at Tappan: that they sent an express to Tappan to inform them:
that he with his company, went to Tappan and found the militia
had gone away: that in the night, they lay on guard at the school
house: that the British came up the next morning, under Colonel
Campbell, to a number, about 1500: that our men retreated to
Clarkstown, & the British followed: but that on account of the
fewness of our men, they did not Engage.[31]

Lieutenant Haring, also of Harrington, had a similar recollec-
tion: "when General Lord Cornwallace made an incursion into that
part of the Country with an Army, as a Foraging party when our
head-quarters was in the south neighborhood of Tappan, and he on
a piquet guard about half a mile distant, when two British deserters came in, who gave notice of the approach of the Enemy, when
they had to retreat before their superior Force to Clarkstown in the
County of Orange."[32] Apprised of the British approach, Cooper
and his men retreated north to Clarkstown. James Vanderbilt, one
of Cooper's militiamen from Haverstraw, reported that the British
followed them to Clarkstown, but no significant action took
place.[33] All the British could do was lament their misfortune in not
surprising the militia post, "which we should certainly have accomplished if it had not been for the Desertion of two Rascals of the
37th Regt. that gave notice of our approach," Captain Lieutenant
Peter Russell of the 64th Regiment wrote home to his sister in
England.[34]

The deserters in question, McCarny and Motisher, disappear
into history after their lifesaving act. Many deserters to the enemy,
from both sides, typically enlisted with the enemy. They were often
career soldiers who simply applied their trade for the other side, as
casually as one might change jobs, but with severe consequences in
case of capture. George Motisher had served in the 37th Regiment
at least since October 1775, while McCarny was drafted (or transferred) from the 16th Foot to the 37th on Christmas Day 1776.
Both were listed on the muster rolls as having deserted from
Captain Henry Savage's company of the 37th on September 28,
1778.[35]

What of Campbell and his corps crossing the Hudson? Thanks to a three-hour delay in crossing, which the army blamed on the Royal Navy and apparently vice versa, the waterborne troops arrived after Cooper's militia had retreated and played no significant role in the operation. With little to do, Campbell's troops helped collect cattle for Cornwallis. "It requires great skill, and still greater attention, to adapt the movements of any embarkation in boats to the tides and shoals of rivers," noted Simcoe on the fruitless expedition.[36] For his part, Campbell was livid when word got back to him that blame was placed on him by naval officers:

> It is with the utmost astonishment and concern I have learnt that certain Gentlemen of the Navy have been pleased to impute my conduct, a loss of time in gaining the Enemy's rear at Tappan on the 27th of Septr.
>
> As this insinuation is of a deliberate nature, and the first instance of the kind I have met with during the course of twenty years Service, duty to my character, and justice to the troops which I have the honour to lead on that day, lay me under the necessity of entreating your Excellency's attention to the inclosed Report, from which simple and impartial state of facts, your Excellency will be able to judge, to whom the loss of a single moment was due.
>
> I shall only beg leave to add, that in corroboration of this statement, your Excellency can only have the testimony of a thousand men and Officers. PS. I forgot to mention, that most of the Midshipmen were sleeping during our passage to the Slote.[37]

Of interest, when Cooper alerted his fellow Orange County Militia colonel, Ann Hawkes Hay, of the British push, he made no mention of Cornwallis but rather alerted him to Campbell:

"This morning at 7 o'clock we were alarmed by the enemies landing a large body of men from about 100 flat boats, at the slote about two miles from Orange Town. A party of light horse came up as far as Orange Town & paraded on the Green. This moment we have information that there are three ships, a sloop & a galley at the Tappan meadows."[38]

Whatever the reason, Cooper was safe for the moment, as neither Cornwallis nor Campbell would be advancing any deeper into
New York in their pursuit. Neither would Cooper loudly celebrate
his escape from almost certain defeat, as there was one more British
column at work that night, and its target would not be as fortunate
as his men were.

Sir Henry Clinton, commander in chief of the British Army in America. (*National Army Museum*)

British lieutenant general Charles, Lord Cornwallis. (*New York Public Library*)

British major general Charles Grey. (*Anne S. K. Brown Military Collection, Brown University Library*)

Lt. Gen. Wilhelm Knyphausen, Hessian commander. (*New York Public Library*)

Above, Lt. Col. John Graves
Simcoe, Queen's Rangers commander. Right, British lieutenant
colonel Banastre Tarleton. (*Library
of Congress*)

Published April 1, 1782, by I. Walker, N.º 76, Pater-noster Row.

Jäger captain Johannes Ewald. (*C.
A. Jenson, 1835, after a drawing by
H. J. Aldenrath*)

American general George
Washington. (*Library of Congress*)

Col. George Baylor, commander of
the Continental 3rd Light
Dragoons. (*New York Public
Library*)

Continental major general William
Alexander, Lord Stirling.
(*Library of Congress*)

"View of Tapen, or Orange-Town taken 28 Septr. 1778 and finished 15 June
1780 on board the *Littledale* transport on the passage from Charles Town
to New-York" by Archibald Robertson. (*New York Public Library*)

British lieutenant colonel Archibald Campbell. (*National Gallery of Art*)

British captain John Peebles. (*Scottish United Services Museum*)

Count Casimir Pulaski, commander, Independent Legion. (*Library of Congress*)

Continental lieutenant colonel Richard Butler (*Yale University Gallery of Art*)

British captain Patrick Ferguson.
(*Private Collection*)

3rd Light Dragoons button excavat-
ed at Baylor Park. (*Courtesy Bergen
County Office of Cultural and
Historic Affairs*)

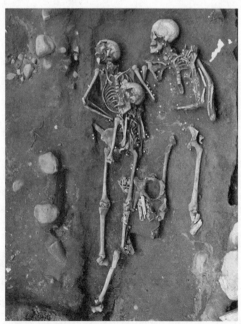

Remains of 3rd Light Dragoons. (*Courtesy
Bergen County Office of Cultural and
Historic Affairs*)

Wortendyke Barn, Park Ridge, New Jersey. A type of barn similar to that used by the 3rd Light Dragoons on the night of September 27, 1778. (*Courtesy Bergen County Office of Cultural and Historic Affairs*)

Mansion house of John Zabriskie at New Bridge, where Cornwallis wrote his report following the attack on Baylor's Dragoons. Photo by Deborah Powell. (*Courtesy Bergen County Historical Society*)

Eight

Bayonets in the Night

WASHINGTON'S ORDERS TO COLONEL BAYLOR AND THE 3RD Light Dragoons to join General Woodford do not appear to have reached the cavalryman at Paramus on September 27, the day Washington sent them. Woodford, as Colonel Cooper quickly discovered, was not yet at Clarkstown, but the distance was short, and it should not have been a difficult march for mounted troops. Even without orders, Baylor was preparing to leave Paramus, but where he went was by no means farther away from British troops under an enterprising commander.

The dragoons were probably relieved to be leaving the area, given their contentious relationship with the inhabitants and militia over the writ for forage and supplies appropriated without payment. While moving off in a rush on the morning of September 27, the corps marched only about six and a half miles, stopping for the night in Old Tappan.[1] "Col. Baylor moved his troops from Hackensac by us & went up to old Taapan without consulting our officers . . . [and] by this were placed for the night in barns at old Taapan," recalled Sergeant Peter Dey, the militia colonel's son.[2] If asked, the militia officers might have suggested getting out of the county, or at least stopping in an area with less of a Loyalist population. Baylor was certainly pleased with his choice of encampments, or as one German diarist put it, the colonel was "Feeling secure and anticipating no enemy."[3] As Baylor explained it to Washington, the area he chose faced little risk:

> On the 26 of Septr. I was at Paramus, with the Regt., where we had been four Days. I directed Major Clough the 26th to send the Quarter Master out to provide Quarters for the Regiment within four or five Miles of Paramus, & the same Distance from the Enemy that we there were, & at the same Time gave him my Reasons for so doing; "which he approved of" they were: that I was apprehensive that the Enemy would, if we remained more than three or four Days in one Place, attempt what they executed in two Days afterwards. On the morning of the 27th I marched the Regt. to the Quarters provided for us at Herringtown, & made it my Business, the Moment I arrived there, to make every necessary Enquiry about the Roads leading from the Enemy's Encampment to our Quarters, & also went out & examined the Country myself. I was of Opinion it was the most secure Place I could have stationed myself in, & that it was convenient to gain the earliest Intelligence of the movement of the Enemy as it would have been had not they received the most particular Intelligence of our Guard & Patrole.[4]

While there is no evidence to implicate any local inhabitant of revealing the encampment of the dragoons, it is quite clear the British had a perfect knowledge of where each troop lay and the quarters of their officers, as well as the guard over the small bridge crossing the Hackensack River. While the officers took quarters among the farmhouses with the inhabitants, the enlisted men that composed the six troops of the 3rd Light Dragoons were put up in the large Dutch barns belonging to the Blauvelt and Haring families along the Overkill Road leading to New York state. A guard was placed over the regiment's forage, and patrols were sent periodically from the guard at the bridge.

After Quartermaster Benjamin Hart had settled the men into their different quarters, the guards had been posted, and the officers made use of whatever comforts the sandstone Dutch farmhouses provided them, events were set in motion that would change all of their lives. To their south, only eight and a half miles away at New Bridge, General Grey was issuing orders to the one thousand five hundred or so men under his command. Sometime between nine and ten that night, Grey's troops marched across New Bridge, past the mansion house of Loyalist John Zabriskie facing the bridge on the west side, and wheeled to the right up Kinderkamack Road, all with unloaded muskets. Grey had defeated the Continental troops under General Wayne the previous September at Paoli, Pennsylvania, using only the bayonet.

Grey's force consisted of the 2nd Battalion of Light Infantry (minus four companies), the 2nd Battalion of Grenadiers, the 33rd and 64th Regiments of Foot, and either fifty or one hundred cavalry from the 16th and 17th Light Dragoons.[5] At Grey's side were at least three Loyalist guides, Weart Banta, Peter Ackerman, and Thomas Hughes, all from Bergen County. Banta was a family man, with a wife and three children to support.[6] A carpenter from Hackensack, he had been an outspoken Loyalist from the beginning of the war, for which he had been imprisoned. Although not (then) a soldier, he certainly acted the part, enlisting sixty-one men for the King's Orange Rangers and the 4th Battalion, New Jersey Volunteers.[7] In October 1777, he was sent out "to reconnoitre Fort Montgomery which he did effectually and afterwards helped to take it."[8] Banta was thrust into the limelight in February 1778, when he and three other Loyalists went from New York City into Bergen County and apprehended Abraham Brower, a Bergen County militiaman implicated in the murder of John Richards, an unarmed Loyalist.[9]

The second guide, Peter Ackerman, was a member of a large Loyalist family from Bergen and Orange counties that contributed no less than thirty-five troops to the British cause. This particular Loyalist, like Banta, was a family man, with a wife and four children to support, and had recruited men (probably family members) for the New Jersey Volunteers.[10] Like many Loyalists who had joined the British on their first arrival in the area in 1776 and early 1777, Ackerman used the opportunity of the foraging to attend the army and take away his family, leaving his property in Harrington Township behind. When informing British claims commissioners of his services during the war, Ackerman prominently mentioned having served on this occasion as a guide against the 3rd Light Dragoons at "tappan wich was Called Lady washentons Lite horse."[11]

The third guide, Thomas Hughes of Barbados Township, was a father of five who had early on joined the British. He later proudly recalled he was "one of those who gave information of Lady Washingtons light Horse . . . and was one of the Guides that conducted the Kings Troops to that Place."[12]

None of the guides would disappoint the British that night, and no fortuitous deserter was making his way to Baylor's quarters.

After proceeding north on the Kinderkamack Road, the column swung east, six companies of light infantry under Major John Maitland of the Corps of Marines leading the column. Sometime between one and two in the morning on September 28, an additional six companies of the 2nd Light Infantry under Major Turner Straubenzee of the 17th Foot silently extended through the fields to the north, making their way to the houses and barns that contained the sleeping officers and men of the 3rd Light Dragoons. The first to discover the British was the patrol of a sergeant and twelve dragoons sent from the bridge, who were quickly cut off by the light infantry advancing through the fields and blocked by the column on the road. No alert or warning came from them. From that point, the six light infantry companies under Straubenzee did all the work. "All Communication being cut off from our Parties they marched up to our Quarters, & executed the horrid Massacre." was all Colonel Baylor would say of the subsequent action.[13]

The British mode of attack this night was similar to Grey's previous victory at Paoli. By forbidding his men to fire and preventing them from having the means to discharge their weapons, the British in the darkness of the night were able to identify the flash of any firearm as belonging to an enemy and dispatch him with bayonets. As was later reported to Washington, "the Charges were drawn from their Firelocks & the Flints taken out that the men might be constrained to use their Bayonets only: This has occasioned the General [Grey] to be nicknamed, among such of the British Officers as can feel the compunctions of humanity, the no Flint General."[14]

After eliminating the dragoons' patrol, the light company of the 71st Highlanders initiated the attack:

> Major Straubenzie moved on with the 71st Light-Company, and in a Small Village surprised a Party of Virginia Cavalry, stiled Mrs. Washington's Guards, consisting of more than an Hundred, commanded by Lieut. Col. Baylor, who, with Major M'Leod [Clough,] and two other Officers, upon forcing the Door of an House, attempted to get up a large Dutch Chimney; the Two former were mortally wounded, the Third killed, and the Fourth made Prisoner; from hence a Part of Sir James Baird's [71st] Company was detached to a Barn where 16 Privates were lodged, who discharged 10 or 12 Pistols, and striking at the Troops sans Effet with their Broad Swords, Nine of them were instantly bayoneted and seven received quarter.[15]

Dismounted cavalry, armed with pistols and swords, fighting in the dark, stood no chance in this battle. Those seeking to surrender met mixed receptions at best. For most, the answer was a bayonet:

> We hear Col. Baylor's regiment of horse, having taken post the beginning of last week at or near Old Tapan, were surprised in the night by means of a tory giving the enemy information, and who conducted them along bye roads into the rear and between our out-centries. These horrible murderers consisted of two regiments of British light-infantry, a regiment and two troops of horse—who made a joint attack, the British officers ordering their men to "give no quarter to the rebels." Our cavalry being in a situation which did not admit of a successful defence, a considerable part of the regiment unavoidably fell a sacrifice to

those cruel and merciless men: Several of our soldiers were murdered after they had surrendered. Col. Baylor, Major Clough,
and Dr. [Thomas] Evans, were dangerously wounded, taken
prisoners, and left on parole; the Major, we hear, has since died
of his wounds.[16]

Some who initially were taken prisoner were later ordered killed.
Thomas Tally of the 2nd Troop was one such soldier. Hearing the
initial alarm raised once the attack commenced, he was ordered by
the British to come out of the barn and surrender. After getting
dressed, he appeared, when he was stripped of his breeches by his
captors but otherwise unharmed. The situation turned bad for Tally
and the others when the light infantrymen guarding them sent for
instructions on what to do with their captives: "That in a few minutes thereafter word was brought that the officer ordered all the
prisoners to be killed upon which the Deponent was ordered into
the said barn, & had no sooner entered the barn than they stuck
him with their bayonets about the breast, upon which he dropt in
the ground, & afterwards found that he had received three more
wounds in the back of which I was then insensible. That the Enemy
held a candle to his face to discover as he believes whether he was
dead, & he supposes left him taking him to be dead or expiring."
    Virginian George Willis, also of the 2nd Troop, told a similar
tale, having initially been taken prisoner but then ordered back into
the barn when he heard orders shouted to kill the prisoners: "he
immediately received two wounds with a Bayonet in his breast, &
in turning about to the other door, he received two more in his
back, & they continued stabbing him till he had received twelve
wounds. That after he had fallen with the wounds, they stripped
him, & by their conversation he understood they left him for dead,
with two more of the said Troop who lay near him."[17]
    Bartlett Hawkins was a twenty-year-old from Orange County,
Virginia, and another who had been granted quarter until a British
officer appeared on the scene. Surrounded by "four of the Enemy
standing about [him] (he having no arms) an officer ordered them
to stab him, upon which two of them immediately stabbed him

with their Bayonets, & left him near the barn door on the ground taking him as he supposed to be dead or expiring."[18] Hawkins was bayoneted a total of eighteen times, disabling him for five months afterward and sporadically thereafter.[19]

Joseph Carrol of the 6th Troop was asleep when he was awakened by the shouting of his sergeant. The groggy dragoon had enough time to dress and make his way to his horse, which he attempted to saddle, however, "at or just out of the barn door seeing him self surrounded by the Enemy, he asked for quarters & surrendered himself a prisoner upon which some of the Enemy, without making him any answer, stuck him with their Bayonets in his left arm & breast & immediately after bayoneted him in his right arm. Upon which the Deponent dropt down in the barn yard & where they left him." Carrol was then stripped of his uniform and left for dead, although five others in the barn were brought off as prisoners.[20]

David Stringfellow was asleep in one of the barns when the clamor about him woke him. Racing from the barn, he had made it forty or fifty yards clear when he was stabbed by a small sword from an officer. Extricating himself from that predicament, he crawled along the ground underneath the horses and into a shed until morning's light revealed the British had gone. Staggering back into the barn that had been his quarters, he retrieved his clothing, which in his haste he had left behind. It was there he found his corporal, Dave Rhore, dying of wounds.[21]

Thomas Benson was a soldier in the 4th Troop, which appears to have been spared. "It appears, indeed, that one of their Lt. Infantry Captains, had the feelings of Remorse, & ventured to disobey his Orders. He gave Quarter to the whole 4th Troop, & not a man of them was hurt, except two that happened to be on guard: For the Honour of Humanity it is to be wished this Gentleman's name had been known."[22] Unfortunately for Benson, he was one of the two on guard from the 4th Troop. A surgeon later informed him he had received a dozen wounds, having been bayoneted in the shoulders, arms, and hips, which, incredibly, did not prevent him from leaping a fence in the barnyard and making his escape.[23]

The most vivid account, and the one that in some respects seems implausible, was given by William Bassett, a twenty-four-year-old private from Bottentout County, Virginia. Bassett, some fifty-five years after the event, not only related his personal experience during the battle but attempted to lay the blame squarely with the inhabitants' getting the dragoons drunk and then alerting the British to their presence. Given that the plans were made for the attack before the regiment even arrived at Old Tappan, and no other survivor (or British account) mentions any frolic or "corrousal" involving the locals (as Bassett's pension application later did), that part of the story does not stand up to scrutiny. It does, however, reveal the rationalization of a survivor about how such a thing could have befallen them. The rest of Bassett's account does correspond in general with those of the other survivors:

> [H]e marched to Old Tappan, and was stationed there in a Stone Barn where the Americans were betrayed by the Torys and all who were stationed there were either Killed, wounded or taken prisoner except Seven exclusive of Capt. [John] Stith. At the time when the afair first spoken of took place Col. Bailors men were quartered at Tappan and the Inhabitants of the place pretended to be very friendly to the cause of the Americans, and some of them made parties for the American soldiers and furnished large quantities of Spirits of the choicest kind for the troops—and the American soldiers supposing themselves safe and in the hands of their friends became merry to excess. In the mean time the Torys sent off runners to New York to inform the Brittish of the situation of the Troops. This applicant was sleeping that night in a Stone Barn at Tappan with many more of the troops. There were troops quartered at almost every house in the place, and he must say it with regret that few of them were in a situation to defend themselves even had they been apprised of the danger which was surrounding them, owing to the corrousal a few hours previous as before stated. He was aroused from his sleep by the breaking of doors without, and the cries of the soldiery for quarters—two men were sleeping close to him under the same cover and he

attempted to awake them, for he knew that the Troops were surprised by the enemy—but he could not succeed in consequence
of the men being insensible through drunkenness. He therefore
thought to make his escape and run to the barn door and sliped
a small sliding door (which was contained in the large door) but
notwithstanding the darkness he could see plainly that the Barn
was surrounded by armed men, he therefore asked for quarters,
they replied to him "God damn your Rebbel Soul we will give
you quarter" and they demanded of him "how many men are in
the Barn"; he answered that he did not know how many. At this
time the men within had become alarmed, except (those who
were drunk) and were runing out at the various places in the
Barn where they could make their escape where upon the Brittish
and Torys cried out "skiver them" "skiver them" (which meant
bayonet them.) The whole party however were killed, wounded,
and taken prisoner except a few of those in the Barn (Eight in all
with Capt. Stith excepted.) This applicant was taken prisoner
and ordered to stand while an armed man stood to guard him.
He took the opertunity when the rest of the Enemy were some
distance off and sprang over a fence to make his excape, the
guard sprang at him, and as he was jumping over the fence he
was stabed in the back by a plunge of his pursuers bayonet
which entered near the back bone which wounded him very bad.
He however made his escape notwithstanding he was almost
fainting under the pain of his wound. The horrors of that night
will never be effaced from his memory. Besides the curses of our
infuriated soldiery we heard the cries and groans of the wounded and dying! Maj. Clough was run through with a bayonet
while asking for quarters![24]

Some later nineteenth-century local accounts provided valuable
information, along with a healthy dose of legend and lore. One of
the farms used for quarters that fateful night was that of Cornelius
D. Blauvelt, a first lieutenant in the Bergen County Militia.[25] Later
generations of Blauvelts would retell the story of how the British
attacked that night, mostly based on a fanciful conversation

between the militia officer and General Grey. While the strict veracity of that part of the story may be in doubt, one part of the legend
would much later be proven true:

> It was not until the next morning that Mr. Blauvelt discovered
> the full extent of the British brutalities. On reaching the stable he
> found five men lying dead on the ground from wounds and
> many more seriously wounded. It appears only a portion of the
> English soldiers entered the house, the remainder being detailed
> for the bloody tragedy in the barn. The wounded ones received
> immediate attention and at night the others were buried under
> the shade of a large tree in the vale opposite the house, near an
> old tannery which was in operation at that time.[26]

The officers among the dragoons certainly suffered as well, starting at the top. The imagery of Colonel Baylor and Major Clough
attempting to hide in a chimney graphically shows the desperation
of the moment. No chimney of any size would have sufficiently hid-
den the two cavalry officers, and their being cut down was
inevitable. While Baylor survived his bayoneting for the present,
Clough succumbed to his wounds the next day. Robert Morrow, a
cornet and adjutant of the corps, "finding himself surrounded in his
Quarters, by the British troops, He offered to surrender himself,
and begged his Life. That they replied 'yes, Damn you, we will give
you Quarters,' then rushed on and stabbed him with their
Bayonets, and Stripped him of all his Cloths." The British stabbed
him several times in the breast and then clubbed him about the head
with the butts of their muskets. Thinking him dead, they left him
there with the dead and dying.[27] Baylor, because of his wounds, was
paroled by the British and left to be treated by Continental doctors
and surgeons. The surgeons tending the wounded also needed to
treat Surgeon George Evans of the dragoons, who was among those
cut down and paroled. Captain John Swan, Lieutenant Peregrine
Fitzhugh, Cornet Francis Dade, Cornet Robert Randolph,
Surgeon's Mate Thomas Evans, Volunteer Baldwin Dade, and
Volunteer John Kelty were the officers taken prisoner and not

wounded, along with three sergeants and thirty-three privates, eight of whom were wounded.[28] An officer of the quartermaster's department, Joseph Shurtliff, was also taken prisoner, although the actual circumstances of this do not seem to have been recorded.[29]

Despite the cries of "no quarter" to the dragoons, more survived the night unhurt than not. According to the subsequent investigation led by Surgeon David Griffith, only "Eleven were killed outright, 17 were left behind wounded, 4 of whom are since dead, 33 are Prisoners in N. York, 8 of them wounded, the rest made their escape."[30] This count differs somewhat from a return made out by Quartermaster Sergeant Charles King on October 23, 1778. That return concurs that thirty-three privates were taken prisoner but notes twenty-two men dead and thirty-four sick or wounded. Seventy-eight horses also appear to have been captured by Grey's troops. Surgeon Griffith indicated that 104 privates were present, which also seems on the low side, as King's return, excluding men on command, shows 129 might have been present at that time.[31] While the number returned as sick may include those men who were in fact suffering from illness and other noncombat-associated ailments, it also may include more men wounded than noted in Griffith's report. General Cornwallis, reporting later on the twenty-eighth after his return to New Bridge, happily informed Clinton, "The whole loss on our side was one Man killed of the Second Battalion of Light Infantry, which Corps had the Principal Share in this Business, and behaved with their usual Spirit and Alacrity."[32]

Grey's work was not done at this point. There were still the columns under Cornwallis and Colonel Campbell to support in their planned surprise of Colonel Cooper's militia at Tappan, at least as far as Grey knew at that point. While the columns of those officers attacked from the south/southeast, Grey wanted to maneuver his force to the northwest and come in from that direction, effectively putting himself between Clarkstown and Tappan, feeling any retreat by the militia would be heading into that area. To accomplish this, Grey's troops continued north, into New York, before cutting back southeast into New Jersey again, as Captain John André explained: "the Column proceeded to the Cackiat

Road where it turned to the Right and crossing the Hackensack at Perrys Mills came to Tapaan. The light Infantry on approaching the Village had been detached to the left in Order to surround any body of the Enemy which might be there. They had however to the number of 200 Escaped an hour or two before."[33] This is not to say, however, that the British met no enemy.

To be sure, not every militiaman escaped death or capture that night. As a prudent commander, Cooper had sent a patrol or scout south across the border into New Jersey to better learn the movements of the enemy. James Quackinbush, a former Bergen County resident who had moved with his grandfather to Clarkstown, New York, in 1776, was now a soldier in the Orange County, New York Militia. Many years later he recalled that fateful night:

> The Company of Captain [Joseph] Crane prepared for a Scouting expedition, and this deponent Volunteered as one to go into New Jersey, and after scouting some time at different places, marched on their return (It being the night that a party of the British under the command of General Gray, as this deponent believes, surprised and took the greater part of Colonel Baylor's Cavalry as they lay asleep at Tappan) as far as the Barn of a person by the name of Hogenkamp, when worn out with fatigue laid all night in the Barn, which was but a few miles south of the place of the massacre, this deponent and the rest of the company slept quietly until morning, when they were alarmed, and informed that the British was above them, Captain Crane immediately paraded his men, and marched upon an eminence, and immediately discovered, that the British had surrounded them, and gave orders for every man to make his escape, when the greater part of the company were killed or wounded. This deponent and few others took a different direction and fortunately escaped, among those that were killed this deponent now remembers the names of John Burges & Jacob Archer, and that Lieutenant Blauvelt was among the wounded.[34]

The barn where the militia was surprised at about sunrise that morning belonged to Lieutenant John Hogenkamp of the Bergen

County Militia.[35] An unnamed British officer, a part of Grey's column, described the aftermath of the attack on Baylor's Dragoons:

> The Troops lay on their Arms till Break of Day, when moving forward, the Light-Infantry fell in with a Volunteer Company of Militia in a very Thick Wood and Swamp, these gave one Fire, which the 40th Company, commanded by Capt. [William] Montgomery, returned, and drove them off, leaving 6 Dead, but afterwards scampering across the Road, in Front of a Company of Grenadiers, three more were killed by them. The Light-Infantry, in pursuing them, up to Tapan, where they were intirely dispersed, took five Prisoners, all of them wounded.[36]

Some escaped, and not for the first time that week. Peter S. Van Orden, the fifteen-year-old from Schraalenburgh who had survived the surprise at Liberty Pole five days earlier, survived this as well, "myself very narrowly escaped to Orangetown, in the State of New York."[37] Abraham Blauvelt of Kakiat, a captain in the Orange County Militia, "finding himself surrounded by a vastly superior force, and a retreat impossible, he offered to surrender himself, but that instead of quarter he was instantly fired upon & wounded in the Thigh & afterwards stabbed in the Breast with a Bayonet and left for Dead. He further Declares that he Heard the British Officers and Soldiers swear that they wou'd give quarter to no Militia man."[38] Even Van Buskirk's New Jersey Volunteers claimed to have taken four prisoners that night, although it is uncertain with whose column these Loyalists were or where exactly the prisoners were taken; militia in the Tappan neighborhood appears most likely.[39]

Despite the light infantry trying to chase down a few of the militia patrol's fugitives, the bloody night's work was at an end. Grey's troops linked up with those of Cornwallis and Campbell; however, there was nothing else to be done but collect some cattle and escort whatever Loyalist families that wished to come within the British lines. One such family was that of Abraham Lent of Orange Town. The owner of a stone house and estate, Lent packed whatever he could onto a borrowed British wagon and went eventually to New York City with a family of six, where he would be reduced to extreme poverty less than a year later.[40] Their story was hardly unique.

For the men engaged in the fight for the new United States, the dawn brought only the sight of the mayhem from hours earlier. Militiaman John A. Haring, then perhaps at Paramus, recalled that they received news of the attack around break of day on the twenty-eighth: "[I] was detailed amongst others to bury the murdered men."[41] David Schofield, an Orange County militiaman retiring from Paramus via Old Tappan, perhaps said it best for many: "at that time I Saw a Number who had been Murderd by the British . . . & there I saw a great deal of human Misery of the Day and those who had been in the night Murderd." And there, some in tanning vats, some in places unknown, the dead would remain nearly forgotten for almost 180 years.

Nine

The Collection

" THE 2ND BATTALION LIGHT INFANTRY WERE THOUGHT TO be active and Bloody on this Service, and it's acknowledged on all hands they might have spared some who made no resistance, the whole being compleatly surprised and all their Officers in bed; this Regiment consisted of 180, and by this rencounter totally disabled from further Service."[1]

So said Lieutenant Colonel Stephen Kemble, a New Jersey Loyalist and the deputy adjutant general of the British army in America. Word of the action the night of September 27 spread on both sides of the lines, and judging by Kemble's thoughts, there was unease over the particulars of the victory. Loyalist Judge Thomas Jones, no fan of virtually any British officer or action, went much further, writing in his history of the war that all of Baylor's men "(a few who concealed themselves excepted) were massacred in cold blood, and to the disgrace of Britons many of them were stabbed while upon their knees humbly imploring and submissively begging for mercy. A merciful mind must shudder at the bare mention of so barbarous, so inhuman, and so unchristian an act. An act inconsis-

tent with the dignity or honour of a British General, and disgrace-
ful to the name of a soldier."[2] Cornwallis publicly showed no signs
of any unhappiness with the night's proceedings, giving full credit
in his public report to General Grey:

"[T]he Left Column, Commanded by General Grey, was so fortunate as not to be discovered, and the Major General conducted
his March with so much Order and so silently, and made so good a
Disposition to surround the Village of Old Taapan, where the
Regiment of Dragoons lay, that he entirely surprized them, and very
few escaped being either Killed or taken; He likewise fell in with a
small Party of Militia, a few of whom were killed and some taken
Prisoners."[3]

News spread through the countryside of Baylor's defeat, sometimes meeting with skepticism. General Putnam, commanding in
the highlands, wrote to Washington at 8:00 PM on the twenty-
eighth:

By Sergeant Robinson of Col. Bailer's Regt. of Lt. Dragoons, I
am this moment inform'd, that this morning just before day, The
Enemy found means to surprise Col. Bailer with his whole
Regiment, then laying at Harring-Town. They came upon them
when they had only one man out to Reconnoiter, which they
took and advanced immediately to where the Regt. lay: They
was so completely surprised, that Sargt. Robinson tells me, only
himself and two officers effected an escape. It is probable he may
exagerate a little, but I believe they have met with a verry severe
blow.[4]

Commissary General Charles Stewart, stationed at King's Ferry,
likewise came across someone fleeing the scene of action, of which
he reported to Washington:

"Judge [John] Herring [Haring], whose residence is near
Tappaan, came here, on his flight nortward, and says, that the principal part of the Light Horse, under Col. Baylor, and the Militia,
who were advanced, near Orange Town, have been surrounded,
and cutt of[f] or taken. That a Body of the Enemy landed at Dobbs

Ferry, last evening and that they are beyond doubt, by this time, at Clarks Town."[5]

Of some immediate concern was the safety of a single regiment that had crossed the river to join the troops intended for Orange County, the Additional Continental Regiment of Colonel Oliver Spencer, a corps of less than 140 officers and men. "I am in froite [fright] least the Colo[nel] should meet poor Baylors fate," wrote General Woodford from Peekskill on the night of the twenty-eighth. His consternation was no doubt increased when some stragglers from Baylor's regiment came his way, going "they knew not where."[6] Despite its proximity to the British, albeit briefly, Spencer's regiment did not make contact with them and lost nothing more than a few deserters.

Once the shock of the defeat had been absorbed, the task at hand for Washington was to assess the situation, move what troops could be spared, and position them in an arc from General Scott's position in Westchester west to Washington's main army in Fredericksburg, then west to Peekskill, crossing the Hudson to Putnam and West Point, then down to Clarkstown in Orange County, stretching west to Kakiat and Ramapo, moving south to Paramus, Acquackanonk, and finally Elizabethtown. The southern end of this defensive line had to concern Washington. The reports coming from General Maxwell still showed his great concern about the threat of a move by British major general John Vaughan on Staten Island. Writing to Washington on September 29, Maxwell informed the commander in chief he was standing fast with his troops in Elizabethtown despite being ordered to Acquackanonk. "I say we think that had Your Excellency been informed with all these circumstances and the likelihood of the Enemy crossing here and pillaging this part of the country, as my last letters has shewn you would not have ordered me up to Acquackinac or in that neighbourhood," Maxwell boldly told his commanding officer.[7]

No British force ever crossed over from Staten Island other than to join Cornwallis's corps on September 22–23. There is evidence to suggest, however, that such a thing may have been contemplated, or at the very least word was spread as a ruse to keep Maxwell's troops in place at Elizabethtown. Captain Peebles of the 42nd Regiment, with Cornwallis, noted in his diary for September 24, 1778, "Vaughan is to cross over to Amboy," but he then or at some later point crossed out that sentence. Two days later, Lieutenant Russell of the 64th Regiment, also with Cornwallis, noted in his writings that "Genl. Vaughan is also said to have taken Possession of Elizabeth Town with ye 1st & 2nd Brigade," but, like Peebles, also crossed out that sentence.[8] On September 28, Chaplain Philip Waldeck of the 3rd Waldeck Regiment, a German unit in British pay, noted in his journal on Staten Island:

> We are still full of good hope and were prepared to break camp at any moment. A general's adjutant came hurrying over from the Jersey shore in a rowboat with eight marines. We were eager to hear something new from him, but he would not engage in a conversation but rather immediately set out on horseback and rode to the general. Two English regiments were commanded to march to Elisabeth Point immediately; Admiral Parker also sent his boat from the men-of-war there, and all was put in readiness to cross over. The enemy on the other side was quite alarmed. Since we had also ridden to that spot and were therefore separated from the enemy by the mere distance of a cannon shot, we were able to observe quite clearly the activities around their batteries which lasted into the night. On our side we made no further movement to cross over and the regiment marched back again. Apparently the intention was to make a feint, so that they would pull up from Hackensack. On our return trip we encountered a number of regiments and the light dragoons were saddled and bridled as if something were still to be undertaken this evening.[9]

Maxwell was certainly suffering from a lack of intelligence coming from the island. With over ten thousand troops deployed in Bergen and Westchester, and others preparing for their different embarkations, the British had precious few troops to launch a third major incursion. Aside from the Waldeckers, Vaughan had at his disposal perhaps some of the 1st and 2nd Brigades of British, the 1st and 3rd Battalions of New Jersey Volunteers, and a small troop of Provincial cavalry with which to threaten Maxwell.[10]

No such threat, real or perceived, faced off against the militia answering Governor Livingston's call at Acquackanonk. Major John Conway of the 4th New Jersey Continentals was Maxwell's eyes and ears at that post, sending him whatever information he could on both the enemy and their own militia. Brigadier General William Winds, commanding the militia, no doubt knew that the longer the British remained in the field, the worse his situation would become. Despite the fact that the militia ordered out by Livingston from the different counties had only just started to gather over the previous few days, there was already chatter about returning home to tend to crops. Conway had rosily estimated Winds's strength at one thousand four hundred or one thousand five hundred men, but in fact it was nowhere near that.[11] On September 29, Winds would attempt to do something with what he had available. Even in that, he apparently felt compelled to ask for volunteers to advance on the British, at least according to Bergen County militiaman Abraham Freeland of Pompton, "to Dislodge the Enemy who had possession of Brower hill in the County of Bergen."[12] Freeland, along with two hundred to five hundred fellow militiamen in and out of the county, crossed the Passaic River and made their way from the southwest, arriving at Hackensack and from there proceeding to New Bridge, where they displayed before the southernmost of the two unfinished British fortifications.

There were probably about one thousand five hundred British and Provincial troops stationed on the west side of the Hackensack River, either working on the forts or covering the area. They had little to fear from Winds's force. New Jersey's militia general marched his men to within three hundred to four hundred yards of the forts, and the British troops simply retired within them and fired some artillery on the militia[13] This put both sides well out of effective musket range. "Received a few shot from the British then retreated into a breas[t] work they had thrown up" was how Samuel Roome of the Eastern Battalion of Morris County Militia described the less-than-heavy fighting that day.[14] Winds reported to Washington that he drove the British pickets in but they would not leave their forts to fight him.[15] British captain Peebles disagreed with his counterpart's interpretation of the action, stating, "A Party of 2 or 300 Rebels came down towards where we are making the work on north side of Newbridge & fired away at a great distance for above an hour when a party of Light Infantry dash'd out after them & drove them off."[16]

Finding nothing further was to be done, Winds led his men back to the area of Slooterdam (modern-day Fair Lawn), on the east side of the Passaic River. Here the troops spent the night, although Winds returned to Acquackanonk to file his reports. There was little to say other than that the tents of one British regiment were gone, although the brush huts of another remained.[17] Winds had an easier time than the troops he left. Peter Van Allen, a thirty-year-old Bergen County militiaman from Franklin Township spent a miserable night with his comrades, recalling "he retreated on to a hill near Slaughter Dam, and lay through the night, during a violent storm, and without shelter."[18] Retiring back to camp across the river the next day, the militia suffered its only recorded casualty, as reported by Aaron Voorhes of the Morris County Militia: "On our homeward march, at Acquackanonk bridge one of our Co[mpany], Jabez Bell, was killed by the discharge of a musket accidently, being shot thro' the brain."[19] American efforts to engage the British army in Bergen County had come to a quiet end.

The British took little notice of Winds's efforts against Brower Hill. Now that Baylor's regiment had been rendered ineffective and Cooper's militia made to retreat, the British wasted no time in foraging in their front, meaning, to the north of their lines. At 7:00 PM on September 29, from his headquarters in Teaneck, Cornwallis issued his orders for sending his troops forward:

The 1st Battalion Grenadiers with 2 6 Pounders, 44th and 46th Regiments and an officer and 20 Dragoons to take Post tomorrow morning at day Break at Cole's House on the Great Road Leading from the Liberty [Pole to] Tappan under the Command of a Senior officer of the whole who is [to] Extend his Post from Right to left in front of the Guards and of the 2 Brigades To Cover a General forage. These Corps to take their Pickets with them, at the same time the Volunteers of Ireland and an officer and 20 Dragoons to take Post at Dwas Brook Bridge, and six Companies of Light Infantry with a three Pounder under the Command of a field officer to march the Road from Schraalenburgh Road to Buskirk's Mill. The Regimental wagons and officers Horses are to forage tomorrow, and no Regiment to forage again, till a Report is made of its being wanted of the Officers Commanding these Brigades. A Rooting Party with arms of 2 men from Each mess under the Command of a Captain and two Subalterns to be sent from Each Regiment who are to Bring Roots Sufficient for 2 days. The Regiment Advanced to Root while they are out for the same time.

The Dragoons are likewise to send for the same Quantity of Roots under the Command of an officer they are to Send their wagons for forage and their Horses, if Provided with forage Cords.

The Officers Commanding Corps and Detachments will be made Responsible for the Behavior of their men if any Irregularities are Committed they Certainly will be Reported to the Commander In Chief.[20]

This method of movement, foraging and covering, would be the chief activity of the British in Bergen County for the next two weeks, particularly on October 2, 5, and 8.[21] The movement of the regiments was often for more than one day with no certainty of early return, hence each corps needed to take its pickets with it. Harvesting crops was not what most new soldiers probably thought of as part of their duty, but veterans recognized that foraging, or rooting, as it was also known, was necessary for the sustenance of almost any army in the field. Captain Peebles recognized the importance of the work and the enormousness of the task before them when he wrote of the foraging of October 2, "Another large foraging party out to day towards Tapan, some Regts. from the Brigades

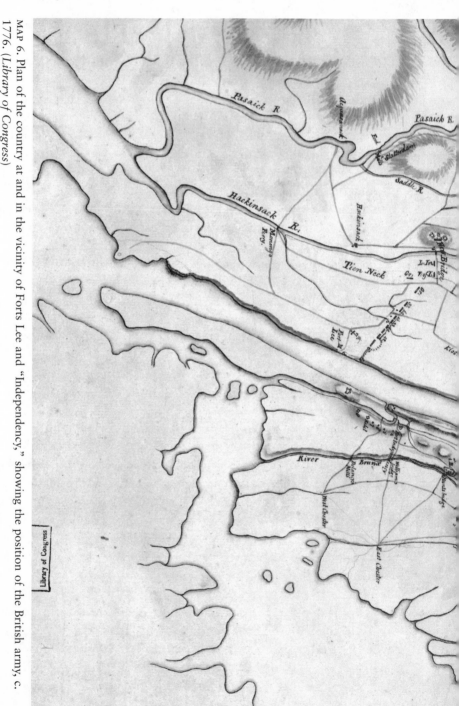

MAP 6. Plan of the country at and in the vicinity of Forts Lee and "Independency," showing the position of the British army, c. 1776. (*Library of Congress*)

cover, they bring the Hay down to the Mill about 5 miles below this in waggons & then put it on board Vessels—it will take a great while to lay in enough at this rate for the Winter—5,000 horses will eat a great deal of hay—1 1/2 tons each."[22]

Shipping the hay, cattle, and produce off to New York City was a monumental task for the Commissary General's Department. The mill that Peebles referred to was at New Bridge on the Hackensack, a river navigable for brigs, sloops, and schooners of sufficient tonnage to transport their acquisitions. The shipping was not that of the Royal Navy but rather privately owned Loyalist vessels operating on a temporary contract basis with the Civil branches of the British army, of which the Commissary General's Department was one. The voyage of these vessels was conducted in safety for the most part. The British occupied all of Bergen Neck, giving them control of the east side of the Hackensack River for the length of the waterway. Detachments of the 57th Regiment had been advanced from their garrison post at Paulus Hook to occupy the few ferries crossing the river, while the infantry of the British Legion occupied "the Heights of Bergen" at the southern end of the neck. Much of the southern part of the river wound its way through what is known today as the Meadowlands, a marshland mostly impassable for infantry. The danger for the British was at the end of the line, where the Hackensack emptied into Newark Bay, an area of great interest to General Maxwell and the Continental troops under his command in the vicinity of Elizabethtown.

The situation at the southern end of the US lines was fluid to an alarming degree. Maxwell had finally obeyed Washington's orders and moved two of his four regiments to Acquackanonk, leaving the remaining two to defend Elizabethtown against any move from Staten Island by General Vaughan. The command at Acquackanonk had been taken over by General Alexander, Lord Stirling, of the Continental army. He had been ordered to New Jersey on September 28, where he was to take command of Maxwell's and Woodford's Continental brigades, all the New Jersey Militia assembled under Generals Winds and Nathaniel Heard, and a force of cavalry and infantry known as Pulaski's Legion, ordered to Acquackanonk from their post in Trenton, New Jersey. Washington's orders to Stirling were straightforward:

> You will make such a disposition of your whole force as shall appear to you best calculated to cover the country, check the incursions of the enemy, and give them annoyance, if any opportunity should offer, which may be, with prudence, embraced. It seems most probable the enemy have nothing more in contemplation than a design against the Posts in the Highlands, you will take such a position as will have an eye to their security, that your Continental troops at least may have an easy communication with and be able to succour them should the enemy make an attempt that way. I have been informed there may be a quantity of stores at Morris Town. I have desired the Commissary if it should be so to have them removed as fast as possible. I wish Yr. Lordships particular attention to this matter.[23]

Upon taking the command, Stirling recognized that the composition of his force was changing hourly. Colonel John Neilson, commanding the militia at Elizabethtown, greeted Stirling's arrival at Acquackanonk by informing him that the regiment of Colonel Frelinghuysen had almost entirely left, while men in his own battalion were "making such constant application for leave to go home that my Patience is Entirely Destroy'd."[24] The militia commanded by General Winds were already leaving before he had even returned from his excursion to Brower Hill, telling Washington "they are Daily going of[f] being Allarmed Men," meaning they had turned out on the first appearance of the British a week earlier.[25] The men called out by Governor Livingston were to at least take their place if not add to their strength. They arrived under the command of New Jersey's other militia general, Nathaniel Heard, but on October 4, Stirling was astonished to find they, too, had an inclination to go home, in their case immediately: "4 oClock this moment General Heard informs me that out of 1000 he marched here yesterday he has not 400 left. It is the Same with Genl. Winds & at New Ark and Elizabeth Town. The Spirit of going home is universal under the pretence of haveing been Called out on a Sudden Alarm for two or three days only."[26] There was no sign or word of Pulaski and his legion.

One small victory Stirling could report was the burning of four Loyalist vessels carrying hay out on the Hackensack River, two of which had been part of a fleet of twenty-three ships, attacked by rebel armed boats coming out of Newark Bay. Not all these vessels were carrying hay for local use, as was reported to Washington on October 9: "One of the Vessels burnt in the Bay by our people, was fitted for the Sea, had 60 puncheons of water on Board, Stalls for 32 horses, and was going to take in her hay."[27] This was almost certainly a small horse transport to accompany one of the British embarkations then forming. Given that no cavalry was included in any of those fleets, this ship probably was to have transported horses for officers, the Royal Artillery, regimental wagons, or the civil branches and hospital. Of the four vessels lost, there was one sloop and three schooners; one of the latter, the *Gage*, was unloaded, while the others were packed with hay.[28]

The British did take some steps to cover their shipping against this threat, but the effort seems to have been insufficient and ill coordinated, leading to the burning of the four vessels. On October 2, 1778, General Vaughan on Staten Island wrote to New York, informing Major General Valentine Jones, commandant of New York City, that nine armed boats had been fitted out by the rebels and might threaten the forage fleet. Vaughan requested that some armed sloops or gunboats be sent to thwart them.[29] Warships were eventually sent, covering the forage ships enough to prevent any further loss, despite the hopes of Colonel Elias Dayton of the 3rd New Jersey Regiment: "The two armed vessels, which anchored the night before last at the mouth of bound-creek to prevent our boats from getting to Newark bay, left their station yesterday, by which means we may have (I hope) an opportunity of burning some more of their foragers."[30]

Other than foraging, there was little to do for the British troops in Bergen, which of course led to problems for the British and Americans alike. Despite all of Cornwallis's warnings of dire consequences to plunderers, large quantities of private property appear to have made their way into soldiers' hands, albeit far less than the widespread losses of the 1776 invasion, when many residents lost property. Most claims submitted at the close of the war list only cattle, crops, and forage, the stated objects of the expedition. Some did have losses that were more extensive and certainly not of a military nature. Daniel Christie of Hackensack Township lost, among other items, a Bible, a Book of Common Prayer, and a spelling book. Abraham Ackerman of Harrington lost five pewter spoons and a spotted rug. Tea kettles, tankards, and sheets were popular items. Martin Poulison of Harrington lost "a grail ful of Soap." Albert C. Zabriskie, Samuel Campbell, James Stagg, and Aury Westervelt, all of Hackensack Township, were unfortunate enough to have British encampments on their property, resulting in the loss of all their fence rails and posts; the cut timber was ready-made firewood. For most of Bergen's rebel inhabitants, the losses were a mix of personal items and foodstuffs. The items taken off the farm of the widow Mary Day of Hackensack Township are an excellent example, with the value she claimed for each in pounds, shillings, and pence:

to 2 gallons of Rum	0. 9. 0.
to half acre Swore of Turnips	1. 0. 0.
to 15 head of Sheep	9. 0. 0.
to 3 yearlings Chalfs [calves]	4. 10. 0.
to 17 pigs Six weeks old	2. 11. 0.
to 20 Turkeys full grown	3. 0. 0.
to 50 Fowls	1. 17. 6.
to 4 Bushels of plantins of potatoes	4. 0. 0.
to 300 of Cabbages	3. 0. 0.
to 70 Bushel of Rey	18. 2. 6.
to 2 Bushel Swore of Oats	3. 0. 0.
to 3 Bushel swore of Wheat	9. 15. 0.
to 4 Loads of hay fresh	6. 0. 0.
to 1 Blanket half worn	0. 6. 0.
to 1 Sheet, to 1 home Spun peticoat	1. 15. 0.

to 1 pewter Dish, 2 pewter plates	0. 10. 0.
to 1 Wagon half worn	8. 0. 0.
to 1 mare, 1 new Saddle & bridle	20. 0. 0.[31]

Military discipline certainly broke down among some units, despite orders and the efforts of officers to contain plundering. Captain Peebles noted in his journal on October 8: "A large foraging Party out to day towards Tapan. I went out with a party for Vegetables of 105 file [that is, soldiers] with arms which passes for a Picquet in this Battn.—got plenty about 4 miles off—a great inclination to plunder & to be licentious among these Grenadrs.—confin'd two."[32] A spy for the United States going by the name John Vanderhoven reported that even some of the Loyalists suffered by the British, noting on October 9:

"I left the army at Newbridge yesterday & am quite asham'd to inform you of the treatment the unhappy people meet with. The whole country stript naked, I saw a poor tory who has been six months in confinement at morristown & the fellow was begging of the soldiers for his children. Thus fare the tories in this quarter."[33]

Desertion was suffered by most of the corps on the expedition, both in Bergen and Westchester. Not all desertions were successful, however, or perhaps even intentional. Take the case of Daniel Marley, a private in the 64th Regiment of Foot, stationed in English Neighbourhood. On September 27, hours before his regiment marched under General Grey to attack Baylor's dragoons at Old Tappan, Marley absconded from camp and was not seen again until apprehended on October 11 at a house not one mile from his camp. When Marley was put on trial, his defense was short and succinct: "that he was in Liquor and lost his way, but that he had not the least intention to Desert or go to the Enemy, and that he lived all the time he was away upon apples and lay upon a Cock of Hay, 'till the night before he was apprehended, when it rained so very hard that he went into the House for shelter." Taking these things into account perhaps, the court found him guilty of desertion but sentenced him to only five hundred lashes on the bare back with a cat-o'-nine-tails.[34]

Theft of rebel property was one thing, but one of the corps involved in the forage suffered a unique loss of its own. The pay and bounty money for a part of the British Legion lay in the tent of one Thomas Miller, a second lieutenant and paymaster of the legion who was responsible for the cash. When Miller was called away to New York City on business, the money was secured in a strongbox and left behind.[35] The next day, October 10, 1778, rain and wind came into the area, intensifying to such a degree at night that the officers ordered their men to abandon their brush huts and occupy the barns of neighboring farms. Not wishing to leave the money unattended, Sergeant Major William Taylor posted a sentry on Miller's tent and had a sergeant lay in the tent with the money. Checking the next morning, Taylor noticed that the sergeant was gone and the sentry was inside by the strongbox, asleep. Finding the sergeant elsewhere in camp, they summoned the sentry with the strongbox, in which there was now just some old clothes. A deserter who came into the British lines the following month informed them he had met with a deserter coming out of the British lines at the time the legion's money was stolen, in possession of upwards of four hundred pounds, approximately the amount stolen. Miller was formally charged and tried for embezzlement that November, even though the prosecution stated only that "duty to the service" obliged them to try Miller, and he was quickly acquitted of the charge.[36]

Aside from keeping an eye on British movements, there was little Stirling could do with the forces at hand. As far as Washington was concerned, his primary worry was the British making a push for the Clove, the strategic pass starting in Suffern, New York, that led through the Ramapo Mountains, providing a back door to the important post and stores at West Point. On September 30, 1778, Washington wrote to General Woodford, at the time still in Orange County:

"That pass is so exceedingly important that they should never be suffered to possess it, and whatever position you take should be calculated to give it perfect security. I have written to Genl. Putnam to send a detachment to occupy the pass leading from Haverstraw through the mountains, by which the Enemy marched to attack Fort Montgomery last year, so that I trust there will be nothing to apprehend from that."[37]

In a few days, Woodford moved with his brigade to Paramus, where he found Colonel Spencer and his regiment along with some militia from Goshen, New York, and a few of Baylor's survivors.[38] Here they remained, within easy striking distance of the British, but neither seemed inclined for any more combat. The British at this point were content to collect their forage, while the Americans collected British deserters from whom they gleaned intelligence. Woodford did his best to keep his men safe, protect the Clove, and get what information he could concerning the enemy, reporting to Washington on October 4:

> The Enemy lay in the same situation they did when my Lord Stirling wrote your Excellency last [October 3, 1778], they appear to be busey at work upon two Redouts on their side the new Bridge, & their Forrageing partys on the other side are very strong. I keep out small scouting partys for the purpose of gaining intelligence, but our numbers will not afford one large enough to cope with those of the Enemy, who are never out of supporting distance, of a Battalion or two of Light Infantry. We have two or three Deserters of a Day, who all agree that ten Regiments are to go immediately to the west Indies. Besides my Brigade, Colo. Spencers Corps & about 150 Militia are here, we shift our Camp every night to guard against a surprise. The [rain] last night gave us a thorough Soaking.[39]

While Washington's concerns were of a purely military nature, Congress turned its attention to the defeat of Colonel Baylor and his regiment. Congress had before turned British actions against civilians into effective propaganda, and the fate of the 3rd Light Dragoons might be of similar value. Henry Laurens, president of Congress, asked Governor Livingston to carry forward a resolve of Congress to investigate the attack. "It has been represented that the unhappy Colonel, several of his Officers, and many of his Troops were Bayonetted in cold blood. Should this be proved, I apprehend suitable retaliation will immediately follow a refusal of satisfaction," Laurens wrote to Livingston on October 6.[40] The depositions collected by Livingston over the next two weeks were published in the newspapers to make the public aware of what it could expect in point of mercy from its enemy.[41]

Ten

Parrying the Thrust
in Westchester

SEPTEMBER 30 DAWNED PLEASANTLY IN WESTCHESTER. FOR THE past week, despite the presence of thousands of British, Hessian, and Provincial troops stretched across the county, neither side seemed inclined for any major action. Washington's main force still remained at Fredericksburg, extending to West Point in the west, and to Danbury in the east, a total of about fifteen thousand men. Small parties from General Scott's Light Infantry and Lieutenant Colonel Ludwig von Wurmb's Jägers occasionally probed each other's lines, but nothing of note had occurred after the latter had taken three prisoners at Tarrytown on September 25. Five days later, however, that changed.

Scott had managed to keep his force relatively safe in the face of so many enemy troops nearby. With about one thousand three hundred infantry and four hundred cavalry at North Castle, his force was a potent tool in the hands of a capable commander.[1] At 3:00 AM on September 30, Lieutenant Colonel Richard Butler of the 9th Pennsylvania Regiment, one of Scott's light infantry commanders, led forward a force of perhaps 450 infantry and cavalry and marched south toward Dobbs Ferry. Butler was a fiery commander, well suited to the task at hand. Private Joseph Plumb Martin, serving under Butler that day, described his commander as "a brave officer, but a fiery, austere hothead. Whenever he had a dispute with a brother officer, and that was pretty often, he would never resort to pistols and swords, but always to his fists. I have more than once or twice seen him with a 'black eye,' and have seen other officers that he had honored with the same badge."[2]

Likewise setting out that morning, advancing in the opposite direction, was a patrol of seventy-two Jägers, twelve of whom were mounted, under the command of Captain Ewald, followed shortly thereafter by a second force of Jägers under Captain Donop of the same composition. Proceeding near Tarrytown, Ewald's patrol found no enemy. Meeting up with Donop on his return, Ewald requested that Donop's force cover his rear and flanks near the Saw Mill River. Ignoring Ewald's warning not to allow his soldiers to pass a defile near a plantation, Donop sent across thirty men under Lieutenant Alexander Wilhelm Bickell right where Butler had placed his men in ambush.[3] Martin best describes the ensuing fight:

> Just at day-dawn we halted in a field and concealed ourselves in some bushes. We placed our sentinels near the road, lying down behind bushes rocks and stoneheaps. The officers had got wind of a party of the enemy that was near us. A detachment of cavalry which accompanied us had taken the same precaution to prevent being discovered that the infantry had. We had not been long in our present situation before we discovered a party of Hessian horsemen advancing up the road, directly to where we were lying in ambush for them. When the front of them had arrived "within hail," our colonel rose up from his lurking place and very civilly ordered them to come to him. The party immediately halted, and as they saw but one man of us, the commander seemed to hesitate, and concluded, I suppose, not to be in too much of a hurry in obeying our colonel's command, but that it was the best way for him to retrace his steps. Our colonel then,

in a voice like thunder, called out to him, "Come here you ras-
cal!" but he paid very little attention to the colonel's summons
and began to endeavor to free himself from what, I suppose, he
thought a bad neighborhood. Upon which our colonel ordered
the whole regiment to rise from their ambush and fire upon
them. The order was quickly obeyed and served to quicken their
steps considerably. Our horsemen had, while these transactions
were in progress, by going round behind a small wood, got into
their rear. We followed the enemy hard up, and when they met
our horsemen there was a trifle of clashing. A part forced themselves past our cavalry and escaped; about thirty were taken and
a number killed. We had none killed and but two or three of the
horsemen slightly wounded. The enemy were armed with short
rifles.[4]

In reality, two parties of Jägers were involved. The initial force
of thirty foot Jägers under Bickell appear to have been caught by
the initial surprise. When the first shots rang out, Donop sent the
twelve horsemen of his force to assist, led by Lieutenant Balthasar
Mertz. Donop himself, much to Ewald's disgust, "took flight with
the rest of his men when he caught sight of several troops of enemy
horse who threatened to cut him off," an assessment with which
Ewald disagreed.[5] Butler had divided his command into three
forces: Major Benjamin Ledyard of the 4th New York Regiment
with two companies of infantry and some cavalry on the right;
Lieutenant Colonel Josiah Harmar of the 6th Pennsylvania
Regiment with two more infantry companies, a party of cavalry
under Captain Alexander Dandridge of the 1st Light Dragoons and
Cornet Ferdinand Neil of Lee's Legion on the left; and the center
force under Butler himself, consisting of a company of infantry
under Captain Charles Graham of the 2nd New York Regiment and
the remainder of Lee's Legion. Lieutenant Bickell, although losing a
number of men, was able to escape along the Hudson and rejoin the
remainder of the patrol that had not been engaged. Lieutenant
Mertz was less fortunate, being slashed about the face and nose
with four saber cuts until forced to surrender.[6]

"I assure you Sir I have never seen Greater bravery displayd. than on this occasion, by both foot & horse . . . the whole in short (that I Saw) in Action would have done honour to any Corps in Europe" was how Butler praised his men to General Scott, adding that only the "Roughness of the Country" prevented all the troops from being engaged and thereby not being able to capture the entire Hessian party.[7] Precise casualty figures for the ambush are difficult to ascertain, for no two sources agree. "Ten were killed, and a Lieutenant and 18 taken prisoners, 15 of whom were Hessian dragoons with their horses and accoutrements. No loss was suffered on our part," said one letter written by a Continental officer from Bedford on October 4.[8] Scott reported to Washington, who had moved his headquarters to Fishkill to better control his troops on both sides of the river, that there were no casualties on their side, but Martin wrote of two or three wounded. A "gentleman from Morristown" reported to a New Jersey newspaper that fifteen Hessians were killed and fourteen wounded, and twenty horses taken, although how he knew this was not mentioned.[9] General Grant of the British noted the loss of one officer and fourteen Jägers. Butler claimed ten killed, along with Mertz and eighteen others captured, three of whom were so badly wounded as to be left behind for humanitarian reasons. Colonel Wurmb wrote that of the mounted men under Mertz, two were killed outright, two died of their wounds, two escaped, and the rest were taken prisoner. No account, however, comes anywhere close to that which Ewald wrote in his diary. Often prone to great exaggeration, he recorded the following the day after the action:

On October 1, General Scott sent back the brave Lieutenant Mertz on parole, accompanied by a trumpeter, with a letter of commendation to General Clinton concerning the extraordinary good conduct of this brave man. The American dragoon captain who delivered him to our post, and who had been in the hand-to-hand fight with this man, was still completely filled with enthusiasm for his heroic deeds. He related that Mertz had killed a dragoon with his own hands, and had seriously wounded one of their bravest officers along with a dragoon. Altogether, he admitted that they had counted twenty-nine killed and wounded by these fourteen courageous men. I have never seen a battlefield on a small scale more horrible than the little spot on which this slaughter had taken place. In a space the length of about 150 paces and the width of a country road, we found twenty-one completely mutilated bodies, counting friend and foe, and seven horses. A loss that was regretted by both sides.[10]

No such letter has been found among Clinton's correspondence, although Wurmb corroborated the account of Mertz's being praised by the enemy. What, if anything, that was communicated to Ewald was truthful in any way is unknown, but it is evident the Jäger captain took it as established fact. One anecdote concerning a Jäger private was related by Private Martin, in what might best be described as a coming-of-age moment for the teenage Continental:

There was an Irishman belonging to our infantry, who, after the affray was over, seeing a wounded man belonging to the enemy lying in the road and unable to help himself, took pity on him, as he was in danger of being trodden upon by the horses, and having shouldered him was staggering off with his load, in order to get him to a place of more safety. While crossing a small worn-out bridge over a very muddy brook, he happened to jostle the poor fellow more than usual, who cried out, "Good rebel, don't hurt poor Hushman." "Who do you call a rebel, you scoundrel?" said the Irishman, and tossed him off his shoulders, as unceremoniously as though he had been a log of wood. He fell with his head into the mud, and as I passed I saw him struggling for life, but I had other business on my hands than to stop and assist him. I did sincerely pity the poor mortal, but pity him was all I could then do. What became of him after I saw him in the mud, I never knew; most likely he there made his final exit. The infantry marched off with the prisoners, and left the horsemen to keep the field, till we were out of danger with our prize; consequently I never heard anything more of him. But the Irishman reminded me "that the tender mercies of the wicked are cruel."[11]

One thing for sure was that Wurmb had tired of Westchester, if not all of America. On October 19, 1778, he wrote home to Germany, "The corps had a great loss on dead and otherwise on captured and the longer I remain at this post I will lose even more. Half of the corps was sick, debilitating dysentery or cold fever, the water is very bad, the fogs are heavy and soon very cool or very warm. I wish we were . . . out of America."[12]

Whatever the actual casualties, a feeling of revenge was perhaps reached by some. "This in some measure Compensates For poor Baylor," General Scott wrote to Washington when he enclosed Butler's report.[13] It was certainly a sentiment touching Washington when he wrote the next day to General Sullivan at Rhode Island, "Colo. Butler with a part of the light Corps retaliated upon the enemy in some measure yesterday morning."[14] Retaliation was also on the minds of Generals Knyphausen and Grant, not on Butler's corps in particular but on any Continental troops within their reach. The day after the defeat of the Jägers, one of the many Loyalist spies employed by the British arrived within their lines in Westchester. Joseph Ayers, a private in the Guides & Pioneers employed in gathering intelligence, reported on the state of affairs in the countryside.[15] The Loyalist reported he had been taken prisoner and brought to the headquarters of Colonel Charles Armand-Tuffin, Marquis de la Rouerie, commanding an independent partisan corps of cavalry and infantry.[16] Armand's corps was a similar, although smaller, version of the British Legion and the other Provincial light corps facing them in Westchester. Armand's corps was formerly raised and commanded by another European, Major Nicholas Dietrich, Baron de Ottendorf. Ayers was able to give information he overheard from Armand's quarters on troop movements to New Jersey and the strength of General Gates's command at Danbury. Of particular interest was the disposition of Scott's force on the lines:

[T]he Rebels had a Guard of 30 men at Burtis's house (6 miles from Hunts Bridge) that Genl. Scot keeps 100 horse & 200 Militia at Wrights mills (3 miles above the Plains to The N. West) from this place they detach 25 Foot & 12 horse to Col. Hammonds [Armand's] 2 miles & a half to the west of Burtis's— Genl. Scot lay between Bedford & N. Castle with about 300 Cavalry & 600 Light Infantry, including the above mentioned detachments; that The Militia is ordered to join him, 500 of them were said to have already assembled.

Some of this Ayers observed after escaping from his sentry while being taken to a guardhouse. Intelligence is best when it comes with corroboration, and that was provided, at least in part, by Solomon Blindberry, a soldier in Colonel Beverley Robinson's Loyal American Regiment.[17]

After confirming Ayers's accounts of the militia and Danbury, Blindberry informed that "at Tom Wrights mills he saw 140 Infantry & 36 Light Horse, The Infantry are chiefly Deserters and The Greatest number of Them Foreigners. 40 odd light horse are billeted at Gilbert Ogdens, Francis Wrights, & Zebulon Dickisons in N[orth] Castle, near four miles further at N Castle Church are betwixt 4 and 500 Light Infantry, there are no cannon at either of those posts nor on this side The Croton River."[18] The British had the information they needed. Grant informed Clinton directly of their plan:

> To return the Compliment if we can, General Kniphausen is to send the Chasseurs [that is, Jägers] to attack the Rebell post at Colonel Hamonds [Armand's]. Wurms will march at Ten at night, and will be at the Place fixed upon before five o'Clock tomorrow morning. Simcoe & Tarlton making a Detour from the Right are to fall in their Rear at the same time they are provided with good Guides. Fires are to be made at the different places where the Rangers have been encamped by way of Deception.[19]

There is but one account of the attempted surprise of Armand's troops, that of Ewald, which is surprising given the number of troops involved. The general plan called for the Jägers, under Wurmb, to advance up the west bank of Saw Mill River to the vicinity of "Watt's house" near Tarrytown while General Grant led the Queen's Rangers, Emmerick's Chasseurs, and the British Legion cavalry up the Mile Square Road to the east to get in Armand's rear and cut off any retreat. The troops set off at about 10:00 PM October 2 and proceeded north to their target. Ewald described what happened next:

> We had just crossed Storm's Bridge to the left when we were attacked by an enemy post which lay at a defile near a plantation. The four jägers of the advanced guard, who were chosen to seize the first sentries by trick or force, were armed only with hunting swords, which they concealed. The four men answered the double enemy sentries that they were deserters, but just as they were about to overpower them by a rush, the enemy sentries smelled a rat, opened fire, and ran back. Thereupon the enemy corps, which was said to consist of a thousand men, grabbed their weapons and took flight, leaving behind their baggage and a part of their arms. The Corps, which immediately followed the four jägers, hurriedly tried to deploy to attack the enemy, and the mounted jägers broke through on the right to take the enemy in the flanks and rear. But the bird had flown the nest. Day broke at this time, the Corps pursued the enemy, and that element under General Grant which was supposed to surround the enemy joined the Jäger Corps beyond Watts's house, having captured only a few stragglers.[20]

Armand's command probably consisted of no more than a few hundred men, nothing close to the thousand guessed at by Ewald. General Scott took virtually no notice of the incident, only writing to Washington probably early in the morning of October 3, "I am informed By an officer of Majr. Lees Corps that the enemy has Returnd, they was about 1 1/2 miles above Tarry Town where they were met by Colo. Gist and exchanged a few Shot and immediately put back."[21]

If the attempted surprise was meant to make Scott's corps pull back or be more cautious, it did not have that effect on the

Continental light corps commander. Colonel Richard Parker of the 1st Virginia Regiment, one of Scott's battalion commanders, had lain close to the British lines for three days until forced to retire on October 4 only for want of provisions. Before withdrawing he attempted to surprise a picket of Emmerick's Chasseurs, in which his infantry was unsuccessful. Captain Dandridge, however, who had taken part in the attack on the Jägers three days earlier, charged his light dragoons at the withdrawing picket, capturing two of Emmerick's infantry and possibly three infantry of other corps. Parker, Dandridge, and the command then withdrew without any casualties.[22]

As was the new routine in Westchester, one insult on the lines produced a retaliatory insult by the opposing side. Unfortunately for the United States, the next excursion launched by the British would be led by John Graves Simcoe. Once again, it was Colonel Sheldon's 2nd Light Dragoons that would be the unfortunate recipients of a visit by Britain's Provincial forces. Simcoe personally led the Queen's Rangers to King Street, near Byram River and the Connecticut border. Here he found a storehouse "with a considerable quantity of merchandize."[23] These stores were accordingly burned, and the troops there, from the 2nd Light Dragoons, were almost entirely taken prisoner "with very good nags and accoutrements."[24] It was left to General Scott to once again inform Washington of the inattention of Sheldon's corps:

> I am Sorry to have occasion to mention to Your Excellency a Second time the loss of a patrol. This morning about 8 oClock I was informd by a Country man that the Enemy wear two miles above Claps tavern, and that the officer and party of horse on that Road had fallen into their hands. I immediately orderd a party down towards the enemy to make What Discoverys he Could, and give me the trooth of the matter. About ten he Sent a horsman up and inform'd me that the whole party was taken and that the enemy had returnd. However about 12 oClock the officer who Commanded the patrol with one man Came in, he is a french Gen[tlema]n and Speaks bad english that I cant very

well understand Him. from the Best Account I can git from him, the hous (meaning Claps tavern) was siroundid before he knew a word of the Enemy. his party Consisted of one officer and Ten Privats nine of which with eleven horses wear taken. This misfortune has again Fallen on Colo. Sheldons Regiment. I have Repietedly orderd that the patrols Should never Stay Four hours at the Same place, but from the best acct. that I can git they, or at least several of the officers take the Best Hous in the neighbourhood of their duty, and there Stay until they are Relieved. I shall order a Court of Inquiry upon this matter Tomorrow. I hope that together with the Surprize will prevent any thing of the kind in Future. The enemy was out on Ward's Road also, this morning Both Horse and foot up as fare as the White Plains they Burnt Several houses on Both Roads, Claps Store among them with a Large Quantity of Rum & Sugar.[25]

Washington's patience with his cavalry had reached its limit. The loss of the better part of Baylor's regiment in one action was one thing, but the 2nd Light Dragoons were losing men piecemeal at an unacceptable rate, and in Washington's view because of the inattention of their officers. He demanded Scott carry through with an investigation:

I learnt with equal chagrin and astonishment, from your letter of yesterday's date, of the new disgrace which has happened to Sheldon's horse; these surprises can only be attributed to the unpardonable inattention of Officers, and their scandalous sacrifice of every other consideration to the indulgences of good Quarters; the frequency of them becomes intolerable and demands some exemplary punishment. I desire that the present case may be very strictly inquired into, and that Col. Sheldon may in my name be desired to address the Officers of horse in such terms as will awaken a sense of their duty. While the Safety of the Army often rests on their vigilance, they neglect the most ordinary precautions for their own security, and risk their own honor, the lives or liberty of their Soldiers, and open an avenue for some more extensive operation of the enemy. If any Officer regardless of his own reputation and the important duty he owes the public, suffers himself to be surprised, he cannot expect if taken, that interest should be made for his exchange, or if he saves his person, to escape the Sentence of a Court Martial.[26]

While no officer of the 2nd Light Dragoons would be charged with negligence, one person did present himself for exemplary punishment. Elisha Smith of Litchfield, Connecticut, enlisted as a soldier in Captain Josiah Stoddard's Troop of the 2nd Light Dragoons in summer 1777.[27] Smith had served previously in other corps and was a veteran of the Battle of Trenton in December 1776. After twelve months' service, for whatever reason, he deserted to the British on August 14, 1778. He met Captain Jacob James two days later and enlisted under him in his troop of the British Legion.[28] Smith, among other deserters in similar circumstances, proved invaluable as a guide for the British, being knowledgeable in the countryside and the whereabouts of his former comrades. Once again, for reasons known only to Smith, he deserted again, this time on September 30, from the British.[29] Returning to his old corps, he found it less than welcoming on his arrival. Brought before a general court-martial, Smith was "tried for deserting to the Enemy last August, for piloting the Enemy in an Incursion into and against the Troops of these States, defrauding the Public by selling his horse, Arms, Accoutrements, Furniture and Cloathing in a treasonable manner to the Enemy and for Mutiny in insulting and menacing his Officers while a Prisoner with them," for which he was found guilty October 10, 1778.[30] The sentence was death. Washington left the details to Scott, explaining, "The example being made where the opportunity to desert is greatest, may have a good tendency in checking so pernicious a practice."[31]

Stoddard appealed to Washington over the sentence, saying Smith was only nineteen, had never been tried for any offense, and had been seduced to desertion by another of the 2nd Dragoons' wayward men, William Patterson, who had likewise enlisted in the legion.[32] Stoddard pleaded for Smith on a personal level, saying the young man was his personal waiter and "of a corrigible Temper, which makes him less desirably an object of Public Justice."[33] Washington was in no mood for leniency, particularly with a member of the regiment that had caused him so much recent unease. Stoddard's request was rejected, Washington informed him, as the execution was "indisputably necessary for the preservation and safety of the army."[34] Smith, a young farmer turned cavalryman from Connecticut, was accordingly executed for the good of the service.

The forage went on. Cornwallis and Knyphausen could concentrate on transport and logistical issues. After Simcoe's capture of the 2nd Light Dragoons at King Street, all was quiet in Westchester, as it had been in Bergen all October. Even Washington could think himself relieved. All the deserters coming in confirmed British plans to embark ten regiments for the West Indies. Two Hessian deserters reported on October 2 that ten thousand men were ordered to the West Indies, with ships wooded and provisioned, ready to sail at any time. The next day two deserters from Emmerick's Chasseurs corroborated the Hessian account and added information concerning the drafting of the 10th, 45th, and 52nd Regiments. Deserters from the 28th and 49th Regiments said the transports intended for their corps were already loaded with baggage, while the forage collected in Bergen County was intended to accompany them.[35] By the end of the first week of October, Washington could breathe easy for the safety of West Point and his army in the Hudson Highlands. His relief might have been somewhat tempered if he had read a journal entry written by Captain Peebles, still tending to his grenadiers under Cornwallis in Bergen, who wrote a simple line for October 2: "A Detachmt. of 500 under Capt. Ferguson gone to Egg harbour."[36] The final phase of Clinton's grand plan had just begun.

Eleven

In Quest of
Pirates and Poles

T HE FINAL PHASE OF CLINTON'S GRAND FORAGE WOULD BE slow to develop but would take him in the direction of the mode of warfare then favored in London, that is, using limited troops in conjunction with the Royal Navy to attack the extensive coastline of America. Indeed, according to Clinton himself, favoring this phase of his operations, the expedition of five hundred British and Provincial troops to South Jersey, was one of the reasons for his movement into Westchester and Bergen: "This position [along the Hudson] was also intended to serve the double purpose of covering a general forage and favoring the operations of a corps I had detached, under Captain [Patrick] Ferguson, to destroy a nest of privateers at Egg Harbor, which had done us a great deal of mischief."[1] Indeed, a naval expedition to Egg Harbor was even suggested by the British peace commissioners, no doubt familiar with Lord Germain's desires concerning the prosecution of the war.[2]

In command of this foray would be one of Great Britain's most energetic and talented officers, Captain Patrick Ferguson of the

Light Infantry Company of the 70th Regiment of Foot. While Ferguson's regiment was stationed in Nova Scotia, the thirty-four-year-old Scotsman had arrived in America in 1777 and was placed in charge of one hundred recruits meant for the different regiments of General Howe's army. These recruits were formed into a temporary corps of riflemen, armed with revolutionary breech-loading rifles capable of being loaded and fired with a fixed bayonet. The corps was to serve during the 1777 campaign and test the rifle, and Ferguson was then to return to England unless Howe judged "it expedient to continue him on this Service in North America," in which case he had leave from the king to remain in America.[3] Dressed in a distinctive green uniform, Ferguson's corps was hotly engaged at the Battle of Brandywine, Pennsylvania, on September 11, 1777, where the captain was seriously wounded in the arm.[4] It was his last action until being selected to lead the Egg Harbor expedition a year later. It was a testament to his leadership that someone of his rank was chosen to lead so many men.

The troops for this expedition came from four corps: at least 161 officers and men from the 1st and 3rd Battalions, New Jersey Volunteers,[5] under the command of Captain Patrick Campbell of the 3rd Battalion and perhaps 150 British regulars from the 5th and 55th Regiments of Foot.[6] All these units were already under orders for embarkation: the two battalions of volunteers to accompany Lieutenant Colonel Archibald Campbell's expedition to Georgia, while the two British regiments were destined for the West Indies under General Grant.[7] The warships carrying the expedition consisted of the sloops *Zebra*, *Nautilus*, and *Greenwich*, and the armed ship *Vigilant*, along with three armed galleys, *Dependence*, *Comet*, and *Cornwallis*, all under the command of Captain Henry Colins.[8] En route they were met by the armed brig *Halifax* cruising nearby to intercept vessels out of Egg Harbor, and Philips ordered it to join the expedition. They were likewise joined by the Loyalist ship *Granby*, one of the new privateers fitted out at New York City that September. It is not certain why the *Granby*, a sloop of ten guns and six swivels commanded by James Bunyan, was part of the flotilla.[9] British general and New York royal governor William Tryon was an enthusiastic supporter of Loyalist privateers, writing to Germain in March 1778:

"Great expectations are form'd of their Success as the Commanders of these Privateers have a perfect knowledge of the Coasts, and will go into Creeks and Harbours, that will not admit of the King's Ships; it is also believed that Numbers of men in the Rebel Ships, will quit that Service, to enter aboard these Privateers."[10]

Egg Harbor was a natural choice as a port of interest for the British. Privateers operating from there could easily prey on British merchant shipping coming into or leaving New York City. It was estimated that in 1778, as many as thirty armed vessels were operating out of Egg Harbor, acting either alone or in groups, ready to intercept valuable cargoes intended for the Loyalist population of New York and convert the captured goods into prize money.[11] The area around the port had prospered as a result, adding new buildings and warehouses. Modest fortifications were thrown up to protect the town and shipping, but no artillery was on hand to arm the works, and no garrison (other than militia guards) was there to man them. The Burlington County seaport would be hard pressed to repulse a determined foe.

The troops for the expedition started boarding from Staten Island on September 28 and two days later set sail.[12] The motions of the British embarkation were noticed on both sides of the Hudson, although the destination was not immediately clear. Lord Stirling, at Acquackanonk on October 7, 1778, wrote to Washington of the confused situation, as it concerned him:

[A]n Expedition has taken place against Egg harbour, Some frigates and Small armed Vessels with some troops from Staten Island under the Command of Courtland Skinner are Sailed for that place. . . . I am much Surprized at Major [Richard] Howels [of the 2nd New Jersey Regiment] Silence. 'Tis possible this Egg Harbour Expedition might have engrossed his attention. A Gentleman I have this moment seen, assures me that all was quiet at Egg harbour on Sunday last. Genl. Maxwell has sent two messengers to Major Howell for Intelligence, I have now desired him to send Col. Forman (who is well acquainted in that Country) to go to Middletown, Neversink &c and get all the Intelligence he can and immediately to return.[13]

Apparently the 2nd New Jersey's major informed his immediate superior, General Maxwell, rather than Stirling directly. Maxwell duly informed Washington (and presumably Stirling) that Howell spotted "on the 1st [October] a Fleet of four Ships & eight Brigs Schooners & Sloops sailed to the Southward, designed as they imagined for Egg harbour."[14] Governor Livingston of New Jersey was also made aware of the situation, about which he could only hope for troops and lament his situation: "I think the Enemy an unconscionable Pack to give this State such a disproportionate share of trouble. Why don't [they] try [their] hands in Connecticut?"[15]

Contrary winds hit the small British fleet almost as soon as it left Staten Island. The six days it took to beat its way south to Little Egg Harbor gave plenty of time to alarm the militia, sail any manned privateers out to safety in open water, move small prizes up the different creeks, and dismantle ships too large to move. That is what Captain Colins found on his arrival off the harbor, taking advantage of the tide to send in two of the galleys and the *Halifax*. The next day, October 6, proving unfavorable, Colins and Ferguson moved the troops onboard into the smaller armed vessels, and by the next day all the vessels were over the shallow offshore sandbar and into the harbor. With all the troops on the smaller vessels, the pursuit of the prizes up the creeks commenced. After several vessels ran aground in the shallow water, the British advanced until they reached Chestnut Neck about 4:00 PM. There, arrayed before them, was Colonel Robert Taylor's 3rd Battalion, Gloucester County Militia, clinging to breastworks built for artillery but of which there was none mounted. One work was built on a hill, while a second was at the water level, and both would have been formidable had artillery been present. Ferguson, however, was unaware of the lack of cannons, making for anxious moments as the British and Provincials approached the shore in open boats:

The Banks of the River below the Works being swampy, rendered it necessary for the Boats with the Troops to pass within Musquet Shot, in order to land beyond them, previous to which Captain Collins advanced with the Galleys to cover our Landing, and as he came to very close to the Works, and the Guns of the Galleys were remarkably well pointed, the Fire from the Rebels was effectually stifled, and the Detachment, landing with Ease, soon drove into the Woods the skulking Banditti that endeavoured to oppose it.[16]

"We were defeated with some loss, and returned [home] after being out one week," is how twenty-three-year-old militiaman Job Weeks glumly but matter-of-factly put it after the war.[17] The battle was over. "One Soldier of the Fifth [Regiment] was wounded through the leg at Chestnut-neck, but we have neither lost a Man by the enemy nor deserting since we set off," Ferguson proudly reported on October 10.[18] It was now time to go to work and destroy, in the words of Britain's commanding officer on the spot, "this nest of pirates."

The sailors and troops methodically went through the village where "they proceeded to destroy the settlements and store houses of the committee-men and every person notoriously concerned in the pyratical vessels, which have greatly annoyed the British commerce from that quarter."[19] Samuel Denike, a local militiaman, could only watch from a distance as the British "burned the village in which all my Father's property was distroy'd."[20] Colins's sailors took charge in examining the vessels and stores found in the harbor on their arrival:

The Vessels at this Place, amounting to Ten in Number, we found were mostly British, which had been seized upon by the Rebel Cruizers; among them was the *Venus of London*, and others of considerable Size, which they could not carry higher up: As all of them were scuttled and dismantled, and some sunk, it was impossible (notwithstanding my Solicitude and Wishes to recover the Property of the King's Subjects) to get them down here; I therefore ordered them to be fired and destroyed. The Storehouses and Settlements here, which seemed so particularly adopted to the Convenience of this Nest of Freebooters, I was also of Opinion, with the Commanding Officer of the Troops, should be destroyed; which was accordingly done, also the Battery before-mentioned, and the Work on the Hill.[21]

At the end of the day on October 6, Ferguson and Colins examined the situation and went over their options. More vessels and stores lay farther inland, but the odds were changing. Continental reinforcements were arriving on the scene, and more militia were being called up. After a week of anticipation as to their whereabouts, over three hundred splendidly equipped lancers and infantry arrived in the neighborhood.[22] It was Count Casimir Pulaski and his legion.

Pulaski was a Polish nobleman born March 4, 1747, at Winiary in the south-central part of his country. By the mid-1760s, Pulaski's father, Josef, along with Casimir and his brothers, Antoni and Franciszek, had become leaders of the Polish rebellion against the Russian-installed monarchy ruling their country. Raising and leading forces into battle against the far more numerous Russian troops, the young count scored several victories but suffered numerous defeats as well. After his capture and parole in July 1768, the Pulaski family raised a new force in Moldavia. After being defeated there, the small force made its way across the Carpathian Mountains back into Poland. With no allies, the rebellion teetered along until finally winning a victory at Czestochowa. Emboldened, Pulaski became involved with an ill-conceived plot to kidnap the king from Warsaw, which was accomplished with much bloodshed the night of November 3, 1771. After bribing a guard, the king quickly returned to Warsaw, and the kidnappers and their movement were branded outlaws throughout Europe. On May 31, 1772, Casimir Pulaski and a handful of staff slipped out of Poland, never to return.[23]

After spending years in exile in France, including a stint in debtors' prison, Pulaski offered his services to American diplomats in Paris, who shipped him off like many others to Congress to add professional European military talent to the fledgling Continental Army. Pulaski's talents as a partisan commander led Congress to appoint him a brigadier general and commander of all Continental cavalry, which was confirmed by Washington shortly after the Battle of Brandywine in September 1777.[24] The officers command-ing the four regiments of light dragoons that made up the Continental army's cavalry never took well to their new Polish com-mander, a man who spoke little English and was considered diffi-cult to get along with. After just six months, Pulaski resigned his commission as general. A new appointment, however, as "Commander of Horse" led Congress to approve of Pulaski's rais-ing a legion of cavalry and infantry in early 1778 that could be a home to the many foreigners offering their services to the new United States. Expending huge sums of money to raise and equip the legion, Pulaski soon became a sore subject to both Congress and Washington, particularly for a corps that by the end of the summer had provided no real service and was still in Trenton, New Jersey, away from any scene of action.

With Cornwallis's entry into Bergen County and the severe loss inflicted on the 3rd Light Dragoons, Washington had little choice but to summon Pulaski and his men to join the army gathering under Stirling. He wrote to Pulaski:

"You are to proceed immediately upon the receipt of this, with your whole Corps both Horse and Foot and put yourself under the command of Major General Lord Stirling, who will be in the neigh-bourhood of Paramus. As the Enemy are out in considerable force in Jersey, near Hackensack, you will make particular enquiry of their situation as you advance, lest you should fall in with their parties."[25]

Still tethered to problems with Congress, including the issuing of commissions to his officers, Pulaski never stirred, although word of his marching to Princeton spread wide and far. The distance between Trenton and Princeton being inconsiderable, it was clear Pulaski was in no hurry in light of his difficulties with Congress. Pressed by Governor Livingston for relief, Congress brushed aside its concerns and at 3:00 PM on October 5, 1778, officially sent

Pulaski a stack of signed commissions for his officers, along with orders to immediately proceed to Egg Harbor.[26] Joining the legion were several pieces of artillery from Colonel Thomas Proctor's 4th Artillery Regiment, giving the Continentals a force greater than Ferguson's land contingent and with cannons to challenge at least the smaller British vessels.

Arriving in the vicinity of what remained of Chestnut Neck on October 8, Pulaski moved the legion to what is now Tuckerton, establishing a large picket of fifty men under Lieutenant Colonel Charles Baron von Bose farther along at the farm of Jeremiah Ridgway.[27] He likewise dispatched Major Julius Count of Montfort into the countryside to coordinate with the militia and announce their arrival. Pulaski happily reported to Congress, "Count Montfort has assured me that the inhabitants towards Leads point are good Whigs and are attached to the common cause and are about 250 Militia all inhabitants, at Big Egg harbour there is 400 Militia."[28] Pulaski's private view of the militia, however, was less than flattering in the same report to Congress, as might be expected from a professional European in dealing with local part-time soldiers: "I beg you would order the Militia to be Obedient, or take them away intirely, for they are so ill inclined that they will only spoil our affairs, besides they disperse and retire when they please and particularly when they are wanted to face the Enemy."[29]

As far as Colins and Ferguson were concerned, their mission was over. Already delayed in its initial arrival because of adverse weather, the fleet needed to return to New York as soon as possible, as all the troops onboard were to be part of the imminent embarkations taking place. On October 7, a day before Pulaski's arrival in the neighborhood, the British flotilla started its retrograde movement to the sea. Before accomplishing that, it first needed to offload the stores from the grounded armed sloops *Greenwich* and *Granby*, thereby lightening them and getting them once again afloat. This presented an opportunity to Ferguson and Colins, as the latter put it:

"During this Delay of the Vessels, the Troops under the Command of Captain Ferguson were employed, under Cover of the

Gun-Boats, in an Excursion on the North Shore, to destroy some principal Salt-Works, also some Stores and Lodgments belonging to the People the most notorious for being concerned in the Privateers, and destroying and oppressing the peaceable and moderate Parts of the King's Subjects."[30]

That night, Ferguson once again led his men ashore:

[A]n opportunity offered, without interrupting our Progress, to make two Descents on the north side of the River, to penetrate some Miles into the Country, destroy three Salt Works, and raze to the ground the Stores and Settlements of a Chairman of their Committees, a Captain of Militia, and one or two other virulent Rebels, who had Shares in the Prizes brought in here, and who had all been remarkably active in fomenting the Rebellion, oppressing the People and forcing them, against their Inclination and better Judgment, to assist in their Crimes. At the same time, be assured, Sir, no manner of Insult or Injury has been offered to the peacable Inhabitants, nor even to such, as without taking a Lead, have been made, from the Tyranny or Influence of their Rulers, to forget their Allegiance.[31]

The destruction of the saltworks, stores, houses, and facilities was, of course, viewed differently by those who owned or benefitted from the structures. One New Jersey newspaper reported that the British had "destroyed a number of vessels, and several houses belonging to Gentlemen who have distinguished themselves by their attachment to the American cause."[32] One side's gentleman was another side's pirate. Pulaski, viewed by the United States as a leader against tyrants, was viewed by the British press as "A Polander, infamous for an attempt to assassinate his King; who if he had not escaped the pursuit of justice, would have ended his villanies on a scaffold, as did several of his accomplices."[33]

It would appear that not everyone serving under Pulaski's command disagreed with that view. With British ships still running aground in narrow, shallow channels, and the weather turning very bad, Colins's fleet was going nowhere anytime soon. This provided opportunities for deserters to attempt to reach the British. On October 10, the day of the big storm that facilitated the robbery of the British Legion's pay in Bergen, five deserters from Pulaski's Legion (at least three of whom were from the elite grenadier company) made their way to the *Nautilus*.[34] Despite a sloop from New York arriving with orders from Admiral Gambier to immediately return, the weather, tides, and wind conspired to keep the small fleet where it was.[35] It was thus that nature played a role in what transpired next.

Before setting off for Egg Harbor, Pulaski's Legion took in a volunteer, at the request of Congress's Board of War. Always eager to encourage desertion among the enemy, particularly the Hessian troops, Congress was well disposed to providing appointments for those they felt trustworthy. And so it was when nineteen-year-old Second Lieutenant Carl Wilhelm Joseph Juliat, who had deserted from the Hessian Landgraf Regiment at Rhode Island, brought before them a letter of recommendation from one of the most prominent foreigners in the service of the United States, Major General Johann Baron de Kalb. The Board of War deliberated on the matter on September 2, 1778:

> The board have considered Genl. de Kalb's letter relative to Lieut. Charles [Carl] Juliat, referred to them by Congress; they have also conversed with Mr. Juliat, and find that Genl. Pulaski would receive him as a volunteer in the infantry of the corps, But he has not the means of subsisting himself in that character: yet from Genl. de Kalb's recommendation, and because encouragement has been given for foreign officers to quit the enemy's service, we are of opinion he should be employ'd. If his services are approved, he may have a commission hereafter either in the legion, or the corps of German volunteers, as Congress shall please to order.[36]

Congress approved Juliat's joining Pulaski's Legion and drawing the pay of a lieutenant, but serving only as a volunteer in the infantry, meaning he acted in the capacity of an officer but without any rank or commission. What exactly transpired after this is not fully clear. Tradition has it that Juliat was part of von Bose's picket detachment at the Ridgway farm. Von Bose, a professional German soldier, was less than welcoming to a fellow German officer who had deserted his colors, and he made his contempt known to Juliat.[37] On October 13, 1778, Juliat, among others, decided that service in the legion was not what he had expected. It is here that accounts significantly differ. Pulaski wrote later to Congress "that one Juliet an Officer Deserter from the Ennemys which was given me by the board of Warr to be at the suite of my Legion Deserted two Days ago with three Men which he debauched and two others whom they forced to follow them."[38] Captain Ewald of the Jägers, certainly no witness to anything that transpired at Egg Harbor, nonetheless recorded the incident in his diary, having similar feelings to von Bose:

"This miserable human being, who had betrayed his friends and served . . . Ferguson as a jackal, was a Mr. von Juliat, who had run away from the Landgraf Regiment at Rhode Island. He took employment with the enemy and was placed with the newly raised Pulaski Corps. After his trick at Egg Harbor, he admitted his perjury to the English . . . who obtained a pardon for him from General Knyphausen by petition of General Clinton."[39]

What is interesting, and what leads to some uncertainty as to the circumstances of the surprise of Pulaski's force, is that neither Ferguson nor Colins mentioned Juliat in their official dispatches. Colins, writing to Admiral Gambier, said simply, "A Captain, Serjeant, and four Men came down to us, the Evening before last [October 13], from the Rebels, and gave us some very satisfactory Intelligence of the Legion of Polaski (to which they belonged)."[40] Ferguson, however, perhaps the person in the best position to know, mentioned someone completely different as providing intelligence on the legion, "a Frenchman, named Bromville," whom he classified as a captain in Pulaski's Legion. Who was this person? A James de Bronville was indeed a lieutenant in the infantry of Pulaski's Legion.[41] Pulaski made no mention of Bronville until October 21, when, without elaboration, he wrote to Congress, "I enclose you the Commission of one of my Lieutenants who thought proper to deliver it to me"[42] and enclosed Bronville's commission.

Regardless of who or where the information came from, it presented another opportunity to strike on land, as the fleet was still stuck in place. Captain Ferguson again went on shore with a force of 250 men made up of the detachments of infantry, joined by some marines of the shipping. Based on the information they received, and with a full knowledge of enemy troop positions, Ferguson's force set out to attack von Bose's infantry picket. At 11:00 PM on October 14, the plan was put in motion, the troops "were embarked with him in the Flat Boats, Gun Boats, &c. under the Command of Captain [Brabazon] Christian, of the *Vigilant*: They arrived at the Place of Landing about Four in the Morning, and the Troops making a quick Movement towards the Enemy, got into their Quarters almost undiscovered."[43] Von Bose appears to have placed only one sentry at the bridge leading from Osborn Island, where Ferguson landed his detachment, to his quarters. After having quickly dispatched the sentry, Ferguson left fifty men to secure the bridge, the only route of escape. At 4:00 AM, the British and Provincials launched their attack.[44]

Much like General Grey's 2nd Light Infantry at Old Tappan, Ferguson's men relied entirely on the bayonet, picking their targets by any flash of a musket firing. "The Colonel the Baron de Bose who headed his Men and fought vigourously was killd with several Bayonet wounds as well as the Lieut. [Joseph] de la Borderie and a small number of soldiers and others were wounded" was how Pulaski initially summed up the encounter.[45] Ferguson's men found Pulaski's picket "cantoned in three different Houses, who are almost entirely cut to pieces."[46] Being alerted to the action at the picket, Pulaski assembled his remaining infantry and saddled his cavalry. They made their way to von Bose's position, but it was too late. Following the route to the bridge, they found the planks removed, the work of Ferguson's men. Pulaski boasted that some of his light infantry and riflemen crossed over on the runners of the bridge to engage the British, but "I would not permit my hunters to pursue any further because I could not assist them, and they returnd again to our line without any loss at that time."[47]

When it was over, there was nothing left to do but count the casualties. Ferguson's force had lost three men missing, two from the 5th Regiment, one a New Jersey Volunteer. Along with two men of the 5th Regiment, slightly wounded was Ensign John Camp of the 3rd Battalion, New Jersey Volunteers, who "received a Stab through his Thigh."[48] For Pulaski's Legion, it was a very different story. Almost echoing General Grey's thoughts, Ferguson reported, "It being a night Attack, little Quarter could, of course, be given." Only five of the legion were taken prisoner. Pulaski counted twenty-five to thirty killed, wounded, and missing, numbers that seem to have grown in the week following: "the number of the Dead may be computed at 10 the wounded 12 and some prisoners, I cannot positively say how many are Dead because those poor wretches have dispersed and every Day we find some killed or wounded, but by my Review I find 30 missing."[49] Pulaski went on making reports to Congress that put himself and his corps in the best possible light, but there was little he could do to mask the fact that his corps had faired very badly in its first fight. In an area where the Revolutionary supporters absolutely held sway, Pulaski blamed not only anyone accused of being a Loyalist, but even the Quakers, long distrusted by the state's authorities for not supporting "The Cause." "I shall be at last forced to search the houses and take the Oath of Fidelity from the Inhabitants otherwise I shall be continually exposed."[50]

The attack on the legion outpost, despite Pulaski's public bravado, sent shivers through the countryside. Gerard de St. Elme, a volunteer commanding a detachment to the north, was typical in his fear: "We are betray'd on all sides, we can't take a step but an hour after the Enemy is informed of it, and know where we go, so that we are extremely fatigued, particularly since the last lesson the Ennemy gave us, we shall be again under Arms this Night, because we know they are to Land."[51] No force came St. Elme's way, but he nonetheless altered his plans and quickly returned to France after the end of the year, having had enough of a revolutionary experience.[52] There were no further attacks by Ferguson's forces, although one wayward New Jersey privateer, "one of the little piratical Crew that infest these Inlets," entered the port and was immediately captured by the Royal Navy.[53] The weather improving, it was time for the British to leave.

It would not have surprised Captain Colins, or perhaps anyone else in the fleet, if one more ship ran aground in the challenging waters around the harbor. Unfortunately for the Royal Navy officer, this time it happened to be his flagship, the *Zebra*, and there was no saving this ship. After transferring the men to other vessels, along with whatever could be salvaged, the ship was torched. "This moment the Frigate [sloop] run on shore is burning and all the rest will sail immediately in my opinion," Pulaski was finally able to report on October 21.[54] This time, he was correct. Colins, Ferguson, and the fleet were finally headed back to New York.

Twelve

Withdrawal

O N OCTOBER 12, 1778, ADMIRAL GAMBIER REPORTED TO
Clinton: "I learn this moment from the *Brune* who pass'd by
Egg harbor & spoke with an Officer of the *Vigilant* that we had
totally destroy'd the Salt works but the privateers had chiefly got
off but some vessels & prizes destroyed & then we may hope
hourly their return safe. This much relieves my anxiety . . . I
thought Even this Imperfect Acct. wou'd give you satisfaction."[1]

Even before this news arrived, Clinton had realized the time was
coming to call in the troops. His objectives had been mostly realized, at least those that were generally given out, but he could not
help feeling a sort of melancholy at what lay before him:

I have in most respectful but most positive terms desired my
recall. I am sure you agree with me, I sought not the Command
as you well know—great good luck & some ill this Campaign,
our arrival at York Was critical. Lord H[owe] assembling his
fleet equally so—he was afterwards out of luck in not intercept-
ing the French in their way to Boston from R[hode] Island. I was

Equally so in not getting in time to R. Island to assist Sulivan in his retreat from thence, I have the Winds alone to blame. Small Strokes against their Sea ports have been successfull & other little Coups de partisan, but Nothing solid. I am now out Ousten[sibly] to seek for forage but in hopes of drawing W[ashington] into a scrape. I am on both sides [of] the North River with a short Communication by boats. Washington's Communication if he passes & approaches us is beyond the Highlands. He does not gudgeon so that as we shall have Collected our forage in 4 days, we shall retire & the army by order broke up into Expedition[s]—to See such an Army dissolved, & I fear to such little purpose heartbreaking.[2]

The least productive part of the foraging had been going on in Westchester, and it was there that Clinton started the process of ending the incursion. General Grant would be leading the most important of the embarkations to the West Indies, and he could not properly plan for his expedition if he was tending to troops in Westchester. Grant planned initially to withdraw his troops October 7 but changed his mind on the arrival of a number of small craft and flat-bottomed boats, vessels used for carrying troops, up the Hudson River. He sent to Clinton, then with Cornwallis in Bergen County, thinking the commander in chief "might possibly have formed some Plan of Embarkation which we were Strangers to, & therefore advised General Kniphausen to send an aid-de-Camp to know your Pleasure before he retired from his present Position."[3] He likewise enclosed some intelligence that was almost certainly given by a double agent, making wild claims of troop strength at Boston in particular, perhaps intended to dissuade the British from attempting to attack the French fleet, which was still there, refitting from the storm damage in late August. Like most false plants, it contained just enough truth to make the whole plausible, such as General Putnam's being at West Point and General Scott's commanding the light infantry, things already well known to the British.[4]

After the momentary confusion over the boats had been

resolved, Knyphausen, Grant, and the troops in Westchester withdrew October 10, and as quickly as that, operations in that area were over. "The Corps which had been advanc'd beyond Kingsbridge, under the Command of Lieutenant General Knyphausen fell back to their old Ground at & near the Bridge," wrote one officer of the Royal Artillery, with no elaboration necessary.[5] Little had occurred in Westchester since the flurry of raids and counterraids at the beginning of October. Scott continued to have small parties snatch up sentries and pickets to help collect intelligence, capturing three Hessians on October 9 but learning nothing new.[6] The light infantry commander's same cast of spies, particularly Captain Eli Leavenworth, were now operating with limited success in New York City and Long Island. The reports submitted, however, only confirmed the most basic information, that major embarkations were preparing, but the spies did not know definitively where they were bound.

Thanks to the torrential rains of October 10, the British withdrawal was cloaked. "Not until the 12th did a strong rebel force patrol as far as the Hessian Jäger Corps's abatis to learn whither we had marched," noted Hessian major Carl Baurmeister.[7] That was not quite the truth. Late on the tenth, the retreat was finally noticed by Scott's advanced corps commanders, notably Colonels Gist and Armand, although only by the word of "a Country man from York."[8] But they informed Scott that all of New York had been evacuated. Major Henry Lee informed Scott of the truth of the matter on October 12: "I am sorry to acquaint you that the intelligence received yesterday from the Colos. Armand & Gist has turned out premature." Lee continued, saying four deserters he examined mentioned an embarkation of three brigades, but that the city was not to be abandoned.[9] Washington probably realized as much by this point and was no doubt relieved simply to have the enemy no longer in close proximity to his lines on that side of the Hudson. The Westchester forage was over.

While things continued apace in Bergen, plans were already in motion to bring activity to an end there as well. On October 9, Cornwallis informed Clinton "our Hay is all embark'd, but the

Southerly wind blew so fresh to day the sloops could not get out of the Creek: I propose if you have no objection to take the position near Fort Lee on Sunday. If anything should happen to make me wish to stay longer here, I will let you know it, but I have taken great pains to inform myself, & I do not see the possibility of striking any blow."[10] There would be no further blows. Stirling's force at Acquackanonk and Woodward's in Paramus kept enough patrols out to avoid a repeat of what befell Baylor. The only enemies the Continentals met with for the most part were deserters coming out of the lines, as Woodward reported from Paramus on October 10:

> The Desertion increases. I had eight come in to this post the Day before yesterday. They all agree that some capital move is in agitation. Those of the 15th Regt. say it is for the West Indies, & that their Regt. being one of the number for that Service, is the cause of their Desertion. A letter from [Lieutenant] Colo[nel] Bayard to Mrs. [Theodosia] Prevost demands a young Gentleman under her care, for whom he has procured a commission in his Regt. & urges his comeing immediately, as he says the Regt. is going to imbark for service.[11]

Scores of vessels were still making their way up and down the Hackensack, although after October 10, the foraging shifted to Secaucus and its vast meadows. Fort Lee likewise became a loading point for forage and cattle to the northeast of the line. Cornwallis delayed moving the whole army on the tenth because of the storm, writing to Clinton, "As the weather looks still very unsettled I shall stay a day or two longer before I fall back, unless I should receive any intelligence that may make me think it adviseable to do it directly." He was still pessimistic, and rightly so, of striking at an unguarded enemy.[12] Washington very strictly ordered Stirling to not become a tempting target to the British, writing to him on October 12:

"As your Lordship's force is so very unequal to that of the Enemy, I would not wish you to remain so near them, as to intice them to aim a blow at you. Keeping their foragers from extending themselves far from their main Body is your object and all that can be expected in your circumstances."[13]

As the British appeared on the verge of withdrawing, some of the Loyalists saw no option but to leave their homes and retire with them to New York City or elsewhere within the lines. Gabriel Van Norden, from the Steenrapie area of New Bridge, was one such Loyalist, leaving behind several lots of land totaling over 240 acres, along with a house, barn, and outbuildings. Van Norden, though a civilian, had been imprisoned for his loyalties in December 1776, and again in July 1777. He was not about to tempt fate a third time:

> He after that remained at his House untill the Earle of Cornwallis entered New Jersey in the Autumn of 1778, he availed himself of the Opportunity and came with his family and such of his Stock and Moveables as he could bring along, within the British Lines, proceeded on to New-York where he settled himself, having left in Possession of the Rebels all his Real Estate Grain of different sorts to the amount of at least a Thousand Bushells, besides Green Corn for the following Years Crop.[14]

Van Norden suffered over 1,100 pounds sterling in losses.

Having the British among them during the forage, some Loyalists took the opportunity to enlist in the Provincial forces. Colonel Van Buskirk's battalion of New Jersey Volunteers enlisted no fewer than eleven men from the county during their three-week visit, including such venerable county names as Ackerman, Wright, Bogert, Kingsland, Blauvelt, Cooper, and Lutkins.[15] These were all men with kin already in the corps, likely to be dependable, rather than deserters like Elisha Smith of the 2nd Light Dragoons who joined the British Legion.

One sure sign the British were leaving, if it hadn't been apparent before, was the west side of the Hackensack River. The twin forts on Brower's Hill, which had taken the better part of a week to make, were demolished the night of October 12. After the last of the troops were across the new bridge early the next morning, that, too, was destroyed to prevent any of Stirling's force from following. General Woodward, keeping an eye on the British proceedings from his post to the north at Paramus, was the first to confirm the enemy pullback, of which he immediately informed Washington:

> The Enemys Rear left the New Bridge this morning after seting Fire to their Redouts & Hutts. They took with them several of the Inhabitants, some by force, & others voluntarily went with them. I have had partys of Horse round them all Day, they are Just return'd & report that they are incamp'd in the English Neighbourhood, their Rear about three & a half miles from the New Brid[g]e. Lt. [Griffin] Fountleroy [1st Light Dragoons] took two of their stragling Refugees, & Genl. Grays waggoner, who was returning to his quarters for a large cheese of the Generals that had been left behind.[16]

The new quarters for the troops would be Fort Lee, particularly the British Grenadiers, who "occupied that ground where the Rebels were Hutted two years ago."[17] British intentions, at this point no great secret among the troops, were being made known to Stirling at Acquackanonk on an almost hourly basis. He informed Washington on October 11:

> I have great reason to believe the Enemy are on the point of leaving Bergen County, the deserters that have Come in this day & yesterday all agree that two Regiments embarked on the 9th Instant, the other Eight for the West Indies were to have embarked this day, but I suppose the Storm will prevent them. The deserters within these three days are about 18, Chiefly from the light Infantry & Grenadier Companies of the Regiments ordered to embark. The Officers of those Regts. Baggage all on board, what little Baggage the Officers of the Army in Bergen County had with them was sent of[f] yesterday. 100 flat Bottomed Boats at the landing near fort Lee. All the forageing Vessels gone down Hackensack River, only three or four Armed Vessels remain in it. Most of these Circumstances are Confirmed

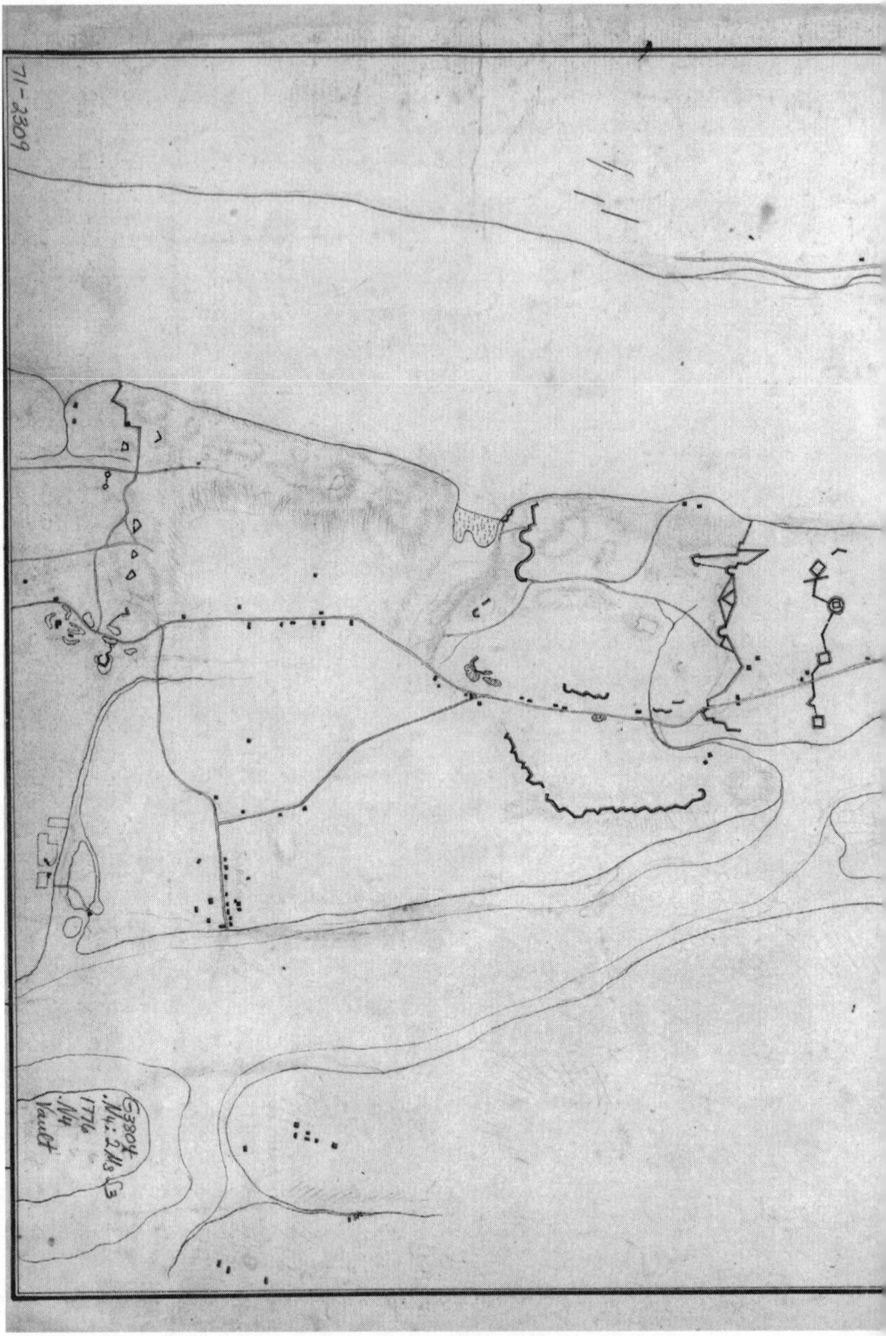

MAP 7. New York Island. Military; unfinished, c. 1776. (Library of Congress)

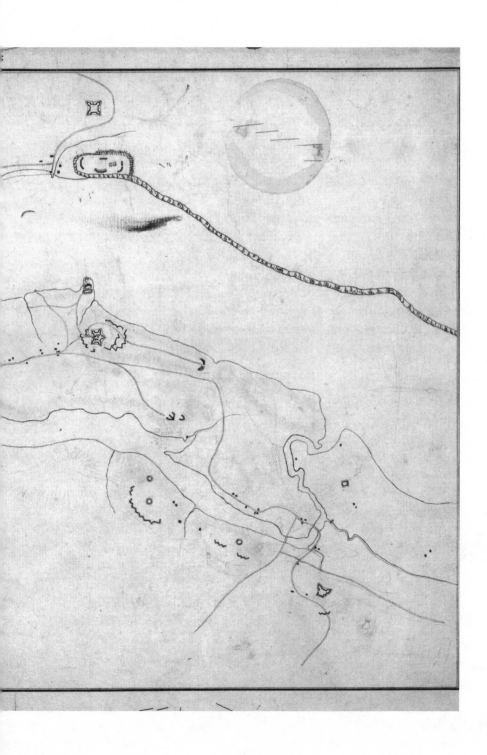

by others who have been among them. Some say ten, others fifteen Regiments are going to the West Indies, others speak of some Regiments going to Halifax.[18]

There was little left for Cornwallis to do other than remove the remaining forage, crops, and cattle, followed by his troops. He sent Clinton word he would "take the position near Fort Lee, & march on Wednesday the 14th to the Neighbourhood of Bergen. I think Paulus Hook will be the most convenient [place] for the embarkation."[19] And so, according to plan, Cornwallis moved his troops on the 14th to Paulus Hook, where they had started three weeks before. Their work in Bergen County being done, "on the 15th crossed from Paulus Hook, to their former Positions on York Island, Long Island, and Staten Island."[20] The Grand Forage in Bergen County was done.

As the British troops started their crossings from Paulus Hook to their different cantonments, Stirling led a large reconnaissance over to Hackensack. Between deserters and spies, Washington finally was getting reliable, continuous intelligence of not only British movements but future plans, and even some accurate insider information. Germain's strategy and Clinton's frustrations were both discovered. How the latter was obtained, only Stirling knew in this instance, as he happily reported to Washington on October 14:

By every Circumstance I can Collect a grand embarkation will immediately take place at New York, but I have within these two hours obtained some particulars which may be depended on vizt. That the ten Regiments so long talked of as under Orders to Embark were really ordered by Ministry four or five months ago, but the Expedition (as its Called) remonstrated against, however a frigate arrived last Satirday with positive Orders for its takeing place, and the embarkation is to be Completed on Friday. Some talk of its being against S. Carolina, but believed more generally to be for the West Indies. A Brigade of Hessians and two Regiments of new Levies are actually embarked for Hallifax, with the remainder of troops they [are] to keep possession of New York & Rhode Island and to do all the mischief they can by detachments along shore & by sudden incursions.[21]

With the British gone, Stirling, Woodward, and the other Continentals witnessed the effects of what six thousand foraging troops could do. Forage had been stripped throughout Hackensack and Harrington townships, supplying both the immediate needs of the horses in the field and a supply for the different embarkations. Crops in the field and those already harvested likewise proved a great acquisition to the commissary magazines, including Indian corn, potatoes, rye, wheat, buckwheat, Indian meal, barley, oats, turnips, and cabbages. Smaller quantities of other items taken, such as salt, butter, honey, smoked pork, cider, and rum, were probably for the immediate use of the troops on the expedition. Livestock taken was probably for short- and long-term use, including cattle, milk cows, hogs, chickens, turkeys, pigeons, and sheep. Dozens of horses also made their way into British service, both temporarily and permanently. Loyalists John Poulison and Dirck Brinkerhoff were still five years later seeking payment for two horses impressed into the Quartermaster General's Department on September 27, 1778.[22]

This is not to say the British stripped the county like a horde of locusts. While the troops were methodical in what they took, the degree to which households lost property seems to have been influenced by their wealth and activism for the rebellion. Militiamen such as Daniel Christie of Hackensack Township lost an immense amount of property, including his blacksmithing tools, a Bible, a Book of Common Prayer, and such household items as jugs, bowls, yarn, and one candlestick. Others, such as John P. Westervelt, probably considered themselves fortunate in giving up just one milk cow and two young pigs, with no loss of private property.[23] The acquisition of some four hundred tons of hay from Bergen, about eight times that collected in Westchester, can only be considered, in terms of the British needs, a successful enterprise.[24]

Loyalist losses were harder to determine. Items taken from abandoned properties would be unknown to the owners and probably

lumped in with overall losses at the end of the war. Some were listed as being taken by the rebels for fear the British in London would
disallow losses they considered should have been settled with the
army before the evacuation of New York. But some Loyalists, particularly those with the army at the time, were present to see what
damage had been done to their land. Isaac Perkins, the ferryman
who guided Cornwallis in the 1776 invasion of Bergen County, saw
the troops take two tons of hay off his land near Fort Lee, valued
at ten pounds New York currency, for which he received no compensation.[25]

Probably no loss of personal property compared to how Clinton
felt over losing so many troops who would now be boarding transports for distant ports. To be sure, he would still be in overall command of the reinforcements going to Pensacola, Bermuda, and
Halifax, along with the expedition to Georgia, but these scattered
forces would be of no use in the longed-for decisive action against
Washington's army. The greatest loss, however, was the ten regiments and artillery detachment sent to the West Indies under
General Grant. The loss was even greater considering that three
additional British regiments were drafted to bring those ten corps
up to strength. Grant's command, including a few men from the
civil branches, numbered over five thousand five hundred officers
and men.[26] The return of the Egg Harbor expedition under Captain
Ferguson on October 24, 1778, completed the troops slated to
embark.[27] That being the case, there was little left for Clinton to do
but three days later formally give over command of the West Indies
expedition to Grant, to which he added his "most hearty Wishes"
for success along with 16,000 pounds sterling in British gold to
carry them over for the time being:

> You will proceed with the Troops Embarked under Your
> Command . . . to the Island of St. Lucia, which you are to Attack
> and if practicable Reduce and take Possesion of, and in case of
> Success, You are to retain such a part of the Force as You shall
> Judge sufficient for the defence thereof, and distribute the
> remainder of the Troops among His Majesty's West India

Islands, in such manner, and in such proportions, as from the information You receive, You shall Judge most proper for their protection and Security, against any Attack of the Enemy.[28]

The fleet, commanded by Commodore William Hotham, assembled at Sandy Hook, then sailed "with a fair wind" on November 3, 1778.[29] Stirling reported the sailing to Washington the same day, adding an economic note that a large supply being needed by the fleets was responsible for "a very Sudden rise in the price of Rum" at New York.[30]

The West India fleet was not the first to depart. Transports carrying the King's Orange Rangers and the Hessian Regiment of Seitz, along with another ship, the *Nancy*, with 205 troops and passengers, made their way out of New York for Nova Scotia in October.[31] As October turned to November, the departures continued. The German Waldeck Regiment and the Provincial battalions of Pennsylvania and Maryland Loyalists were next, off to secure the province of West Florida, an area that extended into modern-day Alabama, Mississippi, and Louisiana.

To reinforce New Providence and the Bahamas, Clinton had formed a new corps consisting of invalids and old soldiers from British regiments who were still capable of limited duty. The Bahamas were a perfect place for such a corps, which he named the Garrison Battalion and put on the same footing as Provincials raised in America.[32] It was put under the command of Major William Sutherland, and Clinton informed Germain on October 3 that he proposed "to send them in a few days to Bermuda and the Bahama Islands, which I hope will meet with His Majesty's Approbation."[33] Clinton sent two companies of the new corps, under Captain John Grant, whose orders were to consult with the civil government on his arrival and concur in "every Measure that can tend to the Benefit of His Majesty's Service."[34]

The last convoy to depart was the Georgia expedition under Lieutenant Colonel Campbell. After the troops embarked at the Watering Place on Staten Island, there was a last-minute change in the composition of the force: the 1st Battalion, New Jersey

Volunteers, was relanded and replaced by the New York
Volunteers. No official reason was ever recorded for why this
change took place, although it is believed there was serious discon-
tent among the New Jersey men about serving so far from home.[35]
After two of the transports had proceeded from New York Harbor
to Sandy Hook, strong winds and rain flung them into the Atlantic
and on their way before the rest of the fleet: the *Young Tom*, with
two companies of DeLancey's Brigade, and the *Neptune*, with 106
men of the 3rd Battalion, New Jersey Volunteers. Worse, the ord-
nance store ship *Betsy*, containing all the artillery along with
ammunition and stores, was driven onshore on Sandy Hook.
Campbell had bitterly complained about the ship from the onset:
"The vessel itself was thought so bad, that the Artillery men &
Officers were placed on board of the men of War."[36]

Since this fleet needed time to refit, Ferguson took the opportunity to lay one more plan in front of Clinton. He proposed taking
eight hundred to one thousand of the men embarked in Campbell's
expedition and launching them swiftly toward Perth Amboy, New
Jersey, where he reported the enemy had "about 1000 men, sickly
half cloth'd, without Discipline, precaution or suspicion of insult,
but lull'd into security from a general reviv'd opinion among them
that we are preparing to quit the Country. They are composed
mostly of the new rais'd Jersey Corps, Moylands horse [4th Light
Dragoons] & Some artillery men."[37] As tempting as it may have
been for the British commander in chief, he would risk no further
delay or mishap in sending Campbell on his way, and nothing came
of the proposed raid. The fleet finally sailed on November 27,
1778, the same day as a ship heading to England carrying its peace
commissioners.[38] Peace in America was as yet nowhere in sight.

Clinton, much against his will and inclination, had fulfilled his
orders. Britain's outposts had been reinforced, and the war would
be brought against the French in their island possessions of the
West Indies. For the remainder of the war, the reluctant British
commander bemoaned his lack of troops and support from home.
France's entry into the war, without firing a shot, had neutralized
major British offensive operations against Washington. While

France would go on to supply the United States with money, arms, uniforms, and other material support, simply the threat of its fleet and army bought Washington precious time to keep his army together, which was the most important (and often daunting) task of his career.

EPILOGUE

I N LATE OCTOBER, A PHILADELPHIA PAPER REPORTED THAT, "ON the 19th inst. two expresses arrived at head-quarters, with the news of the enemy evacuating the city of New York, both accounts agree exactly; in consequence of which, orders were issued the same day for three brigades to hold themselves in readiness to march at a moment's warning. It is expected that our troops will be in possession of New York in six or seven days."[1]

Despite that exciting news, Washington's troops were not in possession of New York six or seven days later. It would take another sixty-one months of war until the actual British evacuation of New York City and the triumphant entry of the Continental army.

Large battles in the north were now few and far between. Clinton utilized what small land forces he had, joined to whatever shipping the Royal Navy would make available when convenient, and followed London's instructions as best as circumstances dictated in attacking from the fleets but never staying in one place long. Even as the British troops were leaving Bergen, Stirling informed Washington that the enemy's "own expression among the facetious ones is 'we are to turn it into a Buccaneering War.'"[2] General Tryon employed this strategy in earnest in July 1779, launching devastating raids along the Connecticut coast,[3] while a small fleet of Loyalist refugee vessels outfitted by Massachusetts native George Leonard operated out of Rhode Island, causing havoc from Martha's Vineyard to Connecticut.[4] This culminated in Brigadier General Benedict Arnold's destruction of New London, Connecticut, on September 6, 1781.[5] To put this last expedition into perspective, during the time of the Grand Forage in 1778, Arnold was a major general in the Continental army and commandant of Philadelphia. The war certainly changed in new and interesting ways over the subsequent three years.

General Grant's expedition to Saint Lucia was successful. His fleet of warships and transports, under the command of Commodore Hotham, was joined to the fleet of Rear Admiral Samuel Barrington and successfully landed the army on Saint Lucia on December 13 and 14, 1778. Barrington spent the next two days fighting the French fleet of Admiral D'Estaing, belatedly arrived from Boston. Barrington's fleet proving victorious, the French troops on the island surrendered to Grant on December 28, 1778. The troops on this expedition soon learned why the West Indies were considered an undesirable theater in which to serve. Within two months of their arrival, nearly 20 percent were sick with a variety of ailments, including nearly half the 35th Regiment. A return from February 1779 showed the following breakdown of ailments: "32 Continued Fevers, 52 Putrid Fevers, 319 Intermittent Fevers, 158 Fluxes, 11 Venereal, 3 Rheumatism, 352 Convalescents, 25 Ulcers, 22 Wounds, 3 Fractures, 1 Dropsical, 1 Scorbutic, 2 Gravel; 981 Total."[6] Contrary to the original expectation of sending several regiments of Grant's force back to New York, nine of the ten units stayed in the West Indies for the rest of the war. Only the 40th Regiment returned to New York, in 1781.[7]

The Hessian Regiment of Seitz and the King's Orange Rangers arrived piecemeal in Nova Scotia between November 15 and 18, 1778. At the end of December, Brigadier General Francis McLean reported to Clinton, "The Hessians are quarter'd upon the Inhabitants and well Satisfied. The Orange Rangers except a Detachment of 1 Captain & 50 Men are in a Barrack which I had repair'd for them at the Eastern Battery; The Detachment was sent to Liverpool, at the Desire of The Lieutenant Governor and Council of the Province."[8] Here they remained, waiting for a French invasion that never came and fending off the occasional New England privateer raid.

The Waldeckers and Provincials heading for West Florida spent some time in Jamaica first, perhaps more preferable than New York in December. A German chaplain described his dining experience on December 3, 1778:

> At noon we all dined in the large room in Howard's Tavern. This is a magnificent house, two stories high, with a wide gallery. The steps, the doors, the floors, all are of mahogany wood. Ovens, and chimneys are not the fashion because snow and winter are not customary here. Instead of windows, there were green painted jalousies through which the sea winds rustled and cooled the rooms. Our table was laden with fresh vegetables, carrots, lima beans, lettuce, pineapple (the most delicate fruit which I have ever eaten, and which grows on what looks like a large cabbage stalk and looks quite lovely), oranges, melons, and Madeira wine. The meal cost not more than a half guinea per person.[9]

After a voyage of an estimated 3,463 miles, the three regiments arrived at Pensacola on January 18, 1779. They remained in the province of West Florida until May 1781, when Pensacola fell to a besieging Spanish army, Spain having declared war on Great Britain in 1779. The survivors were transported to Cuba as prisoners of war.

Lieutenant Colonel Campbell's expedition to Georgia succeeded despite every warning possible to that state that a British expedition was headed its way. In addition to repeated warnings sent from the north, one of the British transport ships, the *Neptune*, carrying three companies of the 3rd Battalion, New Jersey Volunteers, had anchored off Tybee, Georgia, and a sailor who deserted from it gave a full account of the force that was coming.[10] Arriving weeks ahead of the rest of the fleet, the *Neptune* proceeded to Saint Augustine, where it joined an invasion force coming from there under the command of Major General Augustine Prevost. In the end, the sailor's desertion made little difference. Campbell's force routed the Continentals under Major General Robert Howe, killing or capturing over five hundred men at the cost of just twenty-six Crown forces killed and wounded.[11]

Campbell was justifiably proud of his accomplishment, writing home on January 19, 1779, "I have taken a Stripe and Star from the Rebel flag of America."[12] Having secured the province, Campbell almost immediately relinquished command to Prevost and returned to England.

Captain Grant and the two transports carrying the Garrison Battalion arrived at New Providence on December 19, 1778. A week later, the island's governor, Montfort Browne, arrived from New York onboard the *Tartar*.[13] Grant and Browne spent the next few years writing endless letters of complaint about one another.[14]

Juliat, the Hessian and Pulaski's Legion deserter, continued serving in the war, at least for a while. Pardoned by Knyphausen at Clinton's request, Juliat may have taken to a life at sea, enlisting onboard a Loyalist privateer at New York.[15] Having a change of heart, or perhaps not finding merchant raiding to his liking, Juliat petitioned Clinton for permission to serve in the army once more. Knowing the Hessian service per se would not take him back, Clinton, in June 1780, placed the former deserter in a troop of hussars, where he served in the ranks as a private.[16] This cavalry unit consisted of but one troop, the men of which were almost all Germans, primarily escaped prisoners from the Brunswick and Hesse-Hanau troops taken prisoner in 1777 during the Burgoyne Campaign. Its commander, Captain Frederick de Diemar, was a German but of a British unit, the 60th (or Royal American) Regiment of Foot. To make matters even more confusing, the troop was considered a Provincial unit, as no one had the authority to create a new Hessian or other German unit in America. At the intercession of his family in Germany, Juliat was released from further service and in January 1781 sailed for home on the transport ship *Minerva*.[17]

As for George Washington and the Continental army, they had run the gamut of emotions the last few months of 1778. While they had neither won nor lost the major battles of Monmouth and Rhode Island, the *petite guerres* practiced almost daily in Westchester alternately produced minor highs and lows. The experiences of victory and defeat, particularly as they affected the men of General Scott's light infantry, only added to their professionalism in the coming campaigns as the United States continued to build a competent army.

The two corps that suffered the worst at the hands of the British, the 3rd Light Dragoons and Pulaski's Legion, followed different paths after the forage. As severe a blow as Baylor's men had suffered, the one fortuitous aspect was the timing. British and American prisoner-of-war commissioners were in the midst of a massive prisoner exchange that had been under way since the British evacuated Philadelphia in June. It was with relief that a newspaper reported on November 4, "Last week Col. Baylor's cavalry, who were made prisoners by the enemy at Old Tapan, and taken to New-York, were all exchanged, some of whom arrived here [Trenton] on Sunday last [November 1]."[18] The exchange did not include officers, however, there not being an equal number of British officers in American prisons. Those officers would remain as prisoners, mostly on parole on Long Island, until the end of 1780. But the return of the enlisted men at least made it possible to reconstitute the dragoons under a new leader, Lieutenant Colonel William Washington, promoted into the corps from the 4th Light Dragoons. While Baylor remained in nominal command of the 3rd Light Dragoons, he never returned to active duty, dying in 1784 after being promoted to brigadier general at the close of the war.[19] William Washington and the cavalry went on to earn many laurels in the south, their small numbers disproportionate to the many valuable services they performed.

For Pulaski's Legion, the defeat at Egg Harbor was just the start of a string of losses. Sent to the southern theater to help repulse Campbell's Georgia expedition, they no sooner arrived in South Carolina when on May 11, 1779, Pulaski led 120 lancers in an attack on the road to Charleston, then threatened by a British force under Prevost. The lancers ran headfirst into the Georgia Light Dragoons, a Provincial unit one-third the size of Pulaski's. Pulaski's lancers were smashed by the British. When the legion infantry attempted to intervene, they, too, were routed, losing no less than fifty-seven officers and men killed, wounded, and captured compared to a loss of only six British.[20] Five months later, Pulaski was mortally wounded attempting to lead a cavalry attack against the British fortifications at Savannah. The small remains of the legion, commanded by Major Peter de Vernier, was surprised on April 14, 1780 (along with the 3rd Light Dragoons and others) at Monck's Corner, South Carolina, by a Provincial force led by Colonel Banastre Tarleton, who had caused so much grief to Scott and his forces in Westchester in 1778. Vernier was mortally wounded, effectively ending the active existence of the legion. In an unusual coincidence, members of the 3rd Battalion, New Jersey Volunteers, were instrumental in every defeat of Pulaski's forces. What had started in the north ended in the south.

None of the skirmishes throughout the Grand Forage rose to the level of anything like a major battle, actions that are remembered today with battlefield parks, tours, and museums. Two events were remembered enough to warrant a memorial. In 1906, the Bronx chapter of the Daughters of the American Revolution erected a stone cairn bearing a plaque that states in part: "Chief Nimham and seventeen Stockbridge Indians as allies of the Patriots, gave their lives for liberty." The cairn is in Van Cortlandt Park in the Bronx, near 238th Street.

In 1894, the Society of the Cincinnati in the state of New Jersey erected a monument in Little Egg Harbor on the site, or near, where Lieutenant Colonel von Bose and his men were killed by Ferguson's party. Its purpose was "to commemorate the massacre of a portion of the Legion commanded by Brigadier General, The Count Casimir Pulaski of the Continental Army in the Affair at Egg Harbor." In recent times, the monument site and that of Pulaski's headquarters were in danger of being developed commercially. One local resident, George Czurlanis, a retired salesman, partially disabled World War II veteran, and Bronze Star recipient, led a campaign to preserve the sites:

"These are legitimate historic sites that are being taxed by the township as if they were commercial properties," Czurlanis said. "If the taxes aren't paid, the sites can be zoned commercial and auctioned off to the highest bidder, who could do with them as he saw fit. I can't let that happen to these American patriots." The sites were put on the New Jersey list of historic places in 1983, when Czurlanis formed the nonprofit Affair at Little Egg Harbor Society and acquired them for one dollar. But state law defining tax exemptions for historic sites owned by private corporations requires that each site have a building that can be used as a museum or meeting area, or for nonprofit educational purposes.[21]

Putting buildings on the site was well beyond Czurlanis's financial capabilities, but in the end he was successful. Up until his health failed him, George Czurlanis took part in ceremonies at the monument each October. The Little Egg Harbor historian passed away on March 29, 2015, at age ninety-four.[22]

The third of the large defeats suffered by Washington's army during the forage, that suffered by Colonel Baylor and the 3rd Light Dragoons, had no monument, no park, no place of remembrance for the nearly two dozen cavalrymen killed in Bergen County in the early morning of September 28, 1778. The ferocity of the British attack that September morning prompted as much investigation as any loss the Americans suffered. Governor Livingston was charged by Congress to take depositions, and the results were published in the newspapers. Surgeon David Griffith made an extensive report on the casualties to Stirling, which was passed along to Washington. For all the concern at the time, however, the events of that night were largely forgotten. The only physical marker was a 1956 plaque on an eighteenth-century millstone placed in front of nearby Holdrum School, relatively unknown to any but those associated with the building.

In a bit of irony, it was only due to construction and development that the story of what happened in Bergen County in what is modern-day River Vale has been properly remembered. In 1962, historian Adrian C. Leiby published his authoritative *Revolutionary War in the Hackensack Valley*, wherein the story of George Baylor and the events of September 1778 were told in vivid narrative to a wide audience. With the events of 1778 perhaps fresh in people's minds once again, in 1967 local Old Tappan resident Thomas Demarest contacted Bergen County freeholder D. Bennett Mazur, concerned that a new housing development then under construction was about to dig up the burial sight of Baylor's men, which he believed he knew the location of. After interviews by three college students with long-time residents seemed to confirm one spot along the Hackensack River as that of a tannery during the eighteenth century, exploratory digging was started. Demarest and the three students found nothing for two weeks until a human thigh bone was discovered. A professional dig was then sponsored and supervised by the Bergen County Board of Chosen Freeholders and the Bergen County Historical Society.[23]

The dig was led by the historical society's museum director, Wayne Daniels, and the remnants of three tanning vats were located. Inside them were the partial remains of six light dragoons, ranging from 25 percent to 95 percent complete. There was no question as to their being Baylor's men, as the artifacts recovered included buttons marked "LD" for Light Dragoons. One of the skulls had the clear indent of a musket butt, a physical confirmation of some of the dragoons' testimony from the attack. Since the completion of the excavation and the reinterment of the remains, the burial ground has been preserved by the county as a historic park, with suitable plaques and interpretive signage.

The physical reminders of most of the other skirmishes and actions described in this volume have been obscured by modern times. Roads, schools, houses, malls, and other forms of development have covered over scenes of bitter contest from 1778 and the rest of the Revolutionary War. The legacy of these events, however, is the wealth of a society that grew and prospered from these battles. The past and the present still occupy the same ground.

NOTES

ABBREVIATIONS

CL   William L. Clements Library,
University of Michigan
LAC   Library and Archives Canada
LOC   Library of Congress
NA   National Archives (United Kingdom)
NARA   National Archives and Records
Administration (United States)
N-YHS   New-York Historical Society

INTRODUCTION

1. Those seeking books on the Battle of Monmouth may be interested in Brendan Morrissey's *Monmouth Courthouse 1778: The Last Great Battle in the North* (Oxford, UK: Osprey, 2004) and *Monmouth Court House: The Battle that Made the American Army* (Yardley, PA: Westholme, 2010), by Joseph G. Bilby and Katherine Bilby Jenkins. For more information on the Siege of Rhode Island, the author recommends Christian M. McBurney's *The Rhode Island Campaign: The First French and American Operation in the Revolutionary War* (Yardley, PA: Westholme, 2011).

CHAPTER ONE: CLINTON'S CONUNDRUM

1. Germain to Clinton, marked Most Secret, Whitehall, March 8, 1778, Colonial Office, Class 5, Vol. 263, 1–11, National Archives, Kew, Richmond, Surrey, United Kingdon (hereafter cited as NA).
2. Secret instructions from King George III to Sir Henry Clinton, Court of St. James, March 21, 1778, Colonial Office, Class 5, Vol. 263, 13–18, NA.
3. Washington to Congress, Headquarters, 6:00 PM, June 18, 1778, Washington Papers, Series 4, General Correspondence, April 30, 1778–July 23, 1778, Library of Congress (hereafter cited as LOC).
4. Sir Henry Clinton, *The American Rebellion: Sir Henry Clinton's Narrative of His Campaigns, 1775–1782, with an Appendix of Original Documents*, ed. William B. Willcox (New Haven, CT: Yale University Press, 1954), 85–86.
5. Germain to Clinton, marked Most Secret, Whitehall, March 8, 1778, Colonial Office, Class 5, Vol. 263, 1–11, NA.
6. Johann Ewald, *Diary of the American War*, ed. Joseph P. Tustin (New Haven, CT: Yale University Press, 1979), 286.

7. Germain to Clinton, marked Secret, Whitehall, March 21, 1778, Colonial Office, Class 5, Vol. 263, 21–23, NA.
8. Clinton, *American Rebellion*, 87.
9. The other main group was the English, with sixty-five men, "7 & 14 year Servants, transported by the Contractors, conformable to their Sentences at the Old Baily." "A List of Prisoners belonging to the Rebel army; taken the 11th September 1777 at the Battle of Brandywine," Frederick Mackenzie Papers, University of Michigan, William L. Clements Library (hereafter cited as CL).
10. Germain to Clinton, marked Most Secret, Whitehall, March 8, 1778, Colonial Office, Class 5, Vol. 263, 1–11, NA.
11. Clinton to Germain, October 23, 1778, Sir Henry Clinton Papers, Vol. 44, item 7, CL.
12. "Abstract of the Number of Men, Women, Children and Waggoners Victualed at the Commissary Generals Provision Stores between the 17th and 20th July 1778," Clinton Papers, Vol. 37, item 18, CL.
13. Germain to Clinton, Whitehall, March 21, 1778, Colonial Office, Class 5, Vol. 263, 20–21, NA.
14. "List of Promotions and Appointments, by Lieut. Colonel Archibald Campbell, Commanding a detachment of His Majesty's forces for Georgia . . . ," Headquarters Papers, PRO 30/55/9822, NA.
15. "Return of the Number of Men Wagoners Women & Children victualed at Monmouth the 27th & 28th June 1778 inclusive," Clinton Papers, Vol. 36, item 5, CL.
16. Intelligence by unknown to George Washington, June 1, 1778, Washington Papers, Series 4, General Correspondence, April 30, 1778–July 23, 1778, LOC.
17. Captain Charles Feilding to Admiral Lord Howe, Halifax, August 21, 1778, Admiralty, Class 1, Vol. 488, folio 417, NA.
18. Clinton first got official word of the French squadron's approach on July 1, 1778, Clinton, *American Rebellion*, 100.
19. Germain to Clinton, Whitehall, June 5, 1778, Colonial Office, Class 5, Vol. 263, 36, NA.
20. George Germain Papers, Vol. 7, item 46, CL.
21. Court Martial proceedings of Lieutenant John Boswell, Captain Martin McEvoy, and Captain John McKinnon, Flushing Fly, September 5–25, 1778, War Office, Class 71, Vol. 87, 173–181, NA.
22. Clinton, *American Rebellion*, 97.
23. Ibid., 101.
24. "Embarkation Return of the Prince of Wales American Volunteers Commanded by Brigadier General [Montfort] Brown 24th May 1778," Frederick Mackenzie Papers, CL.
25. *Newport Gazette*, July 16, 1779.
26. Rawdon to Grant, New York, July 11, 1778, James Grant Papers of Ballindalloch Castle, Scotland, Library of Congress Microcopy, Reel 38, Army Career Series, Correspondence, Miscellany, July–November 1778.

CHAPTER TWO: WAR IN WESTCHESTER
1. "List of Troops on Rhode Island during the late Siege," Mss of the Duke of Northumberland, Letters & Papers, Jan.–March 1777, The American War, No. 51, 23/3, Page 325, Alnwick Castle.

2. Washington to Sullivan, Headquarters, July 22, 1778, Washington Papers, Series 4, General Correspondence, April 30, 1778–July 23, 1778, LOC.

3. Sullivan to Washington, Portsmouth, Rhode Island, August 10, 1778, Washington Papers, Series 4, General Correspondence, July 24, 1778–September 12, 1778, LOC.

4. "Particular Return of the Continental Army under the Command of His Excellency George Washington," Fredericksburg, October 26, 1778, Revolutionary War Rolls, M246, 1775–1783, RG 93, Reel 137, Folder 14, National Archives and Records Administration (hereafter cited as NARA).

5. After Orders, Headquarters, White Plains, August 8, 1778, Washington Papers, Series 3g, Varick Transcripts, Letterbook 3, 321–323, LOC.

6. General Orders, Headquarters, White Plains, August 14, 1778, Washington Papers, Series 3g, Varick Transcripts, Letterbook 3, 327–328, LOC.

7. Joseph Plumb Martin, *Private Yankee Doodle, Being a Narrative of some of the Adventures, Dangers and Sufferings of a Revolutionary Soldier*, ed. George E. Scheer (1962; repr., Philadelphia: Acorn, 1979), 135–136.

8. Colonel William Lord Cathcart to Sir Henry Clinton, New York, July 26, 1778, Clinton Papers, Vol. 38, item 1, CL.

9. Hurlbut to Washington, New Rochelle, 30 August 1778, Washington Papers, Series 4, General Correspondence, July 24, 1778–September 12, 1778, LOC.

10. Ewald , *Diary of the American War*, 144. Ewald, as events will show, was prone to exaggerate casualties, so his figures cannot be taken as 100 percent accurate. Various New York City newspapers listed the casualties in this action as either thirteen or seven killed, wounded, and taken.

11. The situation with Rogers was unique in that his corps was taken from him without the benefit of a court-martial. About thirty of his officers were likewise removed without facing any formal charges, replaced by others more agreeable to the British. Major Christopher French of the 22nd Regiment was initially given command of the corps after Rogers, replaced a few months later by Major James Wemyss of the 40th. General Orders, New York, January 30, 1777, Sir William Howe Orderly Book, Manuscript Division, New York State Library.

12. Orders issued by Adjutant General Francis Lord Rawdon, New York, July 20, 1778, Simcoe Papers, CL.

13. All of Tarleton's exploits on the capture of Lee were recorded in a letter home, dated Princeton, 17 December 1776. Richard M. Ketchum, ed., "New War Letters of Banastre Tarleton," in *Narratives of the Revolution in New York* (Kingsport, TN: Kingsport Press, 1975), 126–129.

14. *Royal Gazette* (New York), August 8, 1778.

15. John Graves Simcoe, *A History of the Operations of a Partisan Corps called the Queen's Rangers commanded by Lieut. Col. J.G. Simcoe, during the War of the American Revolution* (New York: Bartlett & Welford, 1844), 80.

16. John Pownall to Anthony Todd, Esquire, Whitehall, April 26, 1776, Colonial Office, Class 5, Vol. 251, folio 3, NA.

17. This unit was unique among the Provincials. Although its men were armed, their purpose was more to act as laborers, usually in small detachments. Governor William Tryon to Lord George Germain, New York, December 24, 1776, Colonial Office, Class 5, Vol. 1108, folio 25, NA.

18. William Romer to Germain, St. Alban's Street, March 13, 1777, Colonial Office, Class 5, Vol. 155, folio 30, NA.

19. Germain to Sir William Howe, Whitehall, April 19, 1777, Headquarters Papers of the British Army in America, PRO 30/55/495, NA.

20. Sir Henry Clinton's After Orders, August 21, 1777, Orderly Book of the King's American Regiment, CL.

21. A recruiting notice for the corps particularly encouraged young, out-of-work, single men to join up. Washington Papers, Series 4, General Correspondence, April 30, 1778–July 23, 1778, LOC.

22. "Inspection Roll of the Detachment of the 2nd Battalion of Brigadier Genl. DeLancey's Brigade Commanded By Captain Walter Campbell Incampd, on the Hights Near Kingsbridge Augt. 25th 1778," RG 8, "C" Series, Vol. 1878, Pages 62–62a, Library and Archives Canada (hereafter cited as LAC).

23. *Royal Gazette*, August 26, 1778.

24. Ewald , *Diary of the American War*, 143; "Muster Roll of Captain Van D'Burgh's Company of Light Infantry in His Majesty's Battalion of Chasseurs commanded by Lieut. Colonel Emmerick August 1778," RG 8, "C" Series, Vol. 1891, LAC.

25. Simcoe, *History of the Operations*, 83.

26. Ewald, *Diary of the American War*, 145.

27. Abraham Nimham to the Continental Congress, Philadelphia, no date, Papers of the Continental Congress, M247, Reel 55, Item 42, Vol. 5, Page 451, NARA.

28. Ewald, *Diary of the American War*, 145.

29. Simcoe, *History of the Operations*, 85.

30. Ibid., 85–86.

31. *Royal Gazette*, September 16, 1778.

32. Ewald, *Diary of the American War*, 145.

33. "Return of American officers and others Prisoners on Long Island, August 15th 1778," Revolutionary War Rolls, M246, 1775–1783, RG 93, Reel 135, Folder 4, NARA. The return actually contains information on prisoners taken past the date listed in the title, a mistake in the original document.

34. Johann Heinrichs, "Extracts from the Letter-Book of Captain Johann Heinrichs of the Hessian Jäger Corps, 1778–1780," *Pennsylvania Magazine of History and Biography* 22, no. 22 (1890): 152.

35. Thomas F. Devoe, "The Massacre of the Stockbridge Indians 1778," In *Magazine of American History* 5, no. 3 (1880): 42.

36. "Return of Killed, Wounded & Taken Prisoners [of the Queen's Rangers] to October 25th 1780, Simcoe Papers, CL. Simcoe's wound apparently was near where he received one just months earlier at the Battle of Monmouth. Colonial Office, Class 5, Vol. 96, 65–66, NA.

37. Mullen had enlisted in Captain Richard Hovenden's troop on August 15, 1778, and Wood four days later. "Muster Roll of ye 1st Troop of the Cavalry of ye British Legion Commanded by ye Right Honble Lord Cathcart 1778," RG 8, "C" Series, Vol. 1883, 4, LAC.

38. Discharge of John Crawford, Kingsbridge, October 24, 1779, War Office, Class 121, Vol. 6, No. 256, NA. Crawford was living with his wife and a child in Marysburgh, Upper Canada, in 1797, managing to make a new life for himself despite his severe wound. Memorial of John Crawford to President Peter Russell, Marysburgh, 9 December 1797, Upper Canada Land Petitions, "C" Bundle 3, 1797, RG 1, L 3, Vol. 91, No. 145, LAC.

39. Scott to Washington, 5:30 PM, 31 August 1778, Washington Papers, Series 4, General Correspondence, July 24, 1778–September 12, 1778, LOC.

40. Cornwallis to Clinton, New York, September 2, 1778. Clinton Papers, Vol. 40, item 32, CL.

CHAPTER THREE: THE WOMAN

1. "State of the Troops, British, German & Provincial under the Command of His Excellency General Sir Henry Clinton, New York 15th August 1778," Colonial Office, Class 5, Vol. 96, folio 221, NA.

2. Paulus Hook is now Jersey City, Hudson County, but in the eighteenth century it was a part of Bergen County.

3. Congress would award a gold medal to Wayne for his "coolness, discipline and firm intrepidity" in the attack on Stony Point (and a silver one to Major John Stewart, who had been defeated previously at Valentine's Hill). Washington Papers, Series 4, General Correspondence, July 10, 1779–August 21, 1779, LOC. His loss the following year is best known through the poetry of Major John André, adjutant general of the British army in America, in his three-canto, seventy-two-stanza epic, "The Cow Chase," published in the New York City papers: "All wond'rous proud in arms they came, What hero could refuse? To tread the rugged path to fame, Who had a pair of shoes." *Royal Gazette*, August 16, 1780.

4. For a full biography of this officer, see William L. MacDougall's *American Revolutionary: A Biography of General Alexander McDougall* (Westport, CT: Greenwood, 1977).

5. "Enterprise which was in contemplation but never attempted in the Campaign of 1778 when New Port was invested and Genl. Clinton went with a Force from NY to relieve it," Washington Papers, Series 4, General Correspondence, July 24, 1778–September 12, 1778, LOC.

6. Council of War held at Headquarters, White Plains, September 1, 1778, Washington Papers, Series 4, General Correspondence, July 24, 1778–September 12, 1778, LOC.

7. Brigadier Generals James Clinton and Jedediah Huntington do not appear to have sent written replies, or they have become separated from the rest of the Washington Papers.

8. Lincoln to Washington, White Plains, September 2, 1778, Washington Papers, Series 4, General Correspondence, July 24, 1778–September 12, 1778, LOC. Only Louis Lebègue du Portail and Woodford were for moving any troops east immediately.

9. Stirling to Washington, Camp White Plains, September 2, 1778, Washington Papers, Series 4, General Correspondence, July 24, 1778–September 12, 1778, LOC.

10. Colonel Morris Graham commanded a battalion of nine-month New York State troops then serving under Scott. Scott to Washington, September 3, 1778, Washington Papers, Series 4, General Correspondence, July 24, 1778–September 12, 1778, LOC.

11. Scott to Washington, September 2, 1778. Washington Papers, Series 4, General Correspondence, July 24, 1778–September 12, 1778, LOC.

12. Memorial of Beverley Robinson to the Lords Commissioners of the Treasury, Mortlake, February 12, 1784, Audit Office, Class 13, Vol. 32, folios 430–431, NA.

13. Memorandum Book of the British Army, 1778, Manuscript Division, MSS No. 82750, LOC (hereafter cited as Memorandum Book). "[T]he Congress Regt." refers to Congress's Own or the 2nd Canadian Regiment commanded by Colonel Moses Hazen.

14. Muster Roll of Kane's Company, New York Volunteers, August 27, 1778, RG 8, "C" Series, Vol. 1874, 40–41, LAC.

15. Muster Roll of Barclay's Company, Loyal American Regiment, November 12, 1777, RG 8, "C" Series, Vol. 1867, 4, LAC.

16. Petition of Wynant Williams to the Lords Commissioners of the Treasury, London, March 6, 1790, Audit Office, Class 13, Vol. 67, folios 615–616, NA.

17. Undated petition of Ann Bates, Treasury, Class 1, Vol. 611, folio 196, NA.

18. General Orders, Philadelphia, May 30, 1778, *The Orderly Book of Lt. Col. Stephen Kemble, 1777–1778*, Collections of the New-York Historical Society for 1883 (New York: printed for the society, 1884), 587 (hereafter cited as *Kemble Orderly Book*).

19. Drummond in his debriefing wrote that Chambers went with his regiment from Valley Forge against the Indians, presumably at Wyoming, Pennsylvania, and had probably been killed. Bates, in her memorandum, correctly stated that he had resigned, which occurred on July 1, 1778. It is unknown exactly what Chambers's situation was, but it appears the British felt comfortable that he could be used to advance their interests. Francis B. Heitman, *Historical Register of Officers of the Continental Army during the War of the Revolution* (Washington, DC: Rare Book Shop Publishing, 1914), 149.

20. Memorandum Book.

21. Undated manuscript book of Ann Bates, Treasury, Class 1, Vol. 611, folios 198–205, NA. "Captain James" was Captain Jacob James of Chester County, Pennsylvania. In January 1778 he raised the 2nd Troop, Philadelphia Light Dragoons, which that July became one of the initial troops of cavalry for the newly created British Legion.

22. Washington to Gates, September 12, 1778, Washington Papers, Series 4, General Correspondence, July 24, 1778–September 12, 1778, LOC.

23. "Greens" refers to the uniform coat color worn by some of the Provincial troops at this time, such as the Queen's Rangers and British Legion. Scott to Washington, September 14, 1778, Washington Papers, Series 4, General Correspondence, September 13, 1778–October 10, 1778, LOC.

24. Washington to Scott, September 15, 1778, Washington Papers, Series 4, General Correspondence, September 13, 1778–October 10, 1778, LOC.

25. Memorandum Book.

26. Memorial of John Craig to Lord Sydney, Secretary of State, March 8, 1783, Audit Office, Class 13, Vol. 70A, folio 246, NA.

27. Undated manuscript book of Ann Bates, Treasury, Class 1, Vol. 611, folios 198–205, NA.

CHAPTER FOUR: A TIME FOR LIGHT TROOPS

1. Thomas John Chew Williams, *History of Frederick County Maryland* (Baltimore: Genealogical Publishing, 2003), 1:215.

2. Pension Application of Matthew Patton, January 8, 1834, Collection M-804, Pension and Bounty Land Application Files, No. S31294, Matthew Patton, Maryland, NARA.

3. Heitman, *Historical Register of Officers*, 249.

4. Charles Scott to George Washington, September 15, 1778, Washington Papers, Series 4, General Correspondence, September 13, 1778–October 10, 1778, LOC.

5. Simcoe, *History of the Operations*, 86.

6. An examination of thirty-seven recruits for Emmerick's Chasseurs who enlisted in 1778 for whom a residence is given show twenty-five were from Westchester County. Miscellaneous Manuscripts No. 3616, New York State Library.

7. Simcoe, *History of the Operations*, 87–88.

8. Mordecai Gist to Major William Sterrett, September 15, 1778, Theodorus Bailey Myers Collection, Series 12, Mordecai Gist Letterbook, 1777–1779, New York Public Library.

9. Charles Scott to George Washington, ? Past Seven, September 15, 1778, Washington Papers, Series 4, General Correspondence, September 13, 1778–October 10, 1778, LOC.

10. Charles Scott to George Washington, ? Past Seven, September 16, 1778, Washington Papers, Series 4, General Correspondence, September 13, 1778–October 10, 1778, LOC.

11. *Royal Gazette*, September 19, 1778.

12. Simcoe, *History of the Operations*, 87–88.

13. Gist was happily married to his wife, Mary, at the time, and there is no reason to suspect any dalliance on his part. The legend went on to say that the widow aided the escape of Gist and his men by directing them with a handkerchief from an upper window of her house. Robert Bolton Jr., *History of the County of Westchester from its First Settlement to the Present Time* (New York: printed by Alexander S. Goud, 1848), 2:487–488.

14. Ewald, *Diary of the American War*, 149.

15. Benjamin Tallmadge to Charles Scott, ? Past Ten, September 16, 1778, Washington Papers, Series 4, General Correspondence, September 13, 1778–October 10, 1778, LOC.

16. Benjamin Tallmadge to Charles Scott, Shered's House, September 16, 1778, Washington Papers, Series 4, General Correspondence, September 13, 1778–October 10, 1778, LOC.

17. Charles Scott to George Washington, September 8, 1778, Washington Papers, Series 4, General Correspondence, September 13, 1778–October 10, 1778, LOC. See also *Royal Gazette*, September 16, 1778.

18. *Royal American Gazette* (New York), September 17, 1778; *Royal Gazette*, September 19, 1778.

19. "Return of American officers and others."

20. *Royal Gazette*, September 19, 1778.

21. Charles Scott to George Washington, 11 o'clock, September 16, 1778, Washington Papers, Series 4, General Correspondence, September 13, 1778–October 10, 1778, LOC.

22. Charles Scott to George Washington, White Plains, September 17, 1778, Washington Papers, Series 4, General Correspondence, September 13, 1778–October 10, 1778, LOC.

23. Major-of-Brigade George Benson to Cornet John Hamilton, September 18, 1778, Simcoe Papers 1774–1824, CL.

24. Captain George Beckwith to Lt. Col. John Graves Simcoe, Morris' House, September 18, 1778, Simcoe Papers 1774–1824, CL.

25. Simcoe, *History of the Operations*, 88. Simcoe, although disappointed in not finding any enemy force, amused himself by sketching the ground of the 1776 battlefield.
26. *Royal American Gazette*, September 22, 1778. In addition to the prisoners, another paper mentioned "One Harrison from Rockey-hill was wounded." *Royal Gazette*, September 23, 1778.
27. Charles Scott to George Washington, King Street two miles above Claps, September 20, 1778, Washington Papers, Series 4, General Correspondence, September 13, 1778–October 10, 1778, LOC.
28. Tench Tilghman to Charles Scott, Fredericksburg, September 21, 1778, Washington Papers, Series 4, General Correspondence, September 13, 1778–October 10, 1778, LOC.
29. George Washington to Sir Henry Clinton, Fredericksburg, September 16, 1778, Washington Papers, Series 4, General Correspondence, September 13, 1778–October 10, 1778, LOC.
30. Court Martial Proceedings of Major General Charles Lee, August 12, 1778, Washington Papers, Series 4, General Correspondence, July 24, 1778–September 12, 1778, LOC.
31. Washington to Lee, Headquarters, September 15, 1778, Washington Papers, Series 4, General Correspondence, July 24, 1778–September 12, 1778, LOC. Lee's mood was not improved when Congress confirmed his sentence; and it could not have been made happier with an invitation from Lieutenant Colonel John Laurens, one of Washington's aide-de-camps, to meet at 3:30 in the afternoon of December 23, 1778, in a wood "near the four mile stone on the Point no point road." At that time and place, accompanied by "friends" Major Evan Edwards and Lieutenant Colonel Alexander Hamilton, Laurens sought satisfaction for disparaging remarks made about him, and George Washington, during Lee's court-martial. Laurens's "satisfaction" would come in the form of a duel. At six paces distance the two fired at each other, and Lee announced he was slightly wounded. After much debate on the subject, it was found that honor had been satisfied. In the great formality of such dangerous proceedings, Hamilton and Edwards jointly announced: "Upon the whole we think it a piece of justice to the two Gentlemen to declare, that after they met their conduct was strongly marked with all the politeness generosity coolness and firmness, that ought to characterise a transaction of this nature." "Narrative of an Affair of Honor between General Lee and Colonel Laurens," December 24, 1778, Alexander Hamilton Papers, General Correspondence, 1734–1804, Box 23, LOC.
32. Dr. I. H. Betz, "The Conway Cabal at York, Pennsylvania, 1777–1778," *Pennsylvania German* 9, no. 1 (1908): 252–253.
33. "Gates's pistol flashed in the pan" means that only the priming powder ignited, not the main charge with the ball, generally caused by powder residue clogging the touch-hole into the barrel.
34. *Boston Evening-Post*, October 17, 1778. The matter was only over between the antagonists. Within hours the seconds would be at each other's throats, claiming falsehood and treachery, which soon spread into the newspapers.
35. Thacher's view on dueling would change over the next few years, as he witnessed trivial affairs being settled with pistols, with ever-increasing fatal results. James Thacher, *Military Journal of the American Revolution* (Hartford, CT: Hurlbut, William, 1862), 147.

36. Gist to his wife Mary, Camp at White Plains, September 13, 1778, Theodorus Bailey Myers Collection, Series 12, Mordecai Gist Letterbook, 1777–1779, New York Public Library.

37. General Orders New York, September 20, 1778, Orderly Book of the Guides & Pioneers, 19 August to 6 October 1778, Special Collections Division, United States Military Academy Library, West Point.

38. After the troops embarked, the 1st Battalion, New Jersey Volunteers, were relanded on Staten Island. Ebenezer Bridgham to Muster Master General Edward Winslow, New York, October 10, 1778, Ward Chipman Papers, MG 23, D 1, Vol. 24, 361, LAC. See also "Instructions for Mr. Penman" from Gordon & Crowder, Agents to the Provincial Forces, October 1778, Chancery, Class 106, Vol. 90, NA.

39. General Court Martial Proceedings of Captains John McKinnon and Martin McEvoy, held at Flushing Fly between September 5 & 25, 1778, War Office, Class 71, Vol. 87, 173–178, NA.

40. Edward Winslow to Inspector General Alexander Innes, Long Island, 9 July 1778, Ward Chipman Papers, MG 23, D 1, Vol. 24, 346–347, LAC.

41. Winslow to Innes, 11 August 1778, Ward Chipman Papers, MG 23, D 1, Vol. 24, 354–355A, LAC.

42. Court Martial Proceeding of Lieutenant Colonel John Bayard, New York, March 23 to April 29, 1778, War Office, Class 71, Vol. 54, 155–176, NA.

43. General Orders, Headquarters, New York, October 12, 1778, Early American Orderly Book Collection, *Kemble Orderly Book*, September 11, 1778–October 24, 1778, Microfilm Reel 6, No. 69, New-York Historical Society (hereafter cited as N-YHS).

44. Simcoe, *History of the Operations*, 90–91. By "native Americans," Simcoe meant colonists who were born in America.

45. "Abstract of the Number of Men, Women, Children and Waggoners Victualed at the Commissary Generals Provision Stores between the 23rd and 29th July 1778," Clinton Papers, Vol. 37, item 39, CL.

46. "Return of Provisions Issued at His Majesty's Magazines at King's Bridge from the 23rd to 29th November 1778 both days Inclusive," Clinton Papers, Vol. 46, item 29, CL.

47. "Abstract of disbursements in the Quarter Master Generals department for the hire of Gardiners & Labourers for raising Vegetables for the use of the Army & Navy at New York," March 7, 1779, Clinton Papers, 53:36, CL.

48. Commissary General Daniel Wier to John Robinson, May 20, 1777, Daniel Wier Letterbook, Historical Society of Pennsylvania.

49. General Orders New York, December 19, 1777, Orderly Book of the 3 Battalions of Brigadier General Oliver DeLancey's Brigade, 1776–1778, Early American Orderly Book Collection, Reel 4, No. 44, N-YHS.

50. "State of Provisions on the 14 Septemr. 1778," Clinton Papers, Vol. 41, item 16, CL.

51. Clinton to Germain, New York, September 15, 1778, Clinton Papers, Vol. 41, item 25a, CL.

52. "A List of Persons who draw Forage" by Deputy Commissary George Brinley, New York, December 7, 1777, Clinton Papers, Vol. 28, item 8, CL.

53. "State of Forage 30th Augt. 78," Clinton Papers, Vol. 40, item 28, CL.

CHAPTER FIVE: FOOD AND FORAGE

1. Clinton, *American Rebellion*, 103.
2. Clinton similarly found fault with his subordinate, Lieutenant General Wilhelm von Knyphausen, when he saw an opportunity in 1780 to attack Washington while Clinton was returning from the Siege of Charleston. Frederick Mackenzie, *Diary of Frederick Mackenzie* (Cambridge: Harvard University Press, 1930), 2:391.
3. Clinton to Grey, Rhode Island, September 2, 1778, Clinton Papers, Vol. 40, item 31, CL.
4. Clinton, *American Rebellion*, 103.
5. Sir William Howe to Clinton, German Town, October 8, 1777, Clinton Papers, Letters from Sir William Howe to Sir Henry Clinton, 1777, Vol. 259, CL.
6. Grey's troops destroyed eight large vessels, six armed ships, seventy sloops and schooners, and twenty-three whaleboats; recaptured three ships taken in the weeks before by the French fleet; and then destroyed over twenty-six storehouses filled with rum, sugar, molasses, coffee, tobacco, cotton, tea, medicine, gunpowder, and naval supplies. *The Rembrancer; or, Impartial Repository of Public Events, for the Year 1778, and Beginning of 1779* (London: printed for J. Almon, opposite Burlington House, Piccadilly, 1779), 38.
7. Grey estimated rebel losses at one officer and three men killed by the bayonets of the British Light Infantry. "Return of killed, wounded and missing of the Detachment under the command of Major General Grey," Colonial Office, Class 5, Vol. 1089, folio 86, NA.
8. Grey to Sir Henry Clinton, Whitestone, September 18, 1778. Clinton Papers, Vol. 41, item 40, CL. Holmes Hole Harbor is now known as Vineyard Haven Harbor.
9. Ibid.
10. "Return of Ammunition, Arms, and Accoutrements &c which was brought in by the Militia on the Island of Marthas Vineyard, Agreeable to M. General Gray's Order. Received at Holmes Cove September 12th, 13th & 14th 1778," Clinton Papers, Vol. 41, item 14, CL.
11. Admiral Richard Howe to Sir Henry Clinton, *Eagle* off Staten Island, September 11, 1778, Clinton Papers, Vol. 41, item 5, NA.
12. Clinton to Carpenter, September 21, 1778, Clinton Papers, Vol. 41, item 42, CL.
13. No fewer than 134 Loyalist properties were confiscated in Bergen County during the war, more than even Monmouth County, also a hotbed of Loyalist sentiment and larger than Bergen in size and population. "A list of the names of all those Persons whose property was Confiscated in the Several Counties of the State of New Jersey, for joining the Army of the King of Great Britain &c. as returned to the Auditors Office, previous to the first day of May 1787," Audit Office, Class 12, Vol. 85, folios 43–46, NA.
14. Examination of weekly returns for Colonel Philip Van Cortland's Regiment, Heard's Brigade, September to November 1776, Revolutionary War Rolls, M246, 1775–1783, RG 93, Reel 64, Folder 87, NARA.
15. George Van Buskirk of Closter served in the 3rd New Jersey Battalion under Colonel Elias Dayton for one year, 1776. On discharge, he returned home to Closter and served in the county militia, during which time he was

bayoneted by his former Bergen County Loyalist neighbors in a raid on his town in 1779. Collection M-804, Pension and Bounty Land Application Files, No. S42601, George Van Buskirk, New Jersey, NARA.

16. "Extract of letter from New York, dated Sept. 26 [1776]," *Edinburgh Evening Courant*, November 20, 1776.

17. The ferryman was Isaac Perkins, a Loyalist from the English Neighbourhood, Bergen County. He passed the information to his brother, who informed and led the British on their passage up the river. Narrative of Captain Andrew Snape Hamond, HMS *Roebuck*, October 3 to October 9, 1776, in William James Morgan, ed., *Naval Documents of the American Revolution* (Washington, DC: Naval History Division, Department of the Navy, 1972), 6, 1182–1183.

18. Perkins was one of the three Loyalist guides who led Cornwallis's troops up the Palisades, about seven miles above Fort Lee. Memorial of Isaac Perkins to the Commissioners for American Claims, Burton, March 11, 1786, Audit Office, Class 13, Vol. 19, folio 44, NA.

19. Evidence on the Claim of Abraham Van Buskirk to the Commissioners for American Claims, Halifax, March 31, 1786, Audit Office, Class 12, Vol. 15, folios 105–107, NA.

20. Commission of Lieutenant Colonel Abraham Van Buskirk, November 16, 1776, RG 46, O/S Mss. No. 360, Nova Scotia Archives.

21. Livingston to Washington, Newton, Sussex County, July 11, 1777, Washington Papers, Series 4, General Correspondence, May 30, 1777–July 22 1777, LOC.

22. *New-York Gazette and the Weekly Mercury*, July 21, 1777.

23. Clinton to Howe, Kingsbridge, September 23, 1777, Colonial Office, Class 5, Vol. 94, 683–687, NA.

24. "Return of the Killed, Wounded, Prisoners and Missing of the following Corps during an Excursion to Jersey from the 12th to the 16th Septemr. 1777," Colonial Office, Class 5, Vol. 94, 689, NA.

25. Hotham to Howe, *Preston* off New York, September 23, 1777, Admiralty, Class 1, Vol. 488, folios 46–47, NA.

26. Clinton, *American Rebellion*, 71–72.

27. Tench Tilghman to Hopkins, Haverstraw, July 16, 1778, Washington Papers, Series 4, General Correspondence, April 30, 1778–July 23, 1778, LOC.

28. Moylan to Washington, Tappan, July 23, 1778, Washington Papers, Series 4, General Correspondence, April 30, 1778–July 23, 1778, LOC.

29. Washington to Moylan, White Plains, July 25, 1778, Washington Papers, Series 4, General Correspondence, July 24, 1778–September 12, 1778, LOC.

30. Moylan to Washington, Hackensack, July 29, 1778, Washington Papers, Series 4, General Correspondence, July 24, 1778–September 12, 1778, LOC.

31. Washington to Moylan, White Plains, July 30, 1778, Washington Papers, Series 4, General Correspondence, July 24, 1778–September 12, 1778, LOC.

32. Washington to Clough, White Plains, August 25, 1778, Washington Papers, Series 4, General Correspondence, July 24, 1778–September 12, 1778, LOC.

33. Clough to Washington, August 26, 1778, Washington Papers, Series 4, General Correspondence, July 24, 1778–September 12, 1778, LOC.

34. The last sentence refers to Major Robert Timpany of Bergen County, formerly a schoolmaster at New Bridge. At this point he was a seconded officer

in the 4th Battalion, New Jersey Volunteers. The report of him being ordered to raise a cavalry regiment appears to have been incorrect, as he never attempted such a thing. Clough to Washington, 12 o'clock, September 4, 1778, Washington Papers, Series 4, General Correspondence, July 24, 1778–September 12, 1778, LOC.

35. One enemy soldier referred to them as "Lady Washington's Light-Horse," which was repeated by several other British officers. Petition of William Wright to the New Brunswick House of Assembly, January 17, 1838, Sessional Records of the Legislative Assembly, RS 24, 1838 Petition 277, Provincial Archives of New Brunswick.

36. Moore Furman to Clement Biddle, Acquackanonk, August 26, 1778, Sol Feinstone Collection, Document No. 2472, David Library of the American Revolution.

37. Ibid.

38. Pension Application of Peter Dey, Seneca County, New York, February 5, 1834, Collection M-804, Pension and Bounty Land Application Files, No. S15078, Peter Dey, New Jersey, NARA. "The Sheriff of Bergen" refers to Adam Boyd of Hackensack, who was also a lieutenant in the militia.

CHAPTER SIX: BERGEN COUNTY IN THE CROSSHAIRS

1. Cunningham of Thortoun Papers, 1746–1782, John Peebles Journal, GD 21/492/6, Pages 42–48, Scottish Record Office (hereafter cited as Peebles).

2. The 3rd Brigade consisted of the 15th, 17th, 42nd, and 44th Regiments, while the 4th Brigade was composed of the 33rd, 37th, 46th, and 64th Regiments. The exact numerical strength of the entire force was never given, although period accounts mostly estimated between five thousand and seven thousand. The strength of the different corps on August 15, 1778, present and fit for duty (excluding sick, wounded, men on detached duty, etc.) was in excess of seven thousand, not including the artillery and any of the civil branches of the army that were accompanying the troops. State of the Army, August 15, 1778, Colonial Office, Class 5, Vol. 96, folio 112, NA.

3. Journal of Peter Russell, September 22, 1778, Peter Russell Fonds, F 46, Microfilm MS 75, Reel 3, Archives of Ontario (hereafter cited as Russell).

4. Journal of John André, September 22, 1778, John André Journal, HM 626, Huntington Library (hereafter cited as André).

5. Scott to Washington, King Street, September 23, 1778, Washington Papers, Series 4, General Correspondence, September 13, 1778–October 10, 1778, LOC.

6. Tilghman to Scott, Headquarters, September 24, 1778, Washington Papers, Series 4, General Correspondence, September 13, 1778–October 10, 1778, LOC.

7. Baylor to Washington, Hackensack, September 23, 1778, Washington Papers, Series 4, General Correspondence, September 13, 1778–October 10, 1778, LOC.

8. "Pay Roll of Capt. John Bell's Company of the New York State Regt. in the Service of the United States of America Commanded by Col. Morris Graham for the Months Augt. Sept. Oct. Nov. & Decr. 1778," Revolutionary War Rolls, M246, 1775–1783, RG 93, Reel 74, Folder 106, NARA.

9. Pension application of Abraham Conklin, November 29, 1832, Collection M-804, Pension and Bounty Land Application Files, No. S22699, Abraham Conklin, New York, NARA.

10. The village of Hackensack was on the west side of the river, about three miles below New Bridge, and officially a part of New Barbados Township. Hackensack Township was confusingly located on the east side of the river and included the villages of Schraalenburgh, English Neighbourhood, and Teaneck, but not Hackensack.

11. Benjamin Romaine to Commissioner of Pensions J. L. Edwards, Washington, D.C., June 30, 1834, Collection M-804, Pension and Bounty Land Application Files, No. W18839, Benjamin Romaine, New Jersey, NARA.

12. When the smoke cleared, Sisco was a prisoner. He spent the next fourteen weeks in the Sugar House Prison in New York City. Collection M-804, Pension and Bounty Land Application Files, No. W2360, Peter I Sisco, New Jersey, NARA.

13. Diary of Captain Archibald Robertson, Corps of Engineers, September 23, 1778, in *Archibald Robertson: His Diaries and Sketches in America, 1762–1780*, ed. Harry Miller Lydenberg (New York: New York Public Library, 1930), 182.

14. Pension application of Robert Gould, November 1, 1832, Collection M-804, Pension and Bounty Land Application Files, No. W1270, Robert Gould, New Jersey, NARA.

15. Pension application of Abraham Cisco, September 19, 1832, Collection M-804, Pension and Bounty Land Application Files, No. W12723, Abraham Cisco, New Jersey, NARA.

16. Pension application of Samuel Vervalen, November 29, 1832, Collection M-804, Pension and Bounty Land Application Files, No. W16774, Samuel Vervalen, New Jersey, NARA.

17. Pension application of John D. Haring, February 25, 1833, Collection M-804, Pension and Bounty Land Application Files, No. W16594, John D. Haring, New Jersey, NARA.

18. Pension application of Caroline White, widow of Elias White, December 3, 1838, Collection M-804, Pension and Bounty Land Application Files, No. W22614, Elias White, New Jersey, NARA.

19. Captain John André reported twenty-seven men captured and "a few" killed. André.

20. Pension application of Benjamin Woodruff, December 5, 1832, Collection M-804, Pension and Bounty Land Application Files, No. W26097, Benjamin Woodruff, New Jersey, NARA. "New Milford" is not to be confused with the present town of New Milford, Bergen County. Woodruff was from the area now known as West Milford, Passaic County.

21. A list of American officers who were prisoners with the British in October 1780 included William Rogers, with the notation "taken September 23, 1778 English Neighbourhood." BV Prisoners of War, N-YHS.

22. Interestingly, no other Virginia Continentals were with Rogers, and why he was there remains a mystery. "A Muster Roll of the Lt. Cols. Compy. of the 8th Virginia Regiment of Foot in the service of the United States Commanded by Colo. James Wood, taken for the month of Sepr. 1778," Revolutionary War Rolls, M246, 1775–1783, RG 93, Reel 100, Folder 127, NARA.

23. Pension application of John G. Ryerson, September 23, 1833, Collection M-804, Pension and Bounty Land Application Files, No. S1099, John G. Ryerson, New Jersey, NARA.

24. Pension application of Samuel Helm, August 22, 1832, Collection M-804, Pension and Bounty Land Application Files, No. S10825, Samuel Helm, New Jersey, NARA.

25. Baylor to Washington, Hackensack, September 22, 1778, Washington Papers, Series 4, General Correspondence, September 13, 1778–October 10, 1778, LOC.

26. Peebles, September 23, 1778.

27. Russell, September 23, 1778.

28. Cornwallis to Clinton, English Neighbourhood, 7:00 PM, September 23, 1778, Clinton Papers, Vol. 42, item 2, CL.

29. General Orders, English Neighbourhood, September 2, 1778, Early American Orderly Book Collection, Brigade of Guards Orderly Book, August 7, 1778–December 25, 1778, Microfilm Reel 6, No. 65, N-YHS.

30. Intelligence submitted by Captain Patrick Ferguson, Friday, September 18, 1778, Clinton Papers, Vol. 41, item 33, CL.

31. Baylor to Washington, Paramus, September 24, 1778, Washington Papers, Series 4, General Correspondence, September 13, 1778–October 10, 1778, LOC.

32. Russell, September 24, 1778.

33. "An Account of the Losses and Services of Daniel Isaac Browne First Major of the late Fourth Battallion of the New Jersey Volunteers . . . ," Audit Office, Class 13, Vol. 17, folios 155–156, NA.

34. Cortland Skinner to Sir Henry Clinton, New York, April 13, 1778, Clinton Papers, Vol. 33, item 33, CL.

35. Browne to unknown, Annapolis, Nova Scotia, September 25, 1784, Audit Office, Class 13, Vol. 17, folio 144, NA.

36. The house and farm were sold April 23, 1779, for a little over 1,280 pounds. Certificate of Aaron Dunham, Auditor of Accounts for New Jersey, Audit Office, Class 13, Vol. 17, folio 151, NA.

37. Washington to Henry Laurens, Fredericksburg, September 23, 1778, Washington Papers, Series 4, General Correspondence, September 13, 1778–October 10, 1778, LOC.

38. Putnam to Washington, Peekskill, September 24, 1778, Washington Papers, Series 4, General Correspondence, September 13, 1778–October 10, 1778, LOC. There were actually two churches at that time in Schraalenburgh. It is most likely the South Church, in modern Bergenfield, that is meant here.

39. The deserter Scott interviewed appears to have been the sergeant major of the 2nd Battalion, 71st Regiment of Foot, a Highland unit at Kingsbridge. Scott to Washington, King Street, September 23, 1778, Washington Papers, Series 4, General Correspondence, September 13, 1778–October 10, 1778, LOC.

40. *Connecticut Courant* (Hartford), October 6, 1778.

41. Campbell had spent much of the past two years in captivity in New England. The transport carrying him and some men of the 71st Regiment was among several vessels captured by privateers off Boston in 1776, having not been informed of that city's evacuation by the British. Campbell had been exchanged for the famous Green Mountain Boys leader, Colonel Ethan Allen, in May 1778, and this was his first chance to lead his corps in action. Campbell

to Colonel Elias Boudinot, New York, May 22, 1778, Elias Boudinot Papers, Miscellaneous Manuscript Collection 721, Container 2, LOC.

42. Bernhard A. Uhlendorf, ed., *Revolution in America: Confidential Letters and Journals 1776–1784 of Adjutant General Major Baurmeister of the Hessian Forces* (New Brunswick, NJ: Rutgers University Press, 1957), 217.

CHAPTER SEVEN: THE FOG OF WAR

1. David A. Bernstein, ed., *Minutes of the Governor's Privy Council, 1777–1789* (Trenton: New Jersey State Library Archives and History Bureau, 1974), 90.

2. Cooper and Haring to Thomas Smith, Esquire, Harrington Township, September 25, 1778, in *Public Papers of George Clinton*, ed. Hugh Hastings (New York: Wynkoop Hallenbeck Crawford, 1900), 4:86–87.

3. Scott to Washington, 9:00 o'clock, September 24, 1778, Washington Papers, Series 4, General Correspondence, September 13, 1778–October 10, 1778, LOC.

4. Clinton, *American Rebellion*, 105.

5. Peebles, September 25, 1778.

6. Lydenberg, *Archibald Robertson*, 182–183.

7. Russell, September 25, 1778.

8. "Plan of the country at and in the vicinity of Forts Lee and Independency, showing the position of the British Army," Map No. 71002221, LOC.

9. After Orders, 7 o'clock, Teaneck, September 26, 1778, 17th Regiment of Foot Orderly Book kept by Captain Robert Clayton, AM618, Historical Society of Pennsylvania.

10. Baylor to Washington, Paramus, September 26, 1778, Washington Papers, Series 4, General Correspondence, September 13, 1778–October 10, 1778, LOC.

11. This was probably a reference to the South Church, rather than the North Church about a mile farther on, but given the scanty reference, there is no way to know for sure.

12. Intelligence interview of Hantras Hysonec, enclosed in Baylor to Washington, September 26, 1778, Washington Papers, Series 4, General Correspondence, September 13, 1778–October 10, 1778, LOC. The name of this soldier is badly written in the original document, but it is probably Andreas Eisenach, a German recruit to the 15th Regiment, whose name appears on the rolls of that corps. Muster Rolls of the 15th Regiment of Foot, War Office, Class 12, Vol. 3229, NA. The author thanks Don Hagist for his assistance in helping identify this soldier.

13. "Extract of a letter from an officer in Jersey, dated Aquakanock, October 4, 1778," *New-York Packet, and the American Advertiser* (Fishkill), October 8, 1778.

14. Receipts of Abraham Ely, New Bridge, September 25, 1778, and Teaneck, October 13, 1778, by Major F. E. Gwynn and Captain Thomas Trewren, 16th Light Dragoons, Audit Office, Class 13, Vol. 98, folio 129, NA.

15. Maxwell to Washington, September 27, 1778, Washington Papers, Series 4, General Correspondence, September 13, 1778–October 10, 1778, LOC.

16. Washington to Maxwell, Fredericksburg, September 27, 1778, Washington Papers, Series 4, General Correspondence, September 13, 1778–October 10, 1778, LOC.

17. Washington to Putnam, Fredericksburg, September 27, 1778, Washington Papers, Series 4, General Correspondence, September 13, 1778–October 10, 1778, LOC.
18. Washington to Baylor, Fredericksburg, September 27, 1778, Washington Papers, Series 4, General Correspondence, September 13, 1778–October 10, 1778, LOC.
19. Cornwallis to Clinton, English Neighbourhood, 11:00 AM, September 25, 1778, Clinton Papers, Vol. 42, item 7, CL.
20. Peebles, September 26–27, 1778.
21. Scott to Washington, September 25, 1778, Washington Papers, Series 4, General Correspondence, September 13, 1778–October 10, 1778, LOC.
22. Scott to Washington, ? past 12 o'clock AM, September 26, 1778, Washington Papers, Series 4, General Correspondence, September 13, 1778–October 10, 1778, LOC.
23. Washington to Scott, September 26, 1778, Washington Papers, Series 4, General Correspondence, September 13, 1778–October 10, 1778, LOC.
24. Scott to Washington, September 26, 1778, Washington Papers, Series 4, General Correspondence, September 13, 1778–October 10, 1778, LOC.
25. Scott to Washington, September 27, 1778, Washington Papers, Series 4, General Correspondence, September 13, 1778–October 10, 1778, LOC.
26. Clinton, *American Rebellion*, 105.
27. "Journal of campaign of 1777 under Sir William Howe, 11 June–30 December 1777; and of campaign of 1778 under Sir Henry Clinton, 18 June–15 November 1778" kept by Major General Charles Grey, Archives and Special Collections, GB-0033-GRE-A, Papers of the 1st Earl Grey, A24a, Durham University Library.
28. André, September 27, 1778.
29. *New-York Packet, and the American Advertiser* (Fishkill), October 1, 1778.
30. Cooper to Putnam, Harringtown, September 26, 1778, Washington Papers, Series 4, General Correspondence, September 13, 1778–October 10, 1778, LOC.
31. Pension Application of James Riker, Collection M-804, Pension and Bounty Land Application Files, No. W2573, James Riker, New Jersey, NARA.
32. Pension Application of John D. Haring, Collection M-804, Pension and Bounty Land Application Files, No. W16594, John D. Haring, New Jersey, NARA.
33. Pension Application of James Vanderbilt, Collection M-804, Pension and Bounty Land Application Files, No. S16278, James Vanderbilt, New York, NARA.
34. Peter Russell to Betsey Russell, New York, October 21, 1778, Peter Russell Fonds, F 46, Microfilm MS 75, Reel 3, Archives of Ontario.
35. Muster Roll of Captain Savage's Company, 37th Regiment of Foot, War Office, Class 12, Vol. 5101, NA. The author thanks Don Hagist for his assistance in researching the careers of these two soldiers.
36. Simcoe, *History of the Operations*, 90.
37. Campbell to Sir Henry Clinton, Kingsbridge, October 10, 1778, Clinton Papers, Vol. 43, item 12, CL.
38. Cooper to Hay, Green Bush, September 28, 1778, 19th Century transcription by William B. Sprague, Washington Papers, Series 4, General Correspondence, September 13, 1778–October 10, 1778, LOC.

CHAPTER EIGHT: BAYONETS IN THE NIGHT

1. Old Tappan in 1778 was a large area of Harrington Township. While it is now a town in Bergen County, the area where Baylor and his men spent the night is modern-day River Vale.

2. Pension Application of Peter Dey, Seneca County, New York, February 5, 1834, Collection M-804, Pension and Bounty Land Application Files, No. S15078, Peter Dey, New Jersey, NARA.

3. William E. Dornemann, PhD, "Diary Kept by Chaplain Waldeck during the Last American War," part 2, *Journal of the Johannes Schwalm Historical Association* 2, no. 4 (1998): 50–51.

4. Baylor to Washington, Tappan, October 19, 1778, Washington Papers, Series 4, General Correspondence, September 26, 1778–November 6, 1778, LOC.

5. André, September 27, 1778; Russell, September 27, 1778.

6. Banta to Governor William Tryon, New York, March 7, 1780, Headquarters Papers of the British Army in America, PRO 30/55/2619, NA.

7. Memorial of Weart Banta to Lord Sydney, one of His Majesty's Principal Secretaries of State, London, August 26, 1786, Treasury, Class 1, Vol. 645, folios 139–140, NA. Banta was eventually commissioned a lieutenant, on February 2, 1779, in the King's Militia Volunteers, a refugee corps organized by Governor William Franklin of New Jersey. His career was short lived: he suffered a musket-ball wound in the knee on a raid on Closter less than two months later, leaving him crippled for life. Commission of Weart Banta, February 2, 1779, Treasury, Class 1, Vol. 645, folio 143, NA.

8. "The Memorial of Weart Banta, formerly of Hackinsack in the Province of New Jersey but now of Shelburne in Nova Scotia, Carpenter," Halifax 1786, Audit Office, Class 13, Vol. 17, folios 34–35, NA.

9. *New-York Gazette and the Weekly Mercury*, February 9, 1778.

10. Ackerman to Sir Henry Clinton, New York, October 20, 1779, Headquarters Papers of the British Army in America, PRO 30/55/2375, NA.

11. Memorial of Peter Ackerman to the Commissioners for American Claims, Shelburne, March 1786, Audit Office, Class 13, Vol. 25, folios 5–6, NA.

12. Memorial of Thomas Hughes to the Commissioners for American Claims, no date, Audit Office, Class 13, Vol. 64, folios 382–383, NA.

13. Baylor to Washington, Tappan, October 19, 1778, Washington Papers, Series 4, General Correspondence, September 26, 1778–November 6, 1778, LOC.

14. The firing mechanism of period weapons utilized a highly knapped flint, leading to the firearms being referred to as flintlocks or firelocks. When the trigger was pulled, a series of tensioned springs released, flinging the flint against the steel hammer, creating spark sufficient to ignite the gunpowder in the pan of the lock, which then sent flame through a small touchhole near the breech of the barrel, igniting the main charge which had been loaded down the muzzle and sending the musket ball on its way. Grey's having the men remove the flints from the locks made firing impossible. Surgeon David Griffith to Major General Lord Stirling, Orangetown, October 20, 1778, Washington Papers, Series 4, General Correspondence, September 26, 1778–November 6, 1778, LOC.

15. *New-York Gazette and the Weekly Mercury*, October 5, 1778.

16. *New Jersey Gazette* (Trenton), October 7, 1778.

17. Deposition of Thomas Tally and George Willis, taken before Governor William Livingston, October 22, 1778, Papers of the Continental Congress, M247, reel 66, i53, 125–126, NARA.

18. Deposition of Bartlett Hawkins, taken before Governor William Livingston, October 22, 1778, Papers of the Continental Congress, M247, reel 66, i53, 127, NARA.

19. Pension Application of Bartlett H. Fitzgerald (Bartlett Hawkins), Collection M-804, Pension and Bounty Land Application Files, No. S9562, Bartlett Hawkins, Virginia, NARA.

20. Deposition of Joseph Carrol, taken before Governor William Livingston, October 18, 1778, Papers of the Continental Congress, M247, reel 66, i53, 129, NARA.

21. Deposition of David Stringfellow, taken before Governor William Livingston, October 10, 1778, Papers of the Continental Congress, M247, reel 66, i53, 121, NARA.

22. Griffith to Stirling, Orangetown, October 20, 1778, Washington Papers, Series 4, General Correspondence, September 26, 1778–November 6, 1778, LOC.

23. Deposition of Thomas Benson, taken before Governor William Livingston, October 10, 1778, Papers of the Continental Congress, M247, reel 66, i53, 119, NARA.

24. Pension Application of William Bassett, December 29, 1833, Collection M-804, Pension and Bounty Land Application Files, No. W9739, William Bassett, Virginia, NARA.

25. William S. Stryker, *Official Register of the Officers and Men of New Jersey in the Revolutionary War* (Trenton: Wm. T. Nicholson, 1872), 435.

26. Kevin Wright, "Overkill: Revolutionary War Reminiscences of River Vale," accessed July 23, 2015, http://www.bergencountyhistory.org/Pages/baylormassacre.html.

27. Deposition of Robert Morrow, October 1778, Papers of the Continental Congress, M247, reel 66, i53, 131, NARA.

28. Griffith to Stirling, Orangetown, October 20, 1778, Washington Papers, Series 4, General Correspondence, September 26, 1778–November 6, 1778, LOC.

29. "Return of American officers and others Prisoners on Long Island. August 15th 1778 [*sic*]," Revolutionary War Rolls, M246, 1775–1783, RG 93, Reel 135, Folder 4, NARA.

30. Griffith to Stirling, Orangetown, October 20, 1778, Washington Papers, Series 4, General Correspondence, September 26, 1778–November 6, 1778, LOC.

31. "A Return of the Regt. of L D Commanded By Capt. Stith Octr. 23rd 1778," Revolutionary War Rolls, M246, 1775–1783, RG 93, Reel 115, Folder 13, NARA.

32. Cornwallis to Clinton, New Bridge, September 28, 1778, Colonial Office, Class 5, Vol. 96, folio 96, NA.

33. André, September 27, 1778.

34. Pension Application of James Quackinbush, New York City, September 9, 1836, Collection M-804, Pension and Bounty Land Application Files, No. S15200, James Quackinbush, New Jersey/New York, NARA.

35. C. F. William Maurer, *Dragoon Diary* (n.p.: AuthorHouse, 2005), 493–494.
36. *New-York Gazette and the Weekly Mercury*, October 5, 1778.
37. Pension Application of Peter S. Van Orden, November 28, 1832, Collection M-804, Pension and Bound Land Application Files, No. S11160, Peter S. Van Orden, New Jersey, NARA.
38. Deposition of Abraham Blauvelt, October 1778, Papers of the Continental Congress, M 247, Reel 66, i53, 131, NARA.
39. "List of Rebel Prisoners taken by His Majesty's 4th Battn. NJV since December 1776," Cornwallis Papers, PRO 30/11/2, folio 19, NA.
40. Memorial of Abraham Lent to Sir Henry Clinton, New York, October 21, 1779, Headquarters Papers of the British Army in America, PRO 30/55/2379, NA.
41. Pension Application of John A. Haring, Collection M-804, Pension and Bounty Land Application Files, No. S6980, John A. Haring, New Jersey, NARA.

CHAPTER NINE: THE COLLECTION

1. *Kemble*, 162–164. The published Kemble Papers contain both a journal and an orderly book.
2. Thomas Jones, *History of New York during The Revolutionary War* (New York: New-York Historical Society, 1879), 1:286.
3. Cornwallis to Clinton, New Bridge, September 28, 1778, Colonial Office, Class 5, Vol. 96, folio 165, NA.
4. Putnam to Washington, 8:00 PM September 28, 1778, Highlands, Washington Papers, Series 4, General Correspondence, September 13, 1778–October 10, 1778, LOC.
5. Stewart to Washington, 10:00 AM, King's Ferry, September 28, 1778, Washington Papers, Series 4, General Correspondence, September 13, 1778–October 10, 1778, LOC.
6. Woodford to Washington, Peekskill, September 28, 1778, Washington Papers, Series 4, General Correspondence, September 13, 1778–October 10, 1778, LOC.
7. Three men of one company would desert on September 30. Muster Roll of Lieutenant Uzal Meeker's Company of Spencer's Additional Regiment for the months of October, November & December 1778, Revolutionary War Rolls, M246, 1775–1783, RG 93, Reel 128, Folder 170, NARA.
8. Russell, September 26, 1778.
9. Dornemann, "Diary Kept by Chaplain Waldeck," 50.
10. There were but six British regiments in the New York area not involved in active operations: the 23rd, 27th, 28th, 35th, 40th, and 55th, the last five of which would be embarking under General Grant for the West Indies. Five of these regiments were in the 1st and 2nd Brigades. These two brigades had encamped at the Watering Place, on the east side of Staten Island, after the march from Philadelphia, but had been reduced by regiments being drafted and moved elsewhere. General Orders, Sandy Hook, July 5, 1778, *Kemble Orderly Book*, 602–603.
11. Conway to Maxwell, Acquackanonk, September 30, 1778, Department of Defense, Military Records, Revolutionary War, Revolutionary Manuscripts Numbered, Document No. 2552, New Jersey State Archives.

12. Pension Application of Abraham Freeland, Collection M-804, Pension and Bounty Land Application Files, No. S1002, Abraham Freeland, New Jersey, NARA.

13. Pension Application of Abraham D. Banta, M-804, Pension and Bounty Land Application Files, No. S6575, Abraham D. Banta, New Jersey, NARA.

14. Pension Application of Samuel Roome, Pension and Bounty Land Application Files, No. S4789, Samuel Roome, New Jersey, NARA.

15. Winds to Washington, Acquackanonk, September 30, 1778, Washington Papers, Series 4, General Correspondence, September 13, 1778–October 10, 1778, LOC.

16. Peebles, September 29, 1778.

17. Winds to Stirling, 9:00 PM C-September 29, 1778, Papers of Major General William Alexander, Lord Stirling, Vol. 1, 99, N-YHS.

18. Pension Application of Peter Van Allen, M-804, Pension and Bounty Land Application Files, No. S6301, Peter Van Allen, New Jersey, NARA.

19. Jabez Bell was a corporal in the Morris County Militia. Pension Application of Aaron Voorhes, M-804, Pension and Bounty Land Application Files, No. W122, Aaron Voorhes, New Jersey, NARA.

20. General After Orders, Teaneck, 7:00 PM, September 29, 1778, 17th Regiment of Foot Orderly Book kept by Captain Robert Clayton, AM618, Historical Society of Pennsylvania. The text of these orders has been altered by the author in spelling to make it readable for a modern audience, it being extremely difficult to follow otherwise.

21. André, October 2, 5, and 8, 1778.

22. Peebles, October 2, 1778.

23. Washington to Stirling, September 28, 1778, Washington Papers, Series 4, General Correspondence, September 13, 1778–October 10, 1778, LOC.

24. Neilson to Stirling, Elizabethtown, October 3, 1778, Papers of Major General William Alexander, Lord Stirling, Vol. 1, 137–138, N-YHS.

25. Winds to Washington, Acquackanonk, September 30, 1778, Washington Papers, Series 4, General Correspondence, September 13, 1778–October 10, 1778, LOC.

26. Stirling to Washington, Acquackanonk, October 4, 1778, Washington Papers, Series 4, General Correspondence, September 13, 1778–October 10, 1778, LOC.

27. Stirling to Washington, Acquackanonk, Noon, October 9, 1778, Washington Papers, Series 4, General Correspondence, September 13, 1778–October 10, 1778, LOC.

28. "Return of Vessels loaded with Hay in English Creek and Seacacus," New York, October 20, 1778, Clinton Papers, Vol. 43, item 36, CL.

29. Vaughan to Major General Jones, October 2, 1778, Clinton Papers, Vol. 42, item 29, CL.

30. Dayton to Stirling, Second River, October 6, 1778, Papers of Major General William Alexander, Lord Stirling, Vol. 1, 139, N-YHS.

31. Inventories of Damages by the British and Americans in New Jersey, 1776–1782, Vol. 1, New Jersey State Archives.

32. Peebles, October 8, 1778.

33. It is not known who the individual alluded to was, or the particular circumstances of his children. Presumably all were destitute because of the foraging of the British. John Vanderhoven to Cornelius Vanderhoven, 4:00 PM,

October 9, 1778, Washington Papers, Series 4, General Correspondence, September 13, 1778–October 10, 1778, LOC.

34. Court Martial Proceedings of Daniel Marley, October 15–17, 1778, War Office, Class 71, Vol. 87, 339–340, NA.

35. Certificate of Thomas Miller, New York, May 10, 1782, Headquarters Papers of the British Army in America, PRO 30/55/4580, NA.

36. An examination of the muster rolls of the British Legion show no deserters on the date of the theft. If the money was taken by a deserter, it may have been someone from a different regiment. Court Martial Proceedings of 2nd Lieutenant Thomas Miller, November 15, 1778, War Office, Class 71, Vol. 88, 1–7, NA.

37. Washington to Woodford, Headquarters near Fredericksburg, September 30, 1778, Washington Papers, Series 4, General Correspondence, September 13, 1778–October 10, 1778, LOC.

38. Stirling to Washington, Paramus, 7:00 AM, October 3, 1778, Washington Papers, Series 4, General Correspondence, September 13, 1778–October 10, 1778, LOC.

39. Woodford to Washington, Paramus, October 4, 1778, Washington Papers, Series 4, General Correspondence, September 13, 1778–October 10, 1778, LOC.

40. Laurens to Livingston, October 6, 1778, Papers of the Continental Congress, M247, Reel 23, Item 13, Vol. 2, 99, NARA.

41. The *Pennsylvania Packet* (Philadelphia) of October 26, 1778, was just one of several papers that published the depositions taken by Livingston.

CHAPTER TEN: PARRYING THE THRUST IN WESTCHESTER

1. Council of War, Fredericksburg, September 29, 1778, RG 93, War Department Collection of Revolutionary War Records, Miscellaneous Numbered Records, No. 31,500, NARA.

2. Martin, *Private Yankee Doodle*, 136.

3. Ewald, *Diary of the American War*, 150.

4. Martin, *Private Yankee Doodle*, 136–137.

5. Ewald, *Diary of the American War*, 150.

6. Uhlendorf, *Revolution in America*, 220–221.

7. Butler to Scott, September 30, 1778, Washington Papers, Series 4, General Correspondence, September 13, 1778–October 10, 1778, LOC.

8. *Connecticut Courant* (Hartford), October 13, 1778.

9. *New Jersey Gazette* (Trenton), October 7, 1778.

10. Ewald, *Diary of the American War*, 150–151.

11. Martin, *Private Yankee Doodle*, 137–138.

12. Letter of Lieutenant Colonel Ludwig Johann Adolph von Wurmb, Spuyten Duyvil, October 19, 1778, Freiherr von Jungkenn Papers, Vol. 2, item 24, CL. Translated by Henry Retzer, whom the author thanks.

13. Scott to Washington, North Castle, September 30, 1778, Washington Papers, Series 4, General Correspondence, September 13, 1778–October 10, 1778, LOC.

14. Washington to Sullivan, Fishkill, October 1, 1778, Washington Papers, Series 4, General Correspondence, September 13, 1778–October 10, 1778, LOC.

15. Ayers enlisted January 9, 1778, in 1st Lieutenant Jonathan Williams's Company of the Guides & Pioneers. RG 8, "C" Series, Vol. 1888, LAC.

16. Armand's corps was a similar, although smaller, version of the British Legion and the other Provincial light corps facing them in Westchester. This unit was formerly raised and commanded by another European, Major Nicholas Dietrich, Baron de Ottendorf, until it was placed under Armand's command in 1777. Washington to Armand, June 11, 1777, Washington Papers, Series 4, General Correspondence, May 30, 1777–July 22, 1777, LOC.
17. Blindberry served from 1777 until his death in August 1782. RG 8, "C" Series, Vol. 1867, 19, LAC.
18. Memorandum Book.
19. Both Ayers and Grant used the name "Hammond," and while it may have been assumed they were referencing Lieutenant Colonel James Hamman of the Westchester Militia, Blindberry's statement of the troops being mostly foreigners, and Simcoe in his journal referencing intelligence brought in pinpointing Armand's headquarters, strongly point to the Continental light corps commander. Armand was a part of Scott's command and often mentioned by Ewald as an object of interest to attack. Grant to Clinton, October 1, 1778, Clinton Papers, Vol. 42, item 24, CL.
20. Ewald, *Diary of the American War*, 151.
21. Scott to Washington, North Castle, October 2, 1778, Washington Papers, Series 4, General Correspondence, September 13, 1778–October 10, 1778, LOC.
22. Scott to Washington, near Bedford, October 4, 1778, Washington Papers, Series 4, General Correspondence, September 13, 1778–October 10, 1778, LOC. No deaths appear to have occurred with Emmerick's Chasseurs at this time, although two men, Joseph Tilley and Charles Secard, were listed as being taken prisoner. Muster Roll of Captain Francis Bonapace's Company of Emmerick's Chasseurs, October 24, 1778, RG 8, "C" Series, Vol. 1891, LAC.
23. *Royal American Gazette*, October 13, 1778.
24. *Royal Gazette*, October 10, 1778.
25. Scott to Washington, Bedford, October 7, 1778, Washington Papers, Series 4, General Correspondence, September 13, 1778–October 10, 1778, LOC.
26. Washington to Scott, October 8, 1778, Washington Papers, Series 4, General Correspondence, September 13, 1778–October 10, 1778, LOC.
27. Memorandum Book.
28. Muster Roll of Captain James' Troop, British Legion, September 7, 1778, RG 8, "C" Series, Vol. 1883, 8, LAC.
29. Muster Roll of Captain James' Troop, British Legion, Kingsbridge, October 27, 1778, RG 8, "C" Series, Vol. 1883, 7, LAC.
30. General Orders, Headquarters Fredericksburg, October 10, 1778, Washington Papers, Series 3, Letterbooks, Subseries G, General Orders, Book 3, 384–386, LOC.
31. Washington to Scott, Fredericksburg, October 10, 1778, Washington Papers, Series 4, General Correspondence, September 13, 1778–October 10, 1778, LOC.
32. Muster Roll of Captain Richard Hovenden's Troop, British Legion, 1778, RG 8, "C" Series, Vol. 1883, 4, LAC.
33. Stoddard to Washington, Bedford, October 15, 1778, Washington Papers, Series 4, General Correspondence, September 26, 1778–November 6, 1778, LOC.

34. Washington to Stoddard, Headquarters, October 17, 1778, Washington Papers, Series 4, General Correspondence, September 26, 1778–November 6, 1778, LOC.
35. Memorandum of Intelligence from Deserters, enclosed in Scott to Washington, October 6, 1778, Washington Papers, Series 4, General Correspondence, September 13, 1778–October 10, 1778, LOC.
36 Peebles, October 2, 1778.

CHAPTER ELEVEN: IN QUEST OF PIRATES AND POLES
1. Clinton, *American Rebellion*, 105.
2. William Eden to Clinton, no date, Clinton Papers, Vol. 42, item 21, CL.
3. Barrington to Howe, War Office, March 6, 1777, Headquarters Papers of the British Army in America, PRO 30/55/433, NA.
4. Return of the killed, wounded of the army under Sir William Howe on the Heights of Brandywine, September 11, 1777, Colonial Office, Class 5, Vol. 94, folios 659–660, NA.
5. Muster Rolls of the 1st and 3rd Battalions, New Jersey Volunteers, Staten Island, October 21, 1778, RG 8, "C" Series, Vols. 1851 & 1856, LAC. The exact number of the 1st Battalion is unknown because the muster roll of one company is missing.
6. John Vanderhoven to Cornelius Vanderhoven, 4:00 PM, October 9, 1778, Washington Papers, Series 4, General Correspondence, September 13, 1778–October 10, 1778, LOC.
7. Peter Russell to Betsey Russell, New York, October 21, 1778, Peter Russell Fonds, F 46, Microfilm MS 75, Reel 3, AO.
8. "List, Distribution and Condition of His Majesty's Ships and Vessels employed in America exclusive of the Squadron with Vice Adml. Byron and that under Orders to sail with Comr. Hotham," *Ardent* off New York, October 14, 1778, Admiralty, Class 1, Vol. 489, folio 73–74, NA.
9. "Account of Warrants, issued by Governor Tryon, to the Judge of the Court of Vice Admiralty for the Province of New York, for the purpose of Granting Letters of Marque against the French and Rebels," Colonial Office, Class 5, Vol. 1109, folio 109, NA.
10. Tryon to Germain, New York, March 20, 1778, Colonial Office, Class 5, Vol. 1108, folio 185, NA.
11. William S. Stryker, *The Affair at Egg Harbor, New Jersey, October 15, 1778* (Trenton: Naar, Day & Naar, 1894), 4–5.
12. "Muster-Table of His Majesty's Ship the *Nautilus* between the 1st September and the 31st October 1778," Admiralty, Class 36, Vol. 8261, folio 1, NA.
13. Stirling to Washington, Acquackanonk, 11:00 AM, October 7, 1778, Washington Papers, Series 4, General Correspondence, September 13, 1778–October 10, 1778, LOC. Brigadier General Cortland Skinner, former attorney general of the province of New Jersey, was commanding officer of the New Jersey Volunteers. He was not on the expedition.
14. Maxwell to Washington, Acquackanonk, October 8, 1778, Washington Papers, Series 4, General Correspondence, September 13, 1778–October 10, 1778, LOC.
15. Livingston to Stirling, Princeton, October 5, 1778, Washington Papers, Series 4, General Correspondence, September 13, 1778–October 10, 1778, LOC.

16. Ferguson to Clinton, Little Egg Harbor, October 10, 1778, *Royal Gazette*, March 10, 1779.
17. Pension Application of Job Weeks, M-804, Pension and Bounty Land Application Files, No. S30777, Job Weeks, New Jersey, NARA.
18. *Royal Gazette*, March 10, 1779.
19. Ibid., October 28, 1778.
20. Pension Application of Samuel Denike, M-804, Pension and Bounty Land Application Files, No. S635, Samuel Denike, New Jersey, NARA.
21. Colins to Rear Admiral James Gambier, *Zebra* in Little Egg Harbor, October 9, 1778, *London Gazette*, November 28 to December 1, 1778.
22. While somewhat more common in armies on the continent of Europe, cavalrymen armed with lances instead of merely swords, pistols, and carbines were quite a rarity in America.
23. R. D. Jamro, *Pulaski: A Portrait of Freedom* (Savannah, GA: Printcraft Press, 1979), 11–22.
24. Worthington C. Ford, ed., *Journals of the Continental Congress 1774–1789* (Washington, DC: US Government Printing Office, 1904–37), 8:745.
25. Washington to Pulaski, Fredericksburg, September 29, 1778, Washington Papers, Series 4, General Correspondence, September 13, 1778–October 10, 1778, LOC.
26. Ford, *Journals of the Continental Congress*, 12:983.
27. Jamro, *Pulaski*, 114.
28. Pulaski to Laurens, October 16, 1778, Papers of the Continental Congress, M 247, Reel 181, item 164, 17, NARA.
29. Pulaski to Laurens, October 16, 1778, Papers of the Continental Congress, M 247, Reel 181, item 164, 17, NARA.
30. *London Gazette*, November 28 to December 1, 1778.
31. Ferguson to Clinton, Little Egg Harbor, October 10, 1778, *Royal Gazette*, March 10, 1779.
32. *New Jersey Gazette* (Trenton), October 14, 1778.
33. *Scots Magazine*, January 1781, 29.
34. "Muster-Table of His Majesty's Ship the *Nautilus* between the 1st September and the 31st October 1778," Admiralty, Class 36, Vol. 8261, folio 3, NA.
35. *London Gazette*, November 28 to December 1, 1778.
36. Minutes of the Board of War, September 2, 1778, Papers of the Continental Congress, M 247, Reel 157, item 147, Vol. 2, 251–252, NARA.
37. Jamro, *Pulaski*, 114–115.
38. Pulaski to Laurens, October 16, 1778, Papers of the Continental Congress, M 247, Reel 181, item 164, 17, NARA.
39. Ewald, *Diary of the American War*, 153.
40. *London Gazette*, November 28 to December 1, 1778.
41. Commission of Lieutenant James de Bronville, Pulaski's Legion, October 5, 1778, Papers of the Continental Congress, M 247, Reel 181, item 164, 30, NARA.
42. Pulaski to Laurens, Little Egg Harbor, October 21, 1778, Papers of the Continental Congress, M 247, Reel 181, item 164, 25, NARA.
43. *London Gazette*, November 28 to December 1, 1778.
44. *Royal Gazette*, October 28, 1778.

45. Pulaski to Laurens, October 16, 1778, Papers of the Continental Congress, M 247, Reel 181, item 164, 17, NARA.

46. Ferguson to Clinton, Little Egg Harbor, October 15, 1778, *Royal Gazette*, March 10, 1779.

47. Pulaski to Laurens, October 16, 1778, Papers of the Continental Congress, M 247, Reel 181, item 164, 17, NARA.

48. *Royal Gazette*, March 10, 1779. Camp recovered from his wounds but was wounded again at Musgrove's Mills, South Carolina, August 18, 1780. After recovering from that, he was taken prisoner in December 1780, and along with five of his men was murdered on Christmas Day. Lieutenant Colonel Thomas Brown to Lieutenant Colonel Nisbet Balfour, Augusta, January 23, 1781, Cornwallis Papers, PRO 30/11/62, folios 2–5, NA.

49. Pulaski to Laurens, Stafford, October 19, 1778, Papers of the Continental Congress, M 247, Reel 181, item 164, 43, NARA.

50. Pulaski to Laurens, October 16, 1778, Papers of the Continental Congress, M 247, Reel 181, item 164, 17, NARA.

51. St. Elme to Henry Laurens, Stafford, October 19, 1778, Papers of the Continental Congress, M 247, Reel 181, item 164, 34, NARA.

52. *Journals of the American Congress, from 1774 to 1778, in Four Volumes* (Washington, DC: Way and Gideon, 1823), 3:201.

53. *London Gazette*, November 28 to December 1, 1778.

54. Pulaski to Laurens, Little Egg Harbor, October 21, 1778, Papers of the Continental Congress, M 247, Reel 181, item 164, 25, NARA.

CHAPTER TWELVE: WITHDRAWAL

1. Gambier to Clinton, October 12, 1778, Clinton Papers, Vol. 43, item 34, CL.

2. Clinton to Lieutenant General William Keppel, October 10, 1778, Clinton Papers, Vol. 43, item 13, CL.

3. Grant to Clinton, Mile Square, October 6, 1778, Clinton Papers, Vol. 42, item 38, CL.

4. The informant claimed the French and US forces at Boston numbered twelve thousand men with 180 pieces of artillery emplaced to guard the harbor, numbers far in excess of what was there. Unknown author, Crawford's House, October 5, 1778, Clinton Papers, Vol. 42, item 39, CL.

5. Journal of Military Operations in America from June 17, 1778, to December 31, 1779, Ms. B3/14, Royal Artillery Institution.

6. Scott to Washington, Bedford, October 9, 1778, Washington Papers, Series 4, General Correspondence, September 13, 1778–October 10, 1778, LOC.

7. Uhlendorf, *Revolution in America*, 222.

8. Scott to Washington, near Bedford, October 11, 1778, Washington Papers, Series 4, General Correspondence, September 26, 1778–November 6, 1778, LOC.

9. Lee to Scott, October 12, 1778, Washington Papers, Series 4, General Correspondence, September 26, 1778–November 6, 1778, LOC.

10. Cornwallis to Clinton, English Neighbourhood, 11:00 PM, October 9, 1778, Clinton Papers, Vol. 43, item 9, CL.

11. Woodford to Washington, Paramus, October 10, 1778, Washington Papers, Series 4, General Correspondence, September 13, 1778–October 10, 1778, LOC. Bayard was John Bayard of the King's Orange Rangers. Theodosia

Prevost of Hopperstown (modern-day Ho-ho-kus) was the wife of Lieutenant Colonel James Mark Prevost of the British 2nd Battalion, 60th Regiment of Foot. After his death in Jamaica in 1781, Theodosia married Aaron Burr. It is unknown who the young man was studying at her house (known today as the Hermitage) or if he accepted his ensign's commission in the rangers. This corps soon embarked for Nova Scotia, where it remained for the rest of the war.

12. Cornwallis to Clinton, English Neighbourhood, October 10, 1778, Clinton Papers, Vol. 43, item 14, CL.

13. Washington to Stirling, Fredericksburg, October 12, 1778, Washington Papers, Series 4, General Correspondence, September 26, 1778–November 6, 1778, LOC.

14. Memorial of Gabriel Van Norden to the Commissioners for American Claims, Audit Office, Class 13, Vol. 19, folios 418–419, NA.

15. "Examination of the muster rolls of the five companies of the 4th Battalion, New Jersey Volunteers, October 21, 1778," RG 8, "C" Series, Vol. 1858, LAC.

16. Woodward to Washington, Paramus, October 13, 1778, Washington Papers, Series 4, General Correspondence, September 26, 1778–November 6, 1778, LOC.

17. Peebles, October 13–14, 1778.

18. Stirling to Washington, 3:00 PM, October 11, 1778, Washington Papers, Series 4, General Correspondence, September 26, 1778–November 6, 1778, LOC.

19. Cornwallis to Clinton, English Neighbourhood, October 12, 1778, Clinton Papers, Vol. 43, item 21, CL.

20. André, October 15, 1778.

21. Stirling to Washington, Hackensack, 1:00 PM, October 14, 1778, Washington Papers, Series 4, General Correspondence, September 26, 1778–November 6, 1778, LOC.

22. Claim for losses taken before William Walton, Magistrate of Police, New York, September 2, 1783, Audit Office, Class 13, Vol. 92, folios 173–174, NA.

23. Property losses were determined by extensive examination of claims submitted at the close of the war. Other than testimony or declarations of veracity by friends, neighbors, or relatives, there was no way at the time to verify what was lost. Inventories of Damages by the British and Americans in New Jersey, 1776–1782, Vol. 1, New Jersey State Archives.

24. Russell, October 15, 1778.

25. Claim and evidence of Isaac Perkins to the Commissioners for American Claims, Audit Office, Class 12, Vol. 16, 265–268, NA.

26. "Abstract of the number of Men victualed from the 19th to the 22nd Inst. December inclusive. St. Lucia Decemr. 19th 1778," James Grant Papers of Ballindalloch Castle, Scotland, Library of Congress Microcopy, Reel 38, Army Career Series, Correspondence, Miscellany, December 13–19, 1778.

27. Ewald, *Diary of the American War*, 152–153.

28. Clinton to Grant, New York, October 27, 1778, James Grant Papers of Ballindalloch Castle, Scotland, Library of Congress Microcopy, Reel 38, Army Career Series, Correspondence, Miscellany, July–November 1778.

29. Clinton to Germain, New York, November 8, 1778, Colonial Office, Class 5, Vol. 96, 389, NA.

30. Stirling to Washington, Elizabethtown, November 3, 1778, Washington Papers, Series 4, General Correspondence, September 26, 1778–November 6, 1778, LOC.

31. "Return of the Troops arrived at Halifax in the Ship *Nancy* from New York with the distribution ordered for them, Halifax Octr. 20th 1778," Manuscript No. 13844-4, New York State Library.

32. *Royal American Gazette*, October 6, 1778.

33. Clinton to Germain, New York, October 3, 1778, Clinton Papers, Vol. 42, item 32, CL.

34. Clinton to Grant, New York, November 12, 1778, Headquarters Papers, PRO 30/55/1555, NA.

35. Intelligence by Spy "Z," New York, November 7, 1778, Papers of Major General William Alexander, Lord Stirling, Vol. 1, 185, N-YHS.

36. Campbell to Clinton, on board the *Phoenix*, November 15, 1778, Clinton Papers, Vol. 46, item 10, CL.

37. Ferguson to Clinton, November 9, 1778, Clinton Papers, Vol. 45, item 34, CL.

38. Russell, November 27, 1778.

EPILOGUE

1. *Pennsylvania Evening Post* (Philadelphia), October 26, 1778.

2. Stirling to Washington, Hackensack, 1:00 PM, October 14, 1778, Washington Papers, Series 4, General Correspondence, September 26, 1778–November 6, 1778, LOC.

3. Tryon to Clinton, New York, July 20, 1779, Audit Office, Class 13, Vol. 54, folios 607–610, NA.

4. Memorial of George Leonard to Lord George Germain, enclosed in Germain to Sir Henry Clinton, April 21, 1780, Headquarters Papers, PRO 30/55/2695, NA.

5. Arnold to Clinton, Long Island Sound, off Plumb Island, September 8, 1781, in Clinton, *American Rebellion*, 565–567.

6. "A Report of the Sick and Wounded of the Army under the command of Major General Grant Feby. 27th 1779," James Grant Papers of Ballindalloch Castle, Scotland, Library of Congress Microcopy, Reel 43, Army Career Series, Correspondence, Miscellany, February 5–27, 1779.

7. The 40th Regiment returned to America in August 1781, just in time to take part in Arnold's New London expedition, where it suffered severe casualties in the assault on Fort Griswold. Clinton Papers, Vol. 233, item 39, CL.

8. McLean to Clinton, Halifax, December 28, 1778, Headquarters Papers, PRO 30/55/1634, NA.

9. A British guinea equaled one pound, one shilling sterling. Dornemann, "Diary Kept by Chaplain Waldeck," 56–57.

10. *Pennsylvania Gazette, and Weekly Advertiser* (Philadelphia), February 3, 1779.

11. "Return of the Killed, Wounded and Missing of the Detachment of His Majesty's Forces under the Command of Lieut. Colo. Archibald Campbell, in the action of the 29 Decemr. 1778," Colonial Office, Class 5, Vol. 182, 77, NA.

12. Campbell to William Eden, January 19, 1779, Additional Manuscripts, No. 34,416, folio 246, British Library.

13. *New-York Gazette and the Weekly Mercury*, March 8, 1779.

14. Among the correspondence, Browne wrote of Grant, "A most treasonable and daring attempt has been lately made to subvert this Government and wrest

the reins out of my hands." Browne to Clinton, New Providence, February 1, 1780, Clinton Papers, Vol. 84, item 1, CL.

15. Ewald, *Diary of the American War*, 153.

16. Statement by Francis, Lord Rawdon, London, August 10, 1792, Lloyd W. Smith Collection, LWS No. 209, Morristown National Historic Park.

17. Uhlendorf, *Revolution in America*, 408.

18. *New Jersey Gazette* (Trenton), November 4, 1778.

19. Heitman, *Historical Register of Officers*, 92.

20. Prevost to Clinton, James Island, May 21, 1779, Colonial Office, Class 5, Vol. 98, folio 169, NA.

21. *New York Times*, December 28, 1997.

22. *Asbury Park Press*, April 8, 2015.

23. The complete report of D. Bennett Mazur and Wayne Daniels was published by the Bergen County Board of Chosen Freeholders as the booklet *The Massacre of Baylor's Dragoons*.

BIBLIOGRAPHY

MANUSCRIPT PRIMARY SOURCES

Canada

Archives of Ontario

   Peter Russell Fonds, F 46

Library and Archives Canada

   MG 23, Ward Chipman Papers

      RG 1, Upper Canada Land Petitions

      RG 8, "C" Series

Nova Scotia Archives

   RG 46

Provincial Archives of New Brunswick

   Sessional Records of the Legislative Assembly, RS 24

United Kingdom

Alnwick Castle

   Manuscripts of the Duke of Northumberland, Percy Papers

Ballindalloch Castle

   James Grant Papers

British Library

   Additional Manuscripts

Durham University Library

   Papers of the 1st Earl Grey

National Archives

   Admiralty, Class 1

   Admiralty, Class 36

   Audit Office, Class 12

   Audit Office, Class 13

   Chancery, Class 106

   Colonial Office, Class 5

   Cornwallis Papers, PRO 30/11

   Headquarters Papers of the British Army in America, PRO 30/55

   Treasury, Class 1

War Office, Class 12
War Office, Class 71
War Office, Class 121
Royal Artillery Institution
   Journal of Military Operations in America from June 17, 1778, to
December 31, 1779.
Scottish Record Office
   John Peebles Journal, GD 21

United States
David Library of the American Revolution
   Sol Feinstone Collection
Historical Society of Pennsylvania
   17th Regiment of Foot Orderly Book kept by Captain Robert
Clayton, AM618
   Daniel Wier Letterbook
Huntington Library
   John André Journal, HM 626
Library of Congress
   Elias Boudinot Papers
   Alexander Hamilton Papers
   George Washington Papers
   Memorandum Book of the British Army, MSS No. 82750
Morristown National Historic Park
   Lloyd W. Smith Collection
National Archives and Records Administration
   M246, Revolutionary War Rolls
   M247, Papers of the Continental Congress
   M804, Pension and Bounty Land Application Files
   RG 93, Miscellaneous Numbered Records
New Jersey State Archives
   Department of Defense, Military Records, Revolutionary War,
Revolutionary Manuscripts Numbered
   Inventories of Damages by the British and Americans in New Jersey,
1776–1782
New-York Historical Society
   Brigade of Guards Orderly Book, August 7, 1778–December 25,
1778
   BV Prisoners of War

DeLancey Orderly Book
Kemble Orderly Book
Papers of Major General William Alexander, Lord Stirling
New York Public Library
Theodorus Bailey Myers Collection
New York State Library
Miscellaneous Manuscripts
Sir William Howe Orderly Book
United States Military Academy
Orderly Book of the Guides & Pioneers
William L. Clements Library, University of Michigan
George Germain Papers
Frederick Mackenzie Papers
Orderly Book of the King's American Regiment
Simcoe Papers
Sir Henry Clinton Papers
Von Jungkenn Papers

PUBLISHED PRIMARY SOURCES

Bernstein, David A., ed. *Minutes of the Governor's Privy Council, 1777–1789*. Trenton: New Jersey State Library Archives and History Bureau, 1974.

Clinton, Sir Henry. *The American Rebellion: Sir Henry Clinton's Narrative of His Campaigns, 1775–1782, with an Appendix of Original Documents*. Edited by William B. Willcox. New Haven, CT: Yale University Press, 1954.

Dornemann, William E., PhD. "Diary Kept by Chaplain Waldeck during the Last American War," Part 2. *Journal of the Johannes Schwalm Historical Association* 2, no. 4 (1998): 28–63.

Ewald, Johann. *Diary of the American War*. Edited by Joseph P. Tustin. New Haven, CT: Yale University Press, 1979.

Heinrichs, Johann. "Extracts from the Letter-Book of Captain Johann Heinrichs of the Hessian Jäger Corps, 1778–1780." *Pennsylvania Magazine of History and Biography* 22, no. 22 (1890): 137–170.

Jones, Thomas. *History of New York during The Revolutionary War*. New York: New-York Historical Society, 1879.

Journals of the American Congress, from 1774 to 1778, in Four Volumes. Washington, DC: Way and Gideon, 1823.

Kemble, Stephen. "The Orderly Book of Lt. Col. Stephen Kemble, 1777–1778." In *Collections of the New-York Historical Society for 1883*. New York: Printed for the Society, 1884.

Ketchum, Richard M., ed. "New War Letters of Banastre Tarleton." In *Narratives of the Revolution in New York*. Kingsport, TN: Kingsport Press, 1975.

Lydenberg, Harry Miller, ed. *Archibald Robertson: His Diaries and Sketches in America, 1762–1780*. New York: New York Public Library, 1930.

Mackenzie, Frederick. *Diary of Frederick Mackenzie*. Cambridge: Harvard University Press, 1930.

Martin, Joseph Plumb. *Private Yankee Doodle, Being a Narrative of some of the Adventures, Dangers and Sufferings of a Revolutionary Soldier*. Edited by George E. Scheer. 1962. Reprint, Philadelphia: Acorn Press, 1979.

Morgan, William James, ed. *Naval Documents of the American Revolution*. Washington, DC: Naval History Division, Department of the Navy, 1972.

The Rembrancer; or, Impartial Repository of Public Events, for the Year 1778, and Beginning of 1779. London: Printed for J. Almon, opposite Burlington House, Picadilly, 1779.

Simcoe, John Graves. *A History of the Operations of a Partisan Corps called the Queen's Rangers commanded by Lieut. Col. J.G. Simcoe, during the War of the American Revolution*. New York: Bartlett & Welford, 1844.

Thacher, James, M.D. *Military Journal of the American Revolution*. Hartford, CT: Hurlbut, William, 1862.

Uhlendorf, Bernhard A., ed. *Revolution in America: Confidential Letters and Journals 1776–1784 of Adjutant General Major Baurmeister of the Hessian Forces*. New Brunswick, NJ: Rutgers University Press, 1957.

PUBLISHED SECONDARY SOURCES

Betz, Dr. I. H. "The Conway Cabal at York, Pennsylvania, 1777–1778." *Pennsylvania German* 9, no. 1 (1908): 248–254.

Bolton, Robert, Jr. *History of the County of Westchester from its First Settlement to the Present Time*. New York: Printed by Alexander S. Gould, 1848.

Devoe, Thomas F. "The Massacre of the Stockbridge Indians 1778."
Magazine of American History 5, no. 3 (1880): 38–42.

Ford, Worthington C., ed. *Journals of the Continental Congress 1774–1789*. Washington, DC: Government Printing Office, 1904–37.

Heitman, Francis B. *Historical Register of Officers of the Continental Army during the War of the Revolution*. Washington, DC: Rare Book Shop Publishing, 1914.

Jamro, R. D. *Pulaski: A Portrait of Freedom*. Savannah, GA: Printcraft Press, 1979.

Leiby, Adrian C. *The Revolutionary War in the Hackensack Valley*. New Brunswick, NJ: Rutgers University Press, 1962.

MacDougall, William L. *American Revolutionary: A Biography of General Alexander McDougall*. Westport, CT: Greenwood, 1977.

Maurer , C. F. William. *Dragoon Diary*. N.p.: AuthorHouse, 2005.

Stryker, William S. *The Affair at Egg Harbor, New Jersey, October 15, 1778*. Trenton: Naar, Day & Naar, 1894.

———. *Official Register of the Officers and Men of New Jersey in the Revolutionary War*. Trenton: Wm. T. Nicholson, 1872.

Williams, Thomas John Chew. *History of Frederick County Maryland*. Baltimore: Genealogical Publishing, 2003.

INTERNET SOURCES

Wright, Kevin. "Overkill: Revolutionary War Reminiscences of River Vale." www.bergencountyhistory.org/Pages/baylormassacre. html.

ACKNOWLEDGMENTS

As with all of my previous works, and as I suspect is true for most writers, I had much help along the way on this book, from conception to completion. Working with the family of authors collected within the *Journal of the American Revolution* has allowed me to get a deep appreciation of the logistical, production, and marketing talents of Todd Andrlik. Because of his vision, and that of Bruce Franklin of Westholme Publishing, this book, this series, is possible, for which they have my sincerest thanks.

I am extremely grateful to the person who guided me through this entire process, Don Hagist. Having had the honor of being friends with Don for over thirty-five years, I was extremely gratified to have someone with his breadth of knowledge and good judgment involved in the preparation of the manuscript. Don's selfless giving of his time and knowledge made the preparation of this book much easier than it might have otherwise been. I was also fortunate to have been friends over the same course of time with the man who is truly my mentor in all things research, Don Londahl-Smidt. Don's generosity and patience over the years enabled me to draw on an unparalleled trove of research, while he taught me the skills involved in hunting down every source and using them to best advantage. For all of my research colleagues over the years who have been so generous in their findings and effusive in their support, many thanks.

No good book on the campaigns of the American Revolution can be complete without a thorough search of records in the United Kingdom, and in addition to my own visits to the National Archives there, I had the able assistance of Mr. Fraser's Highlanders himself, Ed Brumby of Scotland, and the indefatigable Michael Barrett, my researcher at Kew. No request went unanswered or unresolved, and in less time than anyone could have a right to expect. As important as the UK records were, US repositories were equally useful, and two in particular deserve special thanks. The William L. Clements Library at the University of Michigan is without question one of the finest places there can be to delve into historical books, maps, and manuscripts. Over the course of my three-plus decades of visits, the staff may have occasionally changed, but every member helped along the way, particularly John Dann, Rob Cox, Brian Leigh Dunnigan, and Don Wilcox. Also, much appreciation to researcher Diana Mankowski for her excellent work in locating documents at the Clements Library in my absence. The number one repository for Revolutionary War documents and publications, without doubt, is the David Library of the American Revolution, located in lovely Washington Crossing, Pennsylvania. Without that library, along with the kindness and indulgence of its staff, particularly Librarian Kathie Ludwig and Chief Operating Officer Meg McSweeney, this book would not exist.

No one individual can know everything on every subject, and that is certainly the case when researching events of over 235 years ago. I am grateful to have had the assistance of the leading authority on the Royal Navy, Bob Brooks, and his encyclopedic knowledge of all things concerning Britain's maritime forces, particularly in figuring out the ships and vessels of the Egg Harbor expedition. As much of the subject matter of this work occurred close to home, it is natural that those around here likewise had a hand in this volume. I am very grateful to the support given me by my friends and colleagues in the Bergen County Historical Society, particularly Kevin Wright and Deborah Powell. No one has a better grasp on local residents, roads, and towns of the past than these folks do. Thanks also to Janet Strom and the Bergen County Division of Cultural and Historic Affairs for their generous assistance concerning the artifacts recovered from the Baylor Massacre burial site, a very tangible connection to some of the events covered in these pages. To my extended family of fellow researchers and friends, thank you for your support and assistance all through the year. From a technological standpoint, most independent writers are at the mercy of their computers and electronic devices to create their work, and like many, I have no special talents in this realm. For that reason I am very grateful to Derek Ramirez, my de facto IT staff, who more than once came to my technology rescue and kept things on track.

Certainly not least of all, my biggest thanks go to my wife, Susan, who endured the better part of a year keeping me sane while I dealt with deadlines and writers block and research obstacles. This book was written in three hotel rooms, two Amtrak trains, a fort, and on the porch of an eighteenth century house, but nowhere more so than at home, where cooperation and support were most needed, and most appreciated.

INDEX

Ackerman, Abraham, 125, 160
Ackerman, Peter, 101-102
Alexander, William (Lord Stirling),
    31, 48, 122-124, 127-128,
    144-145, 148, 159, 161,
    164-165, 167, 170, 176,
    194n14
André, John, 109, 182n3
Archer, Jacob, 110
Armand-Tuffin, Charles, 135, 158,
    199n16, 199n19
Armstrong, Richard, 53
Arnold, Benedict, 6, 171
Ayers, Joseph, 135-136, 198n15,
    199n19

Bahama Islands, 167
Baird, James, 103
Balfour, Nesbit, 36, 202n48
Banta, Weart, 101, 194n7
Baremore, Mansfield, 15
Barnes, John, 73, 76
Barrington, Samuel, 171
Bassett, William, 106
Bates, Ann, 36, 39
Bates, Joseph, 36-37
Baurmeister, Carl, 158
Bayard, John, 51, 159, 202-203n11
Baylor, George, viii, 68, 72, 76-77,
    80-81, 87, 89, 99-100, 102-
    104, 108, 114, 128, 135,
    159, 174, 176-177
Baylor's Dragoons, 68, 111
Bell, Jabez, 118, 197n19
Bell, John, 73

Benson, Thomas, 105
Bergen County Board of Chosen
    Freeholders, 177
Bergen County Historical Society,
    177
Bergen County Militia, 69, 76, 95,
    107
Betsy, 168
Bickell, Alexander Wilhelm, 131-
    132
Biddle, Clement, 68
Bird, William, 51
Blanch, Thomas, 95
Blauvelt, Abraham, 111, 160
Blauvelt, Cornelius D., 107-108,
    110
Blindberry, Solomon, 136
Board of War, 151
Bogert, David Ritzema, 69, 160
Boyd, Adam, 73, 80
Brandywine, battle of, 7, 143, 148,
    179n9
Brinkerhoff, Dirck, 165
Brinley, George, 55
British Legion, 15-16, 18-19, 25,
    42, 50-51, 71, 82, 86, 122,
    127, 135, 137, 140, 160,
    181n37, 183n21, 183n23,
    198n36, 199n16
British War Office, 52
Briton, Joseph, 45
Bronx River, 46, 83
Brooklyn, battle of, 41
Brower, Abraham, 101, 117-118
Brower's Hill, 85-87, 90, 160

Browne, Daniel Isaac, 80
Browne, Montfort, 173
Brune, 156
Bunyan, James, 143
Burges, John, 110
Burgoyne, John, 47, 64, 173
Burr, Aaron, 64, 202-203n11
Butler, Richard, 33, 130-133, 135
Buzzards Bay, 59
Byram River, 138
Byron, John, 36

Campbell, Archibald, 8, 82, 95-98,
    109, 111, 167-168, 173,
    191n41
Campbell, George, 51
Campbell, Patrick, 143
Campbell, Samuel, 125
Camp, John, 154
Carlisle Peace Commission, 4, 47
Carpathian Mountains, 147
Carpenter, Benjamin, 60
Carrol, Joseph, 105
Carter, John, 48
Cathcart, William, 15, 17-18
Chambers, Stephen, 36-37, 183n19
Christian, Brabazon, 153
Christie, Daniel, 125, 165
Cisco, Abraham, 75
Clinton, Henry
    arrival at Rhode Island and, 57-
        58
    as professional soldier and, 4
    battle of Monmouth and, 10
    calling in the troops and, 156-
        157
    Carlisle Peace Commission and,
        47
    commissaries and, 54
    final phase of Grand Forage and,
        142
    giving over command of West
        Indies to Grant and, 166-
        167
    letter from Cornwallis and, 90

letter to Benjamin Carpenter and,
    60
logistical challenges and, 53
Philadelphia Campaign and, 62
promotion to commander in chief
    and, 2
proportion of southern Loyalists
    and, 6
recruiting Irish immigrants and,
    7-8
relief of Rhode Island and, 56
review of the strength of the army
    and, 49-50
Clough, Alexander, 66-69, 71, 80,
    87, 100, 103-104, 107-108
Colins, Henry, 143, 145-147, 149,
    152, 155
Comet, 143
Connecticut Militia, 43
Constitution Island, 65
Continental Army, 7, 12-13, 32,
    38, 40-41, 43, 48, 56, 61,
    65, 74, 90, 94, 122, 148,
    170-171, 174-175
Continental Army Hospital, 48
Conway Cabal, 48
Conway, John, 117
Conway, Thomas, 48
Cooper, Gilbert, 84, 94, 96-99,
    110, 160
Cornwallis, Charles, 26, 62, 71,
    74, 77, 83, 90, 94-95, 97-
    98, 109, 111, 114, 116,
    118, 141, 143, 157-160,
    164, 166
Cornwallis, 143
Craig, John, 39
Crane, Joseph, 110
Crawford, John, 25, 181n38
Croton River, 136
Cunningham, William, 77
Czurlanis, George, 175-176

Dade, Baldwin, 108
Dade, Francis, 108

Dandridge, Alexander, 132, 138
Daniels, Wayne, 177
Daughters of the American
    Revolution, 175
Day, Mary, 125
Dayton, Elias, 124, 187n15
de Diemar, Frederick, 173
de Kalb, Johann Baron, 151
DeLancey, James, 15, 42
Delaware River, 54
Denike, Samuel, 146
Dependence, 143
deserters, 27, 33, 42, 50, 72, 95-
    96, 115, 128, 137, 140-141,
    151, 158-161, 164, 198n36
D'Estaing, Charles Hector, 9-10,
    13, 38
de St. Elme, Gerard, 154
de Vernier, Peter, 175
Devoe, Daniel, 19, 24
Devoe, Frederick, 19, 24
Devoe, Thomas, 24
Dey, Peter, 69, 99, 189n38
Dey, Theunis, 69, 73, 89
Dickison, Zebulon, 136
Dietrich, Nicholas, 135, 199n16
Drake, Joseph, 15
Drummond, Duncan, 36-37, 40,
    183n19

Earl of Carlisle, 3
Eden, William, 3
Edwards, Evan, 185n31
Egg Harbor, 142-145, 149, 151-
    152, 166, 174-176, 212
Eighth Connecticut Regiment, 14
Eighth Pensylvania Regiment, 33
Eighth Virginia Regiment, 75
Eighty-second Regiment, 9
Ellerbeck, Emmanuel, 36
Ely, Abraham, 88
Emmerick, Andreas, 18-21, 24, 42,
    44
Emmerick's Chasseurs, 15-16, 25,
    42, 82, 95, 137-138, 141,
    184n6, 199n22

Episcopal Church of York, 48
Evans, George, 108
Evans, Thomas, 104, 108
Ewald, Johann, 16, 20, 24, 44,
    131-134, 136-137, 152,
    180n10, 199n19

Fell, Peter, 73, 76, 80
Ferguson, Patrick, viii, 141-143,
    145-147, 149-150, 152-155,
    166, 168
Fifteenth Regiment of Foot, 11, 85-
    87, 159
Fifth Massachusetts Regiment, 24
Fifth Regiment of Foot, 11, 143,
    146, 154
Fifty-fifth Regiment of Foot, 11,
    143
Fifty-second Regiment, 50, 64, 141
Fifty-seventh Regiment, 71, 122
First Battalion DeLancey's Brigade,
    50-51
First Battalion of British
    Grenadiers, 70-71, 94, 118
First Battalion of Light Infantry, 71
First Battalion of New Jersey
    Volunteers, 117, 143, 167-
    168
First Dragoon Guards, 17
First Light Dragoons, 132, 161
First Maryland Regiment, 45
First New York Regiment, 29
First Pennsylvania Regiment, 29
First Virginia Regiment, 25, 138
Fitzhugh, Peregrine, 108
Flying Camp, 61
Fort Clinton, 65
Fort Constitution, 61
Fortieth Regiment, 11, 17, 52-53,
    171
Fort Independence, 29, 34
Fort Knyphausen, 15, 29
Fort Lee, 61, 65-66, 73-74, 77, 86-
    87, 90, 159, 161, 164, 166,
    188n18

Fort Montgomery, 65

Fort Ticonderoga, 47

Fort Washington, vi, 15, 28-29, 34, 61, 73

Forty-fifth Regiment, 50, 141

Forty-fourth Regiment, 86

Forty-ninth Regiment of Foot, 11, 83

Forty-second Highlanders, 94

Forty-second Regiment, 70, 85-86, 90, 116

Forty-sixth Regiment, 11, 86

Fountleroy, Griffin, 161

Fourth Artillery Regiment, 149

Fourth Battalion New Jersey Volunteers, 62, 71, 101

Fourth Light Dragoons, 64-65, 168, 174

Fourth Maryland Regiment, 45

Fourth New York Regiment, 132

Fourth Pensylvania Regiment, 33

Fourth Regiment of Foot, 11, 83

Fourth Virginia Regiment, 75

Freeland, Abraham, 117

French and Indian War, 17

Furman, Moore, 68-69

Gage, 124

Gage, Thomas, 2

Gambier, James, 54, 151-152, 156

Gates, Horatio, 38, 48

Georgia Light Dragoons, 175

Germain, George, 2-3, 6-9, 54, 58, 142, 144, 164, 167

Gist, Mordecai, 16, 41, 43-45, 49, 137, 158, 184n13

Gloucester County Militia, 145

Goodale, Nathan, 24

Gould, Robert, 75

Governor's Island, 54

Graham, Charles, 132

Granby, 143, 149

Grant, James, 3, 11, 40, 50, 52-53, 67, 133, 135-137, 143, 157-158, 166-167, 171, 173,

196n10, 199n19, 204n14

Grant, John, 167, 171, 173

Grayham, Morris, 32, 72

Greenwich, 143, 149

Grey, Charles, viii, 29, 59-60, 101, 103, 108-109, 114, 126, 187n7

Griffith, David, 109, 176

Gwynn, F. E., 88

Hackensack River, 60, 73, 85-86, 88-89, 100, 117, 122, 124, 160-161, 177

Halifax, 143, 145

Hamilton, Alexander, 185n31

Hammond, James, 15

Haring, John, 75, 84, 96, 100, 112, 114

Harmar, Josiah, 132

Hart, Benjamin, 101

Hatfield, Isaac, 15

Hawkins, Bartlett, 104-105

Hay, Ann Hawkes, 81, 97

Heard, Nathaniel, 89, 111, 122-123

Heinrichs, Johann, 24

Helm, Samuel, 76

HMS *Phoenix*, 82

Hogenkamp, John, 110

Holdrum School, 176

Hopkins, David, 64

Howard's Tavern, 172

Howels, Richard, 144

Howe, Richard, 13, 28, 60, 64

Howe, Robert, 173

Howe, William, 2, 4-5, 18, 28, 57, 60, 62-64, 67, 143

Hudson Highlands, 27-28, 38, 141

Hudson River, 16, 39, 41, 44, 46, 60-61, 67, 82, 85-86, 157

Hughes, Thomas, 101-102

Hurlbut, George, 16

Hustis, George, 46

Hysonec, Hantras, 87

Jägers, 15-16, 19-20, 24, 42-44, 46, 82-83, 130-133, 135-138, 152
James, Jacob, 140, 183n21
Johnstone, George, 3
Jones, Thomas, 113
Jones, Valentine, 124
Juliat, Carl Wilhelm Joseph, 151-152, 173

Kane, Bernard, 36
Kelty, John, 108
Kemble, Stephen, 113
King, Charles, 109
King's Orange Rangers, 50-51, 101, 167, 171, 202-203n11
Kosciuszko, Thaddeus, 48

Laurens, Henry, 128-129
Leavenworth, Eli, 158
Ledyard, Benjamin, 132
Lee, Charles, 10, 17, 47, 185n31
Lee, Henry, 45, 158
Leiby, Adrian C., 177
Lent, Abraham, 111
Leonard, George, 171
Leslie, Alexander, 6
Levensworth, Eli, 32
Lincoln, Benjamin, 31
Little Egg Harbor Society, 176
Livingston, William, 62, 84, 117, 123, 128-129, 145, 148, 176
Long Island Sound, 16
Lord Percy, 61
Lord Stirling, 31, 122-124, 127-128, 144-145, 148, 159, 161, 164-165, 167, 170, 176, 194n14
Loyal American Regiment, 32, 36, 136

Mackenzie, Frederick, 57
Mackish, John, 33
Maitland, John, 102

Malcom's Additional Continental Regiment, 64
Manhattan Island, 28, 60
Marley, Daniel, 126
Martha's Vineyard, 59-60, 171
Martin, Joseph Plumb, 14, 131, 133-134
Maxwell, William, 84, 88-89, 115-117, 122, 144-145
Mazur, D. Bennett, 177
McCarny, Francis, 95-96
McClachlin, John, 33
McDougall, Alexander, 29
McEvoy, Martin, 51
McKinnon, John, 51
Miller, Thomas, 127, 198n36
Minerva, 173
Mississippi River, 2
Montgomery, William, 111
Morris County Militia, 117-118, 197n19
Morrow, Robert, 108
Motisher, George, 95-96
Moylan, Stephen, 65-66, 69
Muirson, Benjamin Woolsey, 46
Mullen, Thomas, 25, 181n37
mutiny, 140

Nancy, 167
Nautilus, 143, 151
Needham, Francis, 74
Neil, Ferdinand, 132
Neilson, John, 123
Neptune, 168, 172
New Jersey Volunteers, 10, 50-51, 62, 71, 80, 101-102, 111, 117, 143, 154, 160, 168, 172, 175, 186n38, 188-189n34, 200n13
New York Harbor, 10, 168
New York Volunteers, 36, 50, 168
Nimham, Abraham, 20-21, 25, 27, 30, 175
Nimham, Daniel, 20, 24
Ninth Pennsylvania Regiment, 33, 130

North River, 71-72, 82, 86, 157

Odell, John, 43
Ogden, Gilbert, 136
Orange County Militia, 81, 84, 94,
    97, 111

Paoli, battle of, 59
Parker, Richard, 25, 116, 138
Passaic River, 60, 117-118
Patterson, William, 140
Paulus Hook, 28, 61, 70-72, 74,
    76, 78, 86, 90, 122, 164,
    182n2
Peebles, John, 70, 85, 90, 116,
    118-119, 122, 126, 141
Philipse, Frederick, 16
Phillip's Bridge, 43
Pigot, Robert, 12, 15, 57
Poulison, John, 165
Poulison, Martin, 125
Prevost, Augustine, 173
Prevost, Theodosia, 159
Prince Edward Island, 2
Prince of Wales American
    Volunteers, 11
Proctor, Thomas, 149
Provincial King's American
    Regiment, 11
Provincial West Jersey Volunteers,
    10, 50-51, 62, 71, 80, 101-
    102, 111, 117, 143, 154,
    160, 168, 172, 175,
    186n38, 188-189n34,
    200n13
Pulaski, Antoni, 147
Pulaski, Casmir, viii, 124, 147-155,
    174-175
Pulaski, Franciszek, 147
Pulaski, Josef, 147
Pulaski's Legion, 122, 151-152,
    154, 173-174, 201n41
Putnam, Israel, 81, 89, 94, 114-
    115, 127, 191n38

Quackinbush, James, 110
Quaker Hill, battle of, 30
Quakers, 154
Queen's American Rangers, 15-17,
    19-21, 25, 42-43, 51-52, 82,
    95, 137-138, 181n36,
    183n23

Ramapo Mountains, 127
Randolph, Robert, 108
Rawdon, Francis, 7
*Revolutionary War in the
    Hackensack Valley* (Leiby),
    177
Rhore, Dave, 105
Richards, John, 101
Ridgway, Jeremiah, 149, 152
Riker, James, 95
Ritzema, Rudolphus, 50
Rivington, James, 44
Robertson, Archibald, 85
Robinson, Beverley, 32, 136
Rogers, Robert, 17
Rogers, William, 75-76, 180n11,
    190n21-22
Romaine, Benjamin, 73, 75
Romaine, Elias, 73-75
Roman Catholic Volunteers, 9, 51
Roome, Samuel, 117
Ross, John, 21, 52
Royal American Reformees, 50
Royal Artillery, 36, 124, 158
Royal Gazette, Gist's escape and,
    44
Royal Highland Regiment, 70
Royal Navy, 1, 6, 9, 12-13, 28, 31,
    53-54, 58, 61, 64-65, 91,
    97, 122, 142, 155, 170, 212
Russell, Peter, 86, 96, 116
Ryerson, John G., 76

Saint Augustine, 2, 5, 172
Salt Works, 150, 156
Sandy Hook, 10, 28, 91, 167-168,
    196n10

Savage, Henry, 96
Saw Mill River, 131, 136
Schofield, David, 112
Schuyler, Aaron, 47, 69
Schuyler, Philip, 47
Scott, Charles, viii, 13, 25-26, 29,
    31-33, 38-39, 43-46, 67, 71,
    73, 81, 84-85, 90-91, 130,
    133, 135, 137-140, 158,
    175, 182n10, 199n22
Scrolingbour Church, 81
Second Battalion DeLancey's
    Brigade, 19, 42, 50-51
Second Battalion of British
    Grenadiers, 70-71, 86, 101
Second Battalion of British Light
    Infantry, 71, 80, 101, 109,
    113
Second Light Dragoons, 44, 46, 91,
    138-141, 160
Second Light Infantry, 102, 153
Second Maryland Regiment, 21
Second New Jersey Regiment, 144
Second New York Regiment, 132
Seventeenth Light Dragoons, 101
Seventeenth Regiment of Foot, 86,
    102
Seventeenth Regiment of Light
    Dragoons, 8, 11, 17, 46, 71,
    74
Seventh Regiment of Foot, 83
Seventieth Regiment of Foot, 9,
    143
Seventy-first Highlanders, 46, 82,
    95, 103
Seventy-first Regiment of Foot, 82-
    83
Seventy-fourth Regiment, 9
Seven Years' War, 18
Shurtliff, Joseph, 109
siege of Rhode Island, 16
Simcoe, John Graves, 17-21, 24-25,
    42-43, 45-46, 51-53, 83, 97,
    136, 138, 181n36, 199n19
Simms, James, 45
Sisco, Peter I., 74, 190n12

Sixteenth Regiment of Foot, 96
Sixteenth Regiment of Light
    Dragoons, 8, 17, 71, 74,
    101
Sixth Pennsylvania Regiment, 132
Sixtieth Regiment of Foot, 173
Sixty-fourth Regiment of Foot, 86,
    96, 101, 116, 126
Sixty-third Regiment of Foot, 7, 83
Skinner, Cortland, 62, 144, 200n13
Smith, Elisha, 140-141, 160
Spencer, Oliver, 115, 128
Sproat, David, 7
Stagg, James, 125
St. Clair, Arthur, 47
Stewart, Charles, 114
Stewart, John, 21, 27, 30, 175,
    182n3
Stirn, Johann Daniel, 82
Stith, John, 106-107
Stoddard, Josiah, 140
Stony Point, 29, 182n3
Stringfellow, David, 105
Stuart, Walter, 33
Sullivan, John, 12-13, 30, 33, 38,
    56, 58, 135
Sutherland, William, 167
Swan, John, 108

Tallmadge, Benjamin, 44-45
Tally, Thomas, 104
Tarleton, Banastre, 17-19, 21, 24,
    26, 42-44, 46, 175
Tartar, 173
Taylor, Robert, 145
Taylor, William, 127
Tenth Regiment, 50, 141
Thacher, James, 48
Thames River, 59
Thetis, 9
Third Battalion New Jersey
    Volunteers, 50-51, 117, 143,
    154, 168, 172, 175
Third Light Dragoons, 66-67, 77,
    89, 99-100, 102, 128, 148,
    174-176

Third Maryland Regiment, 16, 41
Third New Jersey Regiment, 124
Third New Jersey Volunteers, 50
Third New York Regiment, 50
Third Waldeck Regiment, 116
Thirty-eighth Regiment of Foot, 11
Thirty-fifth Regiment, 171
Thirty-seventh Regiment of Foot,
     86, 94-96
Thirty-third Regiment of Foot, 86,
     101
Thomas, Thomas, 15
Tilghman, Tench, 72
Trenton, battle of, 140
Tryon, William, 28, 39, 55, 143,
     170, 180n17
Twelfth Pennsylvania Regiment, 36
Twenty-eighth Regiment, 11, 141
Twenty-seventh Regiment, 11, 39,
     67
Twenty-sixth Regiment of Foot, 83
Twenty-third Regiment of Foot, 11,
     36

Valentine's Hill, 19, 43, 45-46, 82,
     182n3
Van Allen, Peter, 118
Van Buskirk, Abraham, 62, 80, 160
Van Cortland, Pierre, 15
Vanderbilt, James, 96
Vanderhoven, John, 126
Van Norden, Gabriel, 160
Van Orden, Peter S., 73, 111
Vaughan, John, 115-116, 122, 124
Venus of London, 146
Vervalen, Samuel, 75
Vigilant, 143, 153, 156
Volunteers of Ireland, 8, 51, 71, 76,
     86, 119
Von Bose, Charles, 149, 152-153
von Donop, Carl Moritz, 16, 82,
     131-132
von Hachenberg, Carl Wilhelm, 82
von Knyphausen, Wilhelm, viii, 82-
     83, 135, 141, 152, 158,
     173, 187n2

von Prueschenck, Ernst Carl, 43-44
von Steuben, Friedrich Wilhelm, 8
von Wreden, Carl August, 43-44,
     83
von Wurmb, Ludwig, 130

Waldeck, Philip, 116
Waldeck Regiment, 116, 167
Washington, George
   Baylor's choice of encampments
        and, 100
   bolstering the militia and, 89
   Butler's report and, 135
   Carlisle Peace Commission and,
        47
   Council of Safety and, 62
   council of war at White Plains
        and, 30-31
   defeats against Gage and, 2
   execution of Elisha Smith and,
        141
   expedition against Egg Harbor
        and, 144-145
   inattention of Sheldon's corps
        and, 138-139
   letter to congress and, 3-4
   letter to John Sullivan and, 12-13
   losing patience with his cavalry
        and, 139-140
   orders to David Hopkins and, 64-
        65
   plan to seize northern Manhattan
        and, 27-28
   spy network and, 8-9, 31-32, 67,
        91, 164
   third of the large defeats suffered
        by, 176
   Woodford's report and, 128
Washington, William, 174
Wayne, Anthony, 29, 101, 182n3
Welbank, George, 20
Westervelt, Aury, 125
Westervelt, John P., 165
West Indies, 3, 11, 50, 52, 60, 67,
     128, 141, 143, 157, 159,

161, 164, 166, 168, 171,
196n10
West Jersey Volunteers, 50
West Point, 65, 115, 127, 130,
141, 157
White, Elias, 75
Wilkinson, James, 48
Williams, Wynant, 36
Willis, George, 104
Winds, William, 89, 117-118, 122-
123, 157
Woodford, William, 89, 99, 115,
127-128
Woodruff, Benjamin, 75
Wood, Thomas, 25
World War II, 176
Wright, Francis, 136

Young Tom, 168

Zabriskie, Albert C., 125
Zabriskie, John, 101
Zebra, 143, 155